But What About Your Anger?

*A Biblical Guide to Managing Your Anger
the Way God Intended*

But What About Your Anger?
A Biblical Guide to Managing Your Anger the Way God Intended
Copyright © 2012 by Lee Boger

All rights are reserved. No part of this book may be duplicated, copied, translated, reproduced or stored mechanically, digitally or electronically without specific, written permission of the author and publisher.

Printed in the United States of America.

ISBN: 978-1-939086-09-9

Unless otherwise indicated, all Scripture references are from the Holy Bible, New International Version, copyright ©1973, 1978, 1984, 2011 by Biblica, Inc.. Used by permission. All rights reserved worldwide.

Verses marked NLT are take from the *Holy Bible, New Living Translation*, copyright ©1996. Used by permission of Tyndale House Publishers, Incl, Wheaton, IL 60189 USA. All rights reserved.

Verses marked The Message are take from *The Message*, Copyright ©1993, 1994, 1995, 1996, 2000, 2001, 2002. Used by permission of NavPress Publishing Group.

Verses marked NKJV are taken from the New King James Version, Copyright ©1982 by Thomas Nelson, Inc. Used by permission. All rights reserved.

Cover and book interior design: Toney C. Mulhollan.

A special thanks to Jean Lapeyrolerie for her editorial work.

About the author: Lee and Kathy Boger have three children: twenty-year-old Natalie, sixteen-year-old Mariah and seventeen-year-old David (who they adopted from Romania in 1999). They currently reside in Kokomo, Indiana. Lee works as an engineer for a large industrial company and has a consulting business.

Lee's first book, *But What About The Children?* reveals a dream in God's heart that goes beyond food, clothing and shelter, beyond sports, video games and school, even beyond the traditional bedtime prayer and a once-a-week Sunday school class. It tells the story of how God dreams of seeing his people raise spiritual children from their own vibrant, life-changing walk with the creator of the Universe.

Illumination Publishers International
www.ipibooks.com
6010 Pinecreek Ridge Court
Spring, Texas 77379-2513

Acknowledgements

I cannot write an acknowledgement section for a book on anger without acknowledging that I have anger issues. God reminded me of that fact, typically, on the same day that I finished each chapter. My personality is generally even-keeled and patient, and not easily rattled. My emotions tend to be very steady, not too excited or too depressed. Most people who know me would not think of me as an angry person. The problem with that perception is that it is wrong. I tend to stuff emotions and not display the frustrations or irritations of the day, but the anger is still there. More often than not, it is displayed through passive-aggressive actions such as withdrawal, silence and avoiding conflict, because those responses are easier for me. Reality shows that this reaction is just as destructive, even if objects are not thrown and broken.

I want to thank my friend, Steve Cannon, for his encouragement to finish this book. After a men's midweek service where we broke up into smaller groups for confessions and prayers, Steve commented to me, "Bro, you've got to finish that book. The whole church is angry!"

This book could not have been written without the cooperation and insight from my wife, Kathy, and our three children, Natalie, David, and Mariah. They helped me see my own anger, when my voice became firm or had a higher volume, when my eyes glared, and when my emotions were raw and I became frustrated. God revealed my anger through irritations, frustrations, and circumstances where personal hurt, lack of control, and fatigue fueled my angry responses to life events and people. I never would have made the connections described in this book if not for my family and their help.

Table of Contents

	Acknowledgements	3
	Introduction	7
Chapter 1	Man's Anger	8
Chapter 2	Am I Angry?	17
Chapter 3	Is my Anger Distorted?	33
Chapter 4	God's Anger	41
Chapter 5	God's Anger—Always Justified	47
Chapter 6	God's Anger—Doesn't Show Favoritism	56
Chapter 7	God's Anger—Slow to Develop	64
Chapter 8	God's Anger—Temporary	74
Chapter 9	God's Anger—Often Restrained	79
Chapter 10	God's Anger—Neutralized by Our Repentance	87
Chapter 11	God's Anger—Has a Purpose	98
Chapter 12	God's Anger—Influenced by Prayer	103
Chapter 13	Jesus—God's Anger Walked on the Earth	112

Table of Contents

Chapter 14	Angry Men of God: Naaman—My Way	122
Chapter 15	Angry Men of God: Moses—Double-Edge Sword	126
Chapter 16	Angry Men of God: Job—Angry with God	140
Chapter 17	Angry Men of God: Samson—It's Their Problem	150
Chapter 18	Angry Men of God: Saul—Unresolved	155
Chapter 19	Angry Men of God: David—Passionate	164
Chapter 20	Angry Men of God: Jeremiah—Life's Hard	172
Chapter 21	Angry Men of God: Jonah—They deserve it	182
Chapter 22	Angry Men of God: Nehemiah—It's Personal	187
Chapter 23	Angry Men of God: The Twelve—Pretentious	193
Chapter 24	Someone's Angry With Me	205
Chapter 25	Children's Anger	221
	Epilogue	235
	End Notes	236

Introduction

"A man that does not know how to be angry does not know how to be good."

—Henry Ward Beecher

When I first mentioned the idea of writing a book on anger, a friend of mine asked me what I would title it. When I said, "But What About Your Anger?" he responded, "Well, what about it?" Even though we laughed as we reflected on his comment and the intended sarcasm, it does reinforce the premise that everyone has anger. We experience it more often than we think.

When I observed frequent conflicts within my own family, characterized by increased irritation, frustration, arguments, and occasionally raised voices, I knew there were anger issues that needed to be addressed. The patterns were cyclical with subtle disrespect and some of our discussions were really arguments with unresolved feelings. After reading Stephen Bly's book, *The Surprising Side of Grace, Appreciating God's Loving Anger*, I was drawn to how God's anger is appropriate, yet controlled. It is slow to develop, it has a purpose, and it changes with repentance. I knew that I needed to imitate this characteristic of God, and decided to read everything I could about anger through the Bible and counseling books. Over a period of three years, I read through the entire Bible, taking notes on God's anger, man's anger, and the multiple lessons learned through God's interaction with godly, but angry leaders. During that same time, I read ten books with insight from counselors about how to handle anger in a healthy way through our interaction with people, especially for parents in dealing with their children's anger.

What I learned changed my view of God, my own anger management, and my parenting. It has allowed me to be more self-controlled, better at communicating, and less emotionally charged to everyday irritations and frustrations. God designed us to have the capacity to experience anger, and how we handle it determines whether it brings about change, or more hurt and damage.

My hope and prayer is that through the Scriptures and these counselors' advice, you will not only learn to handle your own anger in a healthy way and parent your children to manage their anger better, but you will also become familiar with and be able to imitate God's anger. God's anger is different than the anger you see in people, and it actually creates more desire and respect for the God who created you. His love comes from a plan to fulfill your dreams and provide blessings for you, a desire to be close to you and share everything, and a willingness to protect you from the devastating consequences of sin. God's anger is necessary to accomplish all of this for you. It is not something to dread, but to embrace, because the heart behind it is good.

CHAPTER ONE

Man's Anger

Holding on to anger is like grasping a hot coal with the intent of throwing it at someone else; you are the one who gets burned.

—Buddha

Anger in Buddhism is defined as "being unable to bear the object, or the intention to cause harm to the object." Anger is viewed as an aversion with stronger exaggeration. Buddhist monks, such as the Dalai Lama, spiritual leader of Tibetans in exile, sometimes get angry. The Dalai Lama once said, "When reason ends, then anger begins. Therefore, anger is a sign of weakness." He was asked the question "Is any anger acceptable in Buddhism?" He answered in this way:

> "Buddhism in general teaches that anger is a destructive emotion and although anger might have some positive effects in terms of survival or moral outrage, I do not accept anger of any kind as a virtuous emotion nor aggression as constructive behavior."[1]

Author and Buddhist practitioner Allan Wallace clarified this perspective:

> "This does not mean that one should never take action against aggression or injustice! Instead, one should try to develop an inner calmness and insight to deal with these situations in an appropriate way. We all know that anger and aggression give rise to anger and aggression. One could say that there are three ways to get rid of anger: kill the opponent, kill yourself or kill the anger - which one makes most sense to you?"[2]

—B. Alan Wallace

In Islam, Muhammad is attributed to have said, "Power resides not in being able to strike another, but in being able to keep the self under control when anger arises."[3]

> "There is not in nature, a thing that makes man so deformed, so beastly, as doth intemperate anger."

—John Webster

You don't have to go very far in the Bible to address the topic of man's anger. It has been an issue ever since God created man. In fact, God only had to create four people in order to see anger surface as an everyday issue in their lives:

> In the course of time Cain brought some of the fruits of the soil as an offering to the LORD. And Abel also brought an offering—fat portions from some of the firstborn of his flock. The LORD looked with favor on Abel and his offering, but on Cain and his offering he did not look with favor. So Cain was very angry, and his face was downcast. Then the LORD said to Cain, "Why are you angry? Why is your face downcast? If you do what is right, will you not be accepted? But if you do not do what is right, sin is crouching at your door; it desires to have you, but you must rule over it." (Genesis 4:3-7)

Have you ever been disappointed when your efforts didn't produce the results you wanted? Ever feel like you'll never overcome your weaknesses? Ever become frustrated when your best intentions achieve the exact opposite effect? Here are a few examples:

- Having a family devotional that ends in an argument
- Making special time with your spouse that ends up hurting each other
- Knocking on a door that you thought God was opening, only to find out it's closed
- Realizing God just added two more responsibilities to your life when you were already feeling overwhelmed

We can all relate to these scenarios, to which we often respond with disappointment, confusion, and even anger. With this all too familiar story in Genesis, how would you respond to Cain, when he didn't like your reaction to his offering? It could be, "I noticed you seemed sad about the offering, what are you feeling?" or, "I know you don't agree with my decision, but that's the way it is" Or, "Do you want to talk?" Do we even pay attention to the response of our closest loved ones when something happens? Our spouse, children and friends have these same feelings and reactions to life events and need our help to process those emotions appropriately. Sometimes similar events happen to us and nobody sees them. Nobody knows. Nobody seems to care.

When God saw Cain, he did care. He did notice, which is why he asked, "Why are you [Cain] angry? Why is your face downcast?" God quickly identified the emotion from what he saw in Cain's face, body language or posture, but especially his heart. Since we can't "see" the heart, sometimes we're not very good at discerning it, so we have to ask, "What's wrong?" This is a good start. God did not need to ask, "Are you angry?" or "Are you sad?" He knew what the emotions were, but he was more interested in Cain being open and admitting

<u>why</u> he was angry and sad. God probably already knew why, but Cain wouldn't find healing and resolution to his feelings unless he talked about them and got help. God reassured Cain, which indicates that God knew Cain was feeling insecure. Maybe Cain thought he would never be accepted, or felt too hurt to ever forgive. It's interesting to me that Cain's downcast face would be coupled with anger.

Gary Chapman in his book, *Anger–Handling a Powerful Emotion in a Healthy Way*, talks about the source of our anger and how to deal with it in a healthy way:

> "We don't sit down and say, 'I think I will now experience anger.' Anger is a response to some event or situation in life that causes us irritation, frustration, pain, or other displeasure... Anger is fed by feelings of disappointment, hurt, rejection, and embarrassment. Anger pits you against the person, place, or thing that sparked the emotion. It is the opposite of the feeling of love. Love draws you toward the person; anger sets you against the person."[4]

Gary makes a great point that anger is a response. One example of distorted anger was when Naaman wanted to be healed of his leprosy, and had the King of Aram send a letter to the King of Israel. Naaman's servant girl had suggested that a prophet in Samaria, who was Elisha, could heal his leprosy:

> The letter that he took to the king of Israel read: "With this letter I am sending my servant Naaman to you so that you may cure him of his leprosy."
> As soon as the king of Israel read the letter, he tore his robes and said, "Am I God? Can I kill and bring back to life? Why does this fellow send someone to me to be cured of his leprosy? See how he is trying to pick a quarrel with me!" (2 Kings 5:6-7)

Instead of asking the King of Aram for clarification, the King of Israel assumed he was supposed to heal Naaman directly. Knowing this would be impossible, he concluded that the King of Aram was picking a fight with him. Both assumptions were wrong, and so his anger was triggered. Maybe he had prior conflicts or negative attitudes toward the King of Aram, and so assumed he wanted to pick a fight. We do the same thing when we simply react to a life event or someone's question without clarifying details, or the person's tone or motive. We react first before listening, or we shut down, withdraw, and avoid responding, because of the past. Often our anger is a reaction, rather than a response that's based on accurate and complete information.

Consider Jacob's response when Laban accused him of stealing his household gods:

> Jacob answered Laban, "I was afraid, because I thought you would take your daughters away from me by force. But if you find anyone who has your gods, that person shall not live. In the presence of our relatives, see for yourself

whether there is anything of yours here with me; and if so, take it." Now Jacob did not know that Rachel had stolen the gods.

So Laban went into Jacob's tent and into Leah's tent and into the tent of the two female servants, but he found nothing. After he came out of Leah's tent, he entered Rachel's tent. Now Rachel had taken the household gods and put them inside her camel's saddle and was sitting on them. Laban searched through everything in the tent but found nothing.

Rachel said to her father, "Don't be angry, my lord, that I cannot stand up in your presence; I'm having my period." So he searched but could not find the household gods. Laban searched through everything in the tent but found nothing.

Jacob was angry and took Laban to task. "What is my crime?" he asked Laban. "How have I wronged you that you hunt me down? Now that you have searched through all my goods, what have you found that belongs to your household? Put it here in front of your relatives and mine, and let them judge between the two of us." (Genesis 31:31-37)

Jacob responded with anger because he knew the accusations were false, and that he was innocent. He didn't know that Rachel had stolen the gods, so the accusations were true. Emotions are not truth, and sometimes even your knowledge of a situation may not be the whole truth.

Consider Potiphar's response when he heard his wife's story:

She kept his cloak beside her until his master came home. Then she told him this story: "That Hebrew slave you brought us came to me to make sport of me. But as soon as I screamed for help, he left his cloak beside me and ran out of the house."

When his master heard the story his wife told him, saying, "This is how your slave treated me," he burned with anger. Joseph's master took him and put him in prison, the place where the king's prisoners were confined. (Genesis 39:16-20)

Potiphar didn't question Joseph, and he seemed oblivious to his wife seducing Joseph over a period of time. Usually there are plenty of signs to indicate that something isn't right in such a situation. How many times did Joseph quickly leave a room when he was alone with Potiphar's wife? How many times did his wife's eyes follow Joseph?

Gary Chapman describes anger as part of God's design. You were created to have the capacity to get angry.

"The human capacity for anger is rooted in the nature of God and is a reflection of his holiness, his love for people and his concern for justice and righteousness. We have that within us since we are made in his image. Our anger comes from a sense of morality or moral concern for right and wrong. When handled properly and in a healthy way, it can bring about good. Human anger is designed by God to motivate us to take constructive or positive action in the face of wrongdoing or when facing an injustice."⁵

Think about the social reforms that have occurred because someone got angry: Mothers Against Drunk Driving (MADD) have caused penalties to be more stringent; the slave trade in England was abolished in the early 1800s; slavery in United States was changed even though it sparked a Civil War; even the racial injustices from the 1960s and prior were greatly alleviated. Without anger, or when one ceases to experience anger, one has lost a sense of moral concern.

> "The world needs anger. The world often continues to allow evil because it isn't angry enough."
> —Bede Jarrett

> "Usually when people are sad, they don't do anything. They just cry over their condition. But when they get angry, they bring about a change."
> —James Russell Lowell

Each of us experiences anger every day. It may not be a fit of rage with objects being thrown, but it can be a lower level of frustration or irritation that is still anger. You may not be yelling in response, but it is still anger. Sometimes you may view your feelings as a progression, such as irritation, then frustration, then anger, then a fit of rage or yelling; but these are all anger, with your response becoming more negative or more distorted about the object of your anger. Remember the Incredible Hulk? The more anger he felt, the stronger he became. His famous quote was, "Don't make me angry. You wouldn't like me when I'm angry." That's true for all of us. The damage usually includes people and sometimes objects. Once your anger takes over, you can't control the effects, just like the Incredible Hulk.

Remember King Herod?

> When Herod realized that he had been outwitted by the Magi, he was furious, and he gave orders to kill all the boys in Bethlehem and its vicinity who were two years old and under, in accordance with the time he had learned from the Magi. (Matthew 2:16)

In his book, *Make Anger Your Ally*, author Neil Clark Warren defines anger:

> "Anger is a physical state of readiness. When we are angry, we are prepared to act... The whole purpose of anger is to give us the wherewithal for managing our environment—particularly those parts which cause us to feel hurt, frustrated, or fearful. If we do that poorly, we will regularly experience a sense of inadequacy and helplessness."⁶

> "We express our anger to manage those internal and external sources of hurt, frustration, and threat and keep inner pain to an absolute minimum."[7]

Another view describes anger as a physical response, when blood pressure rises and the adrenaline starts pumping:

> "Physiologically, it simply doesn't matter whether your anger is justified or not. The body doesn't make moral judgments about feelings; it just responds."
> —Doc Childre and Howard Martin, *HeartMath Solution*

Anger can also be seen as withdrawal or becoming sullen (gloomily or resentfully silent or repressed). That response is also triggered by anger, and can lead to depression or, in the long term, suicide. Not all anger shows itself through an outward response. Sometimes it is an inward response that can't be seen right away, but may come out later. Cain's situation is one example of such a delayed reaction, because he didn't respond to God's question, "Why are you angry?" He calmly spoke to his brother Abel, but then his emotion came out all at once in violence.

God challenged Cain and expected him to master his anger. God didn't accept excuses or allow Cain to be angry because he had a long day. Maybe Cain had an argument with his mom earlier in the day, or worked hard all day in the hot sun to prepare the offering. Either way, God tested Cain to see how he would respond. It's not that much different for us. You may or may not know the reason why you've been a little sensitive lately or on edge, but God still expects you to master your anger. The direction he gave Cain was to talk about it and express why he was feeling that way. Do you express yourself this way when you're irritated, frustrated, or angry? Is there someone in your life whom you trust to confide these feelings? Close relationships are not only essential, but critical for you in order to process your anger in a healthy way. Stuffing those feelings doesn't work. God warns us that giving full vent to them doesn't work either:

> "Fools give full vent to their rage, but the wise bring calm in the end." (Proverbs 29:11)

> "A fool gives full vent to his anger, but a wise man keeps himself under control." (NLT)

That calmness and self-control can only come when you get someone else's perspective and wisdom about your situation and your reaction. Sometimes that different point of view may come from God himself, through the Scriptures or the Holy Spirit. Without that view, you'll be left to your own habitual pattern of dealing with intense emotions. Sometimes calm comes from a good night's sleep, but not before you have "killed", or at least wounded, your own brother, child, spouse, co-worker, or friend with your words, tone of voice, glare, or even physical abuse. You may feel better and apologize in the morning, but the damage has already been done. Usually even a good night's sleep doesn't bring about healing; it just allows the emotions to subside. Whatever triggered the anger will probably be triggered again, because you don't have any new perspective about the perceived injustice to your life. Gary Chapman summarizes it best:

> "Much of our anger grows out of internal emotional and thinking patterns that have developed through the years."[8]

Let's look at how Cain responded:

> Now Cain said to his brother Abel, 'Let's go out to the field.' While they were in the field, Cain attacked his brother Abel and killed him.
> Then the LORD said to Cain, 'Where is your brother Abel?' '
> I don't know,' he replied. 'Am I my brother's keeper?'
> The LORD said, 'What have you done? Listen! Your brother's blood cries out to me from the ground. Now you are under a curse and driven from the ground, which opened its mouth to receive your brother's blood from your hand. When you work the ground, it will no longer yield its crops for you. You will be a restless wanderer on the earth.' (Genesis 4:8-12)

What was the object of Cain's anger? He probably perceived Abel as the object or cause of his anger, so he killed him. Abel was the perceived cause of everything that had gone wrong for Cain, but that's a distorted view. Cain's anger started when he didn't experience what he felt was fair or right when he made his offering. It was really between him and God, but Cain quickly lost that perspective.

> Cain said to the LORD, 'My punishment is more than I can bear. Today you are driving me from the land, and I will be hidden from your presence; I will be a restless wanderer on the earth, and whoever finds me will kill me.'
> But the LORD said to him, 'Not so; anyone who kills Cain will suffer vengeance seven times over.' Then the LORD put a mark on Cain so that no one who found him would kill him. So Cain went out from the LORD's presence and lived in the land of Nod, east of Eden. (Genesis 4:13-15)

Cain didn't even admit to God that he was really angry. That should always be the first step. Sometimes denial is our first step. We think that we are only irritated or frustrated, not angry, because we're not throwing things, or slamming doors, or raising our voices. We even deny that to ourselves when other people have noticed an uptick in volume.

In the movie "Exit Wounds," Steven Seagal's character is forced to go to an anger management class for his lack of discipline, where he's asked to introduce himself to the class and share his struggle with anger. As he rises to get out of his school classroom chair, he gets stuck and breaks the chair into several pieces to free himself. Composing himself, he states without smiling, "I'd like to make something very clear: I don't have rage. I'm a happy guy. You see this face? This is a happy face. You'll be lucky to be as happy as I am."

In the long run, our anger, even if it's coming from a passionate heart that's trying to instill justice doesn't produce the godly life we've been created to have:

> My dear brothers and sisters, take note of this: Everyone should be quick to listen, slow to speak and slow to become angry, because human anger does not produce the righteousness that God desires. (James 1:19-20)

As justified as your anger feels at the moment, unless you control it in a healthy way, it will not make you more righteous. It just doesn't. It didn't produce it in Cain, either. This may seem like a contradiction if God has created us to have the capacity to experience anger, yet James tells us that it doesn't produce the godly life God wants for us. The key to understanding it is realizing that God expected Cain to "master it." To be able to take the appropriate action with a calm and self-controlled approach is not easy, but one of the keys to mastering your angry emotions is to determine the appropriate object of your anger. Mastering your anger allows you to be more holy and your prayers to be more effective.

> Therefore I want the men everywhere to pray, lifting up holy hands without anger or disputing. (1 Timothy 2:8)

If you're tempted to think that some of your anger is "righteous indignation", because your perspective concludes that your anger is definitive, then consider the following passage:

> The acts of the flesh are obvious: sexual immorality, impurity and debauchery; idolatry and witchcraft; hatred, discord, jealousy, fits of rage, selfish ambition, dissensions, factions and envy; drunkenness, orgies, and the like. I warn you, as I did before, that those who live like this will not inherit the kingdom of God.
> But the fruit of the Spirit is love, joy, peace, forbearance, kindness, goodness, faithfulness, gentleness and self-control. Against such things there is no law. (Galatians 5:19-23)

Notice that "fits of rage" is listed as a sin, but "righteous indignation" is not listed as a fruit of the Spirit. Even if your anger is definitive, it's easy to not have self-control in an angry response. God places a high value on controlling anger and cautions us to not be hot-tempered. This control is a qualification for being an elder:

> Since an overseer manages God's household, he must be blameless— not overbearing, not quick-tempered, not given to drunkenness, not violent, not pursuing dishonest gain. Rather, he must be hospitable, one who loves what is good, who is self-controlled, upright, holy and disciplined. (Titus 1:7-8)
>
> An angry person stirs up conflict, and a hot-tempered person commits many sins. (Proverbs 29:22)
>
> Do not make friends with a hot-tempered person, do not associate with one easily angered, or you may learn their ways and get yourself ensnared. (Proverbs 22:24-25)
>
> A hot-tempered person must pay the penalty; rescue them, and you will have to do it again. (Proverbs 19:19)

Sometimes anger looks like passion, so leaders with drive and zeal for change are highly valued in the workplace. Controlled anger can be useful in the military and physical contact sports, but keep in mind God's perspective and values. They are often times quite different than ours. Consider Proverbs 16:32 from different translations:

> Better a patient person than a warrior, one with self-control than one who takes a city. (NIV 2011)
>
> Better a patient man than a warrior, a man who controls his temper than one who takes a city. (NIV 1984)
>
> He who is slow to anger is better than the mighty, And he who rules his spirit than he who takes a city. (NKJV)

God views controlling your anger as better than if you led a military campaign and captured an entire city. Self-control is valued more and accomplishes more for God and his purposes.

CHAPTER TWO

Am I Angry?

> *My uncle Sammy was an angry man. He had printed on his tombstone: What are you looking at?*
>
> —Margaret Smith

A national study of 1,800 Americans aged 18 and older questioned participants on how and when they feel angry, in order to build "a broader social portrait of anger in the United States," said study researcher Scott Schieman. The results of the 2005 survey showed several interesting trends:

- People under 30 experienced anger of all forms or intensities more frequently than older adults. This was mainly due to the fact that young people are more likely to be affected by three core "triggers."

    1. Trigger—Time pressures had the strongest link to anger, especially low-grade versions termed "feelings of annoyance"

    2. Trigger—Economic hardships showed higher levels of anger, particularly among women and younger adults

    3. Trigger—Interpersonal conflict at the workplace

- Having children was also associated with angry feelings and behaviors, particularly in women who frequently deal with discipline and the emotional well-being of the children.
- Those with fewer years of education were also more likely to report feelings of anger, and were less likely to respond proactively in a situation that made them angry. Schieman said, "Education has been linked to feeling more self-control, which could be why those with more education tend to manage their anger more proactively."

There are many triggers to anger, and yours could be completely different than the ones identified in this study. Identifying that you are angry is the first step in dealing with it. In the introduction to Adelaide Bry's book *How to Get Angry Without Feeling Guilty*, clinical psychologist Vivien Wolsk says:

> "It is, in fact, when we don't acknowledge and respect our anger that we

are most likely to express it in inappropriate or damaging ways."⁹

When you think about how our calm and perfect world in the womb gets shattered during the birthing process, you realize that we have to confront frustration and anger from day one! In her book, Adelaide Bry cites a French obstetrician, Frederick Leboyer, who believes that what happens at birth may influence the individual's future emotional well-being.

> "Instead of the abrupt, traumatic exit from the womb into the harshly lit noise and confusion of the ordinary modern-day hospital delivery room, the hasty snipping of the umbilical cord...and the sharp smack on the behind... Leboyer eases the baby's way from womb to world. The delivery area is kept semi-dark, shadowy and silent. The newborn is placed on its mother's stomach, umbilical cord intact and lovingly massaged for five minutes or so, after which the cord is severed and the baby is placed tenderly into a small tub of warm water."¹⁰

The jury is still out on whether this new birthing technique will help people manage their anger, but it does remind me that these emotions get stirred on our first day into this world. Anger and our response to it can take on many different faces. It's easy to identify anger when someone is yelling with a mean looking face, but anger can also be the cause of someone's hurt and withdrawal. Some of us don't like talking about our anger because we view it as wrong, inappropriate, or destructive. Anger can fit all these descriptions if mismanaged and handled in an unhealthy way. But anger can also be a positive force for change, and for stronger and closer relationships, as well as for feelings of more confidence and security.

Some different expressions of anger are as follow: frustration, irritability, annoyance, fretting, withdrawal, grudges, resentment, bitterness, impatience, defensiveness, speech that is stern or insensitive, slander, discouragement, sarcasm, and depression. Anger is also seen through a person blowing off steam, using a persuasive tone of voice, and blaming others.

Let's look at a King of Israel named Ahab and how his anger affected him. In one incident, God showed Ahab his sin:

> The next spring Ben-Hadad mustered the Arameans and went up to Aphek to fight against Israel. When the Israelites were also mustered and given provisions, they marched out to meet them. The Israelites camped opposite them like two small flocks of goats, while the Arameans covered the countryside.
> The man of God came up and told the king of Israel, "This is what the LORD says: 'Because the Arameans think the LORD is a god of the hills and not a god of the valleys, I will deliver this vast army into your hands, and you will know that I am the LORD.'"
> For seven days they camped opposite each other, and on the seventh day the battle was joined. The Israelites inflicted a hundred thousand casualties on the Aramean foot soldiers in one day. The rest of them escaped to the city of Aphek, where the wall collapsed on twenty-seven thousand of them. And

> Ben-Hadad fled to the city and hid in an inner room.
> When Ben-Hadad came out, Ahab had him come up into his chariot.
> "I will return the cities my father took from your father," Ben-Hadad offered. "You may set up your own market areas in Damascus, as my father did in Samaria."
> Ahab said, "On the basis of a treaty I will set you free." So he made a treaty with him, and let him go.
> "...This is what the LORD says: 'You have set free a man I had determined should die. Therefore it is your life for his life, your people for his people.'" Sullen and angry, the king of Israel went to his palace in Samaria. (1 Kings 20:26-30, 33b-34, 42-43)

In this case, Ahab was angry, but he became sullen instead of killing someone. In his mind, an injustice had been committed against him. Maybe he felt God was being unfair to him, or he didn't agree that he had sinned. It look as if Ben-Hadad was trying to make amends with Ahab, based on something his father had done, so it was a win-win scenario for everyone—everyone except God. He had determined that Ben-Hadad was to die. God overruled Ahab and Ahab didn't like it.

In a second situation, Ahab couldn't get what he wanted:

> Sometime later there was an incident involving a vineyard belonging to Naboth the Jezreelite. The vineyard was in Jezreel, close to the palace of Ahab king of Samaria. Ahab said to Naboth, "Let me have your vineyard to use for a vegetable garden, since it is close to my palace. In exchange I will give you a better vineyard or, if you prefer, I will pay you whatever it is worth."
> But Naboth replied, "The LORD forbid that I should give you the inheritance of my fathers."
> So Ahab went home, sullen and angry because Naboth the Jezreelite had said, "I will not give you the inheritance of my fathers." He lay on his bed sulking and refused to eat. (1 Kings 21:1-4)

Ahab sulked again and even refused to eat. Maybe it wasn't very pleasant to be around him, but he was probably withdrawn and depressed. In his mind, an injustice had been committed against him. He was being fair, even offering to pay for the vineyard. He wasn't trying to steal it or cheat Naboth. Yet when he couldn't get it, he was angry, and responded more like a preschool kid who couldn't play with his friend, or didn't get the toy he really wanted for his birthday.

The prophet Ezekiel was angry when God called him to preach to the exiles in Babylon:

> He then said to me: "Son of man, go now to the people of Israel and speak my words to them. You are not being sent to a people of obscure speech and strange language, but to the people of Israel—not to many peoples of obscure speech and strange language, whose words you cannot understand. Surely if I

had sent you to them, they would have listened to you. But the people of Israel are not willing to listen to you because they are not willing to listen to me, for all the Israelites are hardened and obstinate. But I will make you as unyielding and hardened as they are. I will make your forehead like the hardest stone, harder than flint. Do not be afraid of them or terrified by them, though they are a rebellious people."

And he said to me, "Son of man, listen carefully and take to heart all the words I speak to you. Go now to your people in exile and speak to them. Say to them, 'This is what the Sovereign LORD says,' whether they listen or fail to listen."

Then the Spirit lifted me up, and I heard behind me a loud rumbling sound as the glory of the LORD rose from the place where it was standing. It was the sound of the wings of the living creatures brushing against each other and the sound of the wheels beside them, a loud rumbling sound. The Spirit then lifted me up and took me away, and I went in bitterness and in the anger of my spirit, with the strong hand of the LORD on me. I came to the exiles who lived at Tel Aviv near the Kebar River. And there, where they were living, I sat among them for seven days—deeply distressed. (Ezekiel 3:4-15)

Ezekiel's anger led him to be bitter and deeply distressed. Remember, anger isn't just yelling or slamming doors. Let's take a look at the many faces of anger, because identifying anger is the first step toward healing and managing that anger in a healthy, constructive way.

In her book, Adelaide Bry describes twelve different types of people and how they handle their anger. As you read my summary of each one, think about which one most closely describes you or your tendencies in how you handle your own anger and frustrations.

The Actor—creates scenes using the body to dramatize anger. Feels a sense of accomplishment because something has been done, feels relief when it's over. Anger usually takes the form of crying, slamming or throwing things, having a physical release, pointing a finger. Very quick to display and dramatize feelings. First impulse is to do something and feels okay expressing anger this way, while others regret this childishness or damage done to others or to property. These actions frighten some people or cause them anger and lingering negative attitudes toward the actor.

The Big Talker—gets immediate physical and emotional release through verbal explosions. Processes anger as it occurs, usually verbally to whoever will listen, or to the object of their anger, whether or not it's appropriate. Other people are alienated and communication breaks down. Some Big Talkers will repeat the episode several times while others explode only once and forget it.

Author Gary Chapman describes this type of anger as *explosive* anger, which is characterized by slamming doors, throwing objects, or raising the volume of one's voice. He describes the effect:

"Explosive, angry behavior is never constructive. It not only hurts the person at whom it is directed, it destroys the self-esteem of the person who is out of control. No one can feel good about themselves when they think about what they have done. In the heat of such angry explosions, people say and do things they later regret. Undisciplined anger that expresses itself in verbal and physical explosions will ultimately destroy relationships. The person on the receiving end loses respect for the person who is out of control and will eventually just avoid them."[11]

In their book *The Anger Workbook*, authors Les Carter and Frank Minirth call this angry response open aggression and clarify it with an explanation as to its cause:

> "Open Aggression—includes explosiveness, rage, blame, intimidation, bickering, criticism, griping and sarcasm. It's a self-preserving stand at someone else's expense. It's a focus that so strongly emphasizes personal needs that there is a powerful insensitivity to the needs of others. Two major explanations: (a) emotional energy is expended on nonessentials, which are trivial imperfections or problems that simply won't go away and that we cannot live with. People are different and we cannot force them into our mold. It's hard to accept these facts emotionally in a way that keeps us composed. (b) deep insecurity causes increased efforts to be heard. Their emotional stability hangs by a thread, dependent upon others' cooperation to respect them and their needs."[12]

The Blamer—blames anger on someone else or on the circumstances, and will not accept responsibility for own angry response. Has the view that the other person "made me" do it or say it. The Blamer often uses the term "if only" to qualify how better life would be if the other person would simply change, or would have reacted differently in the past.

The Body Person—desperately wants to maintain a good, sweet, kind and lovable self-image, so cannot accept any angry feelings; creates psychosomatic symptoms that play out as real physical ailments, such as headaches, rashes, diarrhea, constipation, asthma, etc. The "fight or flight" mechanism in our bodies that causes adrenaline secretion and raising of blood pressure and heart rate when we are fearful or angry, can cause common illnesses when we suppress strong emotions because we think they are inherently wrong. The physiochemical reactions are real as the mind-body war that ensues.

The Comedian—manages to deflect the anger and pain felt at viewing life's inequities, converting them instead into wisecracks, satiric anecdotes, puns, clever retorts, and jokes. These statements are used to spar and sting the object of anger with humor. Animated talk keeps things lively and fun, but if questioned about the underlying anger or bitterness, the comedian challenges that person's ability to take a joke.

Sarcasm can be expressed as a form of humor, but it can also hurt. The prophet Elijah used it as an instrument of truth when he mocked the priests of Baal (1 Kings 18:27). Jesus addressed the Pharisees' focus on the law rather than the heart (Matthew 23:24). Cain used sarcasm to justify himself (Genesis

4:9). If you study sarcasm throughout the Bible, it's never used against the weak, timid or humble. It's never unleashed upon a child. Rather, it was used against people who were stubborn, self-righteous or arrogant.

Sarcasm often hides undisclosed anger, annoyance or even jealousy. It provides someone the dishonest opportunity to wound without looking like they are wounding. Later, they can fall back on the age-old cop-out, "I didn't mean it. Can't you take a joke?" For those who are quick-witted and proficient at sarcasm, it can be used as a form of bullying. Sarcasm must be used with great skill and careful thought or people get hurt. Some people do not have this skill, so they should not use sarcasm at all. Sharp words, even when said with a smile, can still leave a wound. Remember, it's only funny when both people are laughing.

The Corner Person—learned at an early age that expressing anger was bad and suffered punishment for it; therefore, as an adult, "hides in a corner" or finds some quiet environment of solitude to avoid confrontation, guilt, and increased feelings of being a bad person. Has a hard time accepting anger, handling conflict or even differences of opinion. Sometimes sulks, or stifles ideas or feelings to comply with the other person. Sometimes turn to drugs or alcohol, unable to confront anger and feelings of worthlessness and self-hate that go along with it.

The Creator—needs an outlet for anger and sometimes welcomes a fight or looks for an excuse to let off some steam. Has a large amount of generalized or "free floating" anger. The tension of that anger is present all of the time and it is regularly unloaded. If everything is going well for too long, the Creator begins to feel uncomfortable, and begins to look for a fight or something to which the anger can be directed, unaware of the effect on others. Usually started as a youngster full of constant anxiety due to frequent moves, divorce, financial problems, or abandonment. The Creator can also be a young mother who constantly gives and has no outlet for her anger. She can work herself into a frenzy before a conversation begins, because she "creates" the negative response she anticipates receiving.

The Daydreamer—releases anger through imagined fantasies and plays out all the scenarios with whatever situation or person made them angry. Usually wins in these mind games, but the process is also therapeutic, because the anger can be processed in a safe environment, and the Daydreamer leaves those moments feeling better, relieved, and vindicated. Sometimes these thoughts can come from unrecognized anger which can be troubling. These negative images and role-playing can frighten some people until they connect with the suppressed anger. Sometimes the Daydreamer confuses the anger issue with reality, convinced that the real issue is resolved when, in fact, it's only resolved in the daydreamer's mind. This can lead to escape from the uncomfortable confrontation, preferring to deal with it only in a fantasy world.

The Doer—uses physical, strenuous activity as a good, healthy way to get rid of the poisons of accumulated anger. These physical actions do not provide "permanent" relief unless accompanied by some new insight and understanding. This is a healthy way to drain away the anger because it connects the angry emotion with the body, which is exactly how anger affects us. Your body reacts to the angry emotions and needs an outlet.

The Saboteur—is not conscious of anger and doesn't realize that habitual lateness, broken promises, broken objects, forgetfulness, or apathy are actually anger or resentment, which causes other people discomfort or anger. Everyone experiences anger this way occasionally, but the Saboteur has a chronic problem with a sincere apology and a promise to do better. Doesn't feel responsible for the behavior and quickly blames circumstances or explains, "I'm just that way." Sabotage is a sneaky way to get the anger message across.

The Sexed-Up Angry Couple—sometimes resolve their anger toward each other with an aggressive, sexual time together, but anger remnants usually remain.

The Stuffer—may be aware of anger, but suppresses any outward expression, either verbally or physically, because it is viewed as bad and damaging to others, or as making one's own situation worse. Sometimes doesn't feel the right to express any negative emotion. Stuffing is a protective mechanism that keeps a person from being hurt. Sometimes the Stuffer is aware of anger, which is too dangerous to reveal, but many stuffers are not even aware that they are angry.

Authors Les Carter and Frank Minirth describe **The Stuffer**:

> "Suppression – people view all anger as bad or not moral, so they avoid it at all costs and will not admit to themselves that they are angry."[13]

The last type, **The Stuffer**, best represents my natural reaction to my own anger. Author Gary Chapman refers to this response as implosive anger.[14] Similar to imploding a building or structure, implosive anger destroys from within. It begins with silence or withdrawal, but leads to resentment, bitterness, and eventually hatred. It progresses in steps:

- **Denial**—Says or thinks, "I'm not angry, but I am frustrated" or "I'm just upset" or "I am disappointed" or "I just don't like it when _____". The anger will grow until denial is no longer an option.

- **Withdrawal**—Not in denial, but keeps distance and spends time away; then may display passive-aggressive behavior such as not cooperating, avoiding eye contact, or being disrespectful. Sometimes the anger is redirected toward another person or object (i.e., kicking the dog, or picking on a sibling or co-worker, or complaining about everything). My own thinking would be, "I don't want to be around this person", so I would minimize contact or look forward to time away.

- **Brooding**—Replays the situation over and over again, leading to bitterness, resentment or hatred. If left unresolved, brooding can also lead to depression, emotional breakdown, suicide, or an outward explosion triggered by a minor issue. Usually my brooding would create less patience for any issue with this person and I would be quickly provoked again.

Bitterness is destructive. There are many Scriptures that warn us about its effect:

> And do not grieve the Holy Spirit of God, with whom you were sealed for the day of redemption. Get rid of all bitterness, rage and anger, brawling and slander, along with every form of malice. Be kind and compassionate to one another, forgiving each other, just as in Christ God forgave you. (Ephesians 4:30-32)
>
> Do not hate a fellow Israelite in your heart. Rebuke your neighbor frankly so you will not share in their guilt. Do not seek revenge or bear a grudge against anyone among your people, but love your neighbor as yourself. I am the LORD. (Leviticus 19:17-18)
>
> Make every effort to live in peace with everyone and to be holy; without holiness no one will see the Lord. See to it that no one falls short of the grace of God and that no bitter root grows up to cause trouble and defile many. (Hebrews 12:14-15)

God clearly directs us to get rid of all bitterness; otherwise, we will grieve the Holy Spirit and the bitter root will cause trouble for a lot of people. Naomi said, "Call me Mara", which means bitter (Ruth 1:20-21), because of the hard life and tragic circumstances she had to endure by losing her husband, and then both her sons ten years later. Herod's wife "nursed a grudge against John the Baptist" (Mark 6:19-22) because he preached that her adultery was wrong. When she had the opportunity, she manipulated King Herod and had him killed.

Bitterness doesn't necessarily come from tragic circumstances or our lack of humility. It can also come because someone has hurt us, as in Joseph's response to his brothers, after forgetting about their hatred toward him and the fact that they sold him as a slave. Joseph had completely forgotten about his painful past and associated trials in prison. Pharaoh's blessings and a new life allowed him to adjust:

> Before the years of famine came, two sons were born to Joseph by Asenath daughter of Potiphera, priest of On. Joseph named his firstborn Manasseh (means to forget) and said, "It is because God has made me forget all my trouble and all my father's household." The second son he named Ephraim (means twice fruitful) and said, "It is because God has made me fruitful in the

land of my suffering." (Genesis 41:50-52)

Then he saw his brothers again, and the pain came back as fresh as the day he was sold as a slave:

> Now Joseph was the governor of the land, the person who sold grain to all its people. So when Joseph's brothers arrived, they bowed down to him with their faces to the ground. As soon as Joseph saw his brothers, he recognized them, but he pretended to be a stranger and spoke harshly to them. "Where do you come from?" he asked. "
> From the land of Canaan," they replied, "to buy food."
> Although Joseph recognized his brothers, they did not recognize him. Then he remembered his dreams about them and said to them, "You are spies! You have come to see where our land is unprotected." (Genesis 42:6-9)

Bitterness can also come from envy, as shown by Simon the Sorcerer (even after he became a Christian):

> When Simon saw that the Spirit was given at the laying on of the apostles' hands, he offered them money and said, "Give me also this ability so that everyone on whom I lay my hands may receive the Holy Spirit."
> Peter answered: "May your money perish with you, because you thought you could buy the gift of God with money! You have no part or share in this ministry, because your heart is not right before God. Repent of this wickedness and pray to the Lord in the hope that he may forgive you for having such a thought in your heart. For I see that you are full of bitterness and captive to sin." (Acts 8:18-23)

Even if we can't see our own bitterness, as in Simon's case, other people can see it and they can help us. The reason other people can see it is because we will talk about it. As Jesus says in Matthew 12:34, "For the mouth speaks what the heart is full of." Consider Esau's bitterness toward Jacob when he took both his birthright and his blessing:

> Esau held a grudge against Jacob because of the blessing his father had given him. He said to himself, "The days of mourning for my father are near; then I will kill my brother Jacob."
> When Rebekah was told what her older son Esau had said, she sent for her younger son Jacob and said to him, "Your brother Esau is planning to avenge himself by killing you. (Genesis 27:41-42)

If Esau said these bitter thoughts "to himself", then how did Rebekah hear about it? He obviously told someone during a meal or while working the fields. You just can't keep those angry, bitter thoughts and emotions to yourself.

Which angry person are you? You may have the tendency to be more than one. If you're married, which one is your spouse? It would be interesting to see if your choice agrees with your spouse's choice, and vice versa. It's important to understand how you deal with your own anger, but it also helps to know how the people close to you handle their anger. This information can provide you with insight that will give you more patience and direction in responding to them. In her book, Adelaide Bry discusses a more humanistic approach in dealing with these responses, and encourages the reader to understand his or her type, apply new ways to handle this type, and so grow in handling anger. She doesn't really offer a spiritual perspective.

Using a different approach, Gary Chapman talks about the steps necessary to deal with our anger, regardless of which type we are:[15]

1. **Consciously acknowledge to yourself that you are angry**—Acknowledgement sets the stage for applying reason to your anger. It may be an irritation or a little frustration, but it is anger nonetheless and it is okay to experience anger.

2. **Restrain your immediate response**—Restraint allows you to change your habit whether the response is a verbal and physical response or withdrawal and silence. Sometimes counting or taking a timeout allows you time to identify the cause of your anger. Taking a break to collect your thoughts helps engage your brain and respond instead of react. Ask yourself, "Do I have all the facts?"

3. **Locate the focus of your anger**—What specifically was said or done that made you angry? What's the injustice or perceived sin against you? A situation may remind you of an injustice from the past or something that happened earlier in the day, which is totally unrelated to the current situation. Then you should evaluate whether the offense is serious or small, which should affect your response. You could rate it from 1 to 10 with 10 being the most serious offense.

4. **Analyze your options**—Does the action I am considering have any potential for dealing with the wrong and helping the relationship? And is it best for the person at whom I am angry? The two most constructive options are either to confront the person in a helpful way, or to consciously decide to overlook the matter.

5. **Take constructive action**—If you choose to overlook the offense, confess your anger to God and release it to Him. If you choose to confront the person, then do so gently and listen carefully to any explanation and ask questions to clarify. It may give you a different perspective on the person's actions and intentions.

These steps work. They have allowed me to respond better and to change some old habits. People use different techniques to deal with anger. Some techniques were learned as children, while others were developed through years of experimenting, based on what was perceived as helpful. You may have heard that physical, aggressive behavior can be an appropriate outlet for your anger. Jim Messina, Ph.D. psychologist and co-founder of Coping.org says:

> "Constructive ways of letting your anger out include focused actions such as beating on a weight bag, using a hammer to hammer nails, breaking glass jars or other objects in sealed paper or cloth bags, beating on pillows or mattresses, yelling in an empty car or outside in a vacant lot or park or engaging in other activities conducive to contained emotional release."[16]

Gary Chapman talks about a different perspective:

> "Some years ago it was popular in certain psychological circles to believe that releasing anger by aggressive behavior could be a positive way of processing anger, if the aggression was not toward a person. Thus, angry people were encouraged to beat pillows, punching bags, and dolls, or to take their aggression out on a golf ball. However, almost all research now indicates that the venting of angry feelings with such aggressive behaviors does not drain a person's anger, but actually makes the person more likely to be explosive in the future."[17]

If you don't find ways to handle your anger appropriately, it doesn't take a PhD to know that it will produce more strife and damage to you and your family, neighbors, or co-workers. For example, if you stop and visualize someone who's angry and shouting, do you think raising his voice will help his communication or his situation? Probably not. In fact, a study conducted by the Speech Research unit at Kenyon College in Ohio found that when you shout at someone else, they literally can't help but shout back. This is true even when the "shoutee" couldn't see the "shouter", and even when the subjects being discussed were neutral[18].

Take a look at a few examples in Scriptures to see the effect of unresolved anger:

Consider again Ahab King of Israel...

> So Obadiah went to meet Ahab and told him, and Ahab went to meet Elijah. When he saw Elijah, he said to him, "Is that you, you troubler of Israel?" "I have not made trouble for Israel," Elijah replied. "But you and your father's family have. You have abandoned the LORD's commands and have followed the Baals. (1 Kings 18:16-18)

> Ahab said to Elijah, "So you have found me, my enemy!" "I have found you," he answered, "because you have sold yourself to do evil in the eyes of the LORD. (1 Kings 21:20)

> But Jehoshaphat asked, "Is there no longer a prophet of the LORD here

whom we can inquire of?"
> The king of Israel answered Jehoshaphat, "There is still one prophet through whom we can inquire of the LORD, but I hate him because he never prophesies anything good about me, but always bad. He is Micaiah son of Imlah." "The king should not say such a thing," Jehoshaphat replied. (1 Kings 22:7-8)

> When he arrived, the king asked him, "Micaiah, shall we go to war against Ramoth Gilead, or not?" "
> Attack and be victorious," he answered, "for the LORD will give it into the king's hand."
> The king said to him, "How many times must I make you swear to tell me nothing but the truth in the name of the LORD?"
> Then Micaiah answered, "I saw all Israel scattered on the hills like sheep without a shepherd, and the LORD said, 'These people have no master. Let each one go home in peace.'"
> The king of Israel said to Jehoshaphat, "Didn't I tell you that he never prophesies anything good about me, but only bad?" (1 Kings 22:15-18)

Ahab didn't resolve his anger, and he constantly had a negative attitude towards people, even godly people, because anger clouds spiritual perspective and will "give the devil a foothold" in life, as described in Ephesians 4:27.

Consider Asa King of Judah when he first became king…

> Asa did what was good and right in the eyes of the LORD his God. He removed the foreign altars and the high places, smashed the sacred stones and cut down the Asherah poles. He commanded Judah to seek the LORD, the God of their ancestors, and to obey his laws and commands…Then Asa called to the LORD his God and said, "LORD, there is no one like you to help the powerless against the mighty. Help us, LORD our God, for we rely on you, and in your name we have come against this vast army. LORD, you are our God; do not let mere mortals prevail against you." The LORD struck down the Cushites before Asa and Judah. (2 Chronicles 14:2-4, 11-12)

But 35 years later…

> At that time Hanani the seer came to Asa king of Judah and said to him: "Because you relied on the king of Aram and not on the LORD your God, the army of the king of Aram has escaped from your hand. Were not the Cushites and Libyans a mighty army with great numbers of chariots and horsemen? Yet when you relied on the LORD, he delivered them into your hand. For the eyes of the LORD range throughout the earth to strengthen those whose hearts are fully committed to him. You have done a foolish thing, and from now on you will be at war."
> Asa was angry with the seer because of this; he was so enraged that he put him in prison. At the same time Asa brutally oppressed some of the people. The

events of Asa's reign, from beginning to end, are written in the book of the kings of Judah and Israel. In the thirty-ninth year of his reign Asa was afflicted with a disease in his feet. Though his disease was severe, even in his illness he did not seek help from the LORD, but only from the physicians. Then in the forty-first year of his reign Asa died and rested with his ancestors. (2 Chronicles 16:7-13)

Asa's anger was a proud response after hearing the truth. He directed his anger toward the messenger, rather than God. Three years later, he developed an illness and still wouldn't seek God. Two years later, he died. Sometimes when we have spiritual victories, we can become proud and view ourselves as always right. Staying humble will allow those spiritual success stories to keep coming into our lives. Asa's anger should have been a warning to him to at least consider what the other person was saying. It's obvious from our perspective that Asa was wrong, but it's not so clear when it's happening to us.

Consider Joab, one of David's commanders…

Joab avenged his brother Asahel's death by murdering Abner in 2 Samuel 3. David didn't agree with this action or condone it, but rather honored Abner. In 2 Samuel 18, Joab didn't have the patience or respect for the king's orders to bring Absalom back safe, so he killed Absalom and ignored King David's wishes. In the next chapter, he corrected David for grieving over Absalom instead of celebrating the army's victory. Joab made a judgment on David's behavior, and responded with his own anger as he had done before. In the next chapter, Joab killed his cousin Amasa for leading Absalom's army (i.e., he lumped him in with Absalom and against King David).

When the time drew near for David to die, he gave a charge to Solomon his son:
"Now you yourself know what Joab son of Zeruiah did to me—what he did to the two commanders of Israel's armies, Abner son of Ner and Amasa son of Jether. He killed them, shedding their blood in peacetime as if in battle, and with that blood he stained the belt around his waist and the sandals on his feet. Deal with him according to your wisdom, but do not let his gray head go down to the grave in peace. (1 Kings 2:1, 5-6)

So Benaiah entered the tent of the LORD and said to Joab, "The king says, 'Come out!'"
But he answered, "No, I will die here."
Benaiah reported to the king, "This is how Joab answered me."
Then the king commanded Benaiah, "Do as he says. Strike him down and bury him, and so clear me and my whole family of the guilt of the innocent blood that Joab shed. The LORD will repay him for the blood he shed, because without my father David knowing it he attacked two men and killed them with the sword. Both of them—Abner son of Ner, commander of Israel's army, and Amasa son of Jether, commander of Judah's army—were better men and more upright than he. May the guilt of their blood rest on the head of Joab and his descendants

forever. But on David and his descendants, his house and his throne, may there be the LORD's peace forever."

So Benaiah son of Jehoiada went up and struck down Joab and killed him, and he was buried on his own land in the desert. (1 Kings 2:30-34)

Joab didn't resolve his anger and he felt justified in his killings, but God saw the situation differently. David saw it differently, too.

Abner served Saul, who tried to kill David; Abner fought against David's men and killed Joab's brother, Asahel, after warning him to stop his pursuit of Abner. He fought as an enemy of David. But as Saul's house grew weaker, Abner began to change:

> During the war between the house of Saul and the house of David, Abner had been strengthening his own position in the house of Saul…
>
> May God deal with Abner, be it ever so severely, if I do not do for David what the LORD promised him on oath and transfer the kingdom from the house of Saul and establish David's throne over Israel and Judah from Dan to Beersheba."…
>
> Then Abner sent messengers on his behalf to say to David, "Whose land is it? Make an agreement with me, and I will help you bring all Israel over to you." "Good," said David. "I will make an agreement with you." (2 Samuel 3:6, 9-10, 12-13a)

Maybe Joab held a grudge against Abner for killing Asahel, and it wouldn't matter what Abner did for David; Joab was going to get his revenge. If someone sinned against Joab, he would get even once the time was right. Have you ever had a conflict with someone that caused you hurt and made you angry? Then later on, even years later, you see them again. Was your anger stirred again? Do you still feel the same toward them, even if they've changed? If so, then you can relate to Joab, who dealt with Amasa in the same way. Joab and Amasa were sons of David's sisters, making both of them David's nephews. Maybe because he was family, David was more willing to overlook Amasa's brief allegiance with Absalom.

> And say to Amasa, 'Are you not my own flesh and blood? May God deal with me, be it ever so severely, if you are not the commander of my army for life in place of Joab.' (2 Samuel 19:13)

Maybe Joab heard that Amasa was going to lead the army instead of Joab, and that made him angry. Joab had no grace or willingness to spare Absalom or anyone who had joined Absalom, even if King David told him otherwise. What if your conviction is different than the leader in your own congregation? What if your perspective and judgment decide that justice needs to be demonstrated for a given situation? Do you take matters into your own hands? How much mercy do you have toward someone who has sinned against you?

> Speak and act as those who are going to be judged by the law that gives freedom, because judgment without mercy will be shown to anyone who has not been merciful. Mercy triumphs over judgment. (James 2:12-13)

Joab not only acted against the king's wishes, but he also thought the king wasn't clear-minded and decisive when dealing with Absalom. I'm not sure Joab would have agreed with any of King David's decisions during this time. This wasn't David's best time spiritually, but did Joab rely on God on how to proceed? There's no indication that he even prayed about his decisions or his perspective. When we perceive an injustice, and those involved do not act according to what we think is appropriate, our anger can be stirred. Be careful how you respond, though, because God may want to deal with it differently.

All of these examples show the importance of resolving anger. Resolving it helps you mature, enables you to "overlook" an offense, and keeps anger from being triggered as often. When Joseph saw the good God had done through his trials, his bitterness changed to joy:

> Joseph said to his brothers, "I am Joseph! Is my father still living?" But his brothers were not able to answer him, because they were terrified at his presence.
> Then Joseph said to his brothers, "Come close to me." When they had done so, he said, "I am your brother Joseph, the one you sold into Egypt! And now, do not be distressed and do not be angry with yourselves for selling me here, because it was to save lives that God sent me ahead of you. For two years now there has been famine in the land, and for the next five years there will be no plowing and reaping. But God sent me ahead of you to preserve for you a remnant on earth and to save your lives by a great deliverance. (Genesis 45:3-7)

Resolving your anger also helps you respond to someone else's anger in a healthy way and not allow your emotions to escalate.

Jesus views unresolved anger seriously:

> You have heard that it was said to the people long ago, 'You shall not murder, and anyone who murders will be subject to judgment.' But I tell you that anyone who is angry with a brother or sister will be subject to judgment. (Matthew 5:21-22a)

Controlling your emotions allows you to interact better with someone who is emotionally charged, as Paul counseled Timothy:

> Don't have anything to do with foolish and stupid arguments, because you know they produce quarrels. And the Lord's servant must not be quarrelsome

but must be kind to everyone, able to teach, not resentful. Opponents must be gently instructed, in the hope that God will grant them repentance leading them to a knowledge of the truth. (2 Timothy 2:23-25)

CHAPTER THREE

Is My Anger Distorted?

> *Anyone can become angry–that is easy, but to be angry with the right person at the right time, and for the right purpose and in the right way–that is not within everyone's power, and that is not easy.*
>
> —Aristotle

Gary Chapman in his book, *Anger–Handling a Powerful Emotion in a Healthy Way*, describes two types of anger. The first type he calls definitive anger, which is anger at someone doing something wrong. This is the only kind of anger God ever experiences because he is holy and perfect, and he always has the right perspective. His anger is valid and is aroused by moral transgression. The second type of anger Chapman calls distorted anger, which is a mere disappointment, an unfulfilled desire, a frustrated effort, or a bad mood. It comes from a situation that made life inconvenient for us, or touched one of our emotional "hot spots," or happened at a time when we were extremely tired or stressed. Distorted anger results from a perceived wrong and therefore, it is distorted from reality. The alleged wrong is only in our perception; there is no real wrongdoing. Most of the time we experience distorted anger every day.[19]

Authors Les Carter and Frank Minirth describe when our anger is triggered:

"Anger comes when you feel the need to clearly communicate that your personal boundaries have been violated."

Anger is defined as an intent to preserve:

(1) **Personal worth**—person perceives rejection or invalidation;

(2) **Essential needs**—person perceives lack of respect or appreciation;

(3) **Basic convictions**—other people differ or don't feel as strongly as we do on a particular issue."[20]

Because our anger is often triggered by hurt to us or others, frustration toward what we are trying to accomplish, or simply irritation at other people's incompetence, from our perspective it always seems justified and definitive. That's why it's not natural to stop and ask yourself a few questions before unleashing your emotions toward the offending party:

- Why am I angry? (What specifically triggered it?)
- What wrong or sin has been committed? (If you can't identify it, then your anger's probably distorted.)
- Do I have all the facts? (Additional information can change our perspective and response.)
- Would I react the same way if this person was a stranger? (Our history with people can influence how we react.)

Les Carter and Frank Minirth also share a couple of spiritual reasons our anger is stirred:

> "Pride is more than just arrogance or conceit. It is at the core of virtually any unhealthy, nonproductive emotion or behavior... If pride has gained a foothold on your emotions, anger is inevitable... While anger is not the only way pride is revealed, you can get a good idea of how strong your pride is by recognizing how anger reflects self-preoccupation. Whether it's open aggression or passive aggression your mind is focused on you, your rights or your preferences."[21]

> "Inferiority feelings or low self-esteem – The more you have been weighed down by reminders of your inadequacies, the more inclined you will be to harbor anger. As anger festers, an inner thought grows: "I'm really tired of being looked down upon. Something's got to give." Some suppress this anger until depression or apathy sets in, whereas others develop a cynical edge that prompts adversarial remarks such as sarcasm or condescension. Sometimes when feelings of inferiority come upon us, we look for a way out. The most common escape is to seek an edge of superiority such as tone of voice, rebuttal, defensiveness or 'digging our heels in'."[22]

Let's look at a few examples in the Scriptures.

Jeremiah was misunderstood...

> After the Babylonian army had withdrawn from Jerusalem because of Pharaoh's army, Jeremiah started to leave the city to go to the territory of Benjamin to get his share of the property among the people there. But when he reached the Benjamin Gate, the captain of the guard, whose name was Irijah son of Shelemiah, the son of Hananiah, arrested him and said, "You are deserting to the Babylonians!"
> "That's not true!" Jeremiah said. "I am not deserting to the Babylonians." But Irijah would not listen to him; instead, he arrested Jeremiah and brought him to the officials. They were angry with Jeremiah and had him beaten and imprisoned in the house of Jonathan the secretary, which they had made into a prison.
> Jeremiah was put into a vaulted cell in a dungeon, where he remained a long time. (Jeremiah 37:11-16)

Jeremiah was legitimately leaving to handle some personal real estate issues back home, but Irijah saw his actions differently. Irijah had already made up his mind, and wouldn't even listen to Jeremiah. This kind of response is a clear warning sign that your anger may be distorted—if you aren't willing to listen to the other person. In Jeremiah 28, there was a false prophet named Hananiah, who was challenged by Jeremiah for lying to the Israelites. Jeremiah predicted that Hananiah would die, and later that same year, he did die. What if Irijah was Hananiah's grandson, and held a grudge against Jeremiah for possibly causing his grandfather's death? That could easily lead to a preconceived, critical heart toward Jeremiah, and cause Irijah's reaction when Jeremiah was leaving Jerusalem. It's obvious that other people were angry with Jeremiah, too, so Irijah wasn't alone in feeling this way, even if he wasn't related to Hananiah.

A king changes his mind…

> Amaziah called the people of Judah together and assigned them according to their families to commanders of thousands and commanders of hundreds for all Judah and Benjamin. He then mustered those twenty years old or more and found that there were three hundred thousand men fit for military service, able to handle the spear and shield. He also hired a hundred thousand fighting men from Israel for a hundred talents of silver.
> But a man of God came to him and said, "Your Majesty, these troops from Israel must not march with you, for the LORD is not with Israel—not with any of the people of Ephraim. Even if you go and fight courageously in battle, God will overthrow you before the enemy, for God has the power to help or to overthrow."
> Amaziah asked the man of God, "But what about the hundred talents I paid for these Israelite troops?" The man of God replied, "The LORD can give you much more than that."
> So Amaziah dismissed the troops who had come to him from Ephraim and sent them home. They were furious with Judah and left for home in a great rage.
> Amaziah then marshaled his strength and led his army to the Valley of Salt, where he killed ten thousand men of Seir. The army of Judah also captured ten thousand men alive, took them to the top of a cliff and threw them down so that all were dashed to pieces.
> Meanwhile the troops that Amaziah had sent back and had not allowed to take part in the war raided towns belonging to Judah from Samaria to Beth Horon. They killed three thousand people and carried off great quantities of plunder. (2 Chronicles 25:5-13)

Amaziah should have gotten advice from a spiritual prophet before paying the troops from Israel, but at least he listened after the fact. Was the anger in the men of Israel definitive? If they had a spiritual perspective and asked Amaziah for more details, they could have accepted the change in plans as God's will, gone home content, and even prayed for their brothers to be successful in battle. Maybe a follow-up discussion with God or the prophet would have helped the troops understand that "God is not with Israel," and then become aware of their own sin and the need to repent. Without that perspective, though, they became angry and caused more damage. Their anger was distorted. Do you ever react without knowing all the facts? Do you simply rely on your own perspective and insight, assuming you are always right?

A proud king...

> Uzziah was sixteen years old when he became king, and he reigned in Jerusalem fifty-two years. His mother's name was Jekoliah; she was from Jerusalem. He did what was right in the eyes of the LORD, just as his father Amaziah had done. He sought God during the days of Zechariah, who instructed him in the fear of God. As long as he sought the LORD, God gave him success.
> ...But after Uzziah became powerful, his pride led to his downfall. He was unfaithful to the LORD his God, and entered the temple of the LORD to burn incense on the altar of incense. Azariah the priest with eighty other courageous priests of the LORD followed him in. They confronted King Uzziah and said, "It is not right for you, Uzziah, to burn incense to the LORD. That is for the priests, the descendants of Aaron, who have been consecrated to burn incense. Leave the sanctuary, for you have been unfaithful; and you will not be honored by the LORD God."
> Uzziah, who had a censer in his hand ready to burn incense, became angry. While he was raging at the priests in their presence before the incense altar in the LORD's temple, leprosy broke out on his forehead. When Azariah the chief priest and all the other priests looked at him, they saw that he had leprosy on his forehead, so they hurried him out. Indeed, he himself was eager to leave, because the LORD had afflicted him.
> King Uzziah had leprosy until the day he died. He lived in a separate house—leprous, and banned from the temple of the LORD. Jotham his son had charge of the palace and governed the people of the land. (2 Chronicles 26:3-5, 16-21)

When King Uzziah sought the Lord, he was humble, and he let Zechariah teach him and show him how to fear God. After the Lord gave him victories and success, Uzziah became proud, and decided he too could burn incense in the temple. When confronted about his sin, he became angry, and raged at the priests. What do you think Uzziah said to them? How could he justify his right to burn incense? Maybe he felt a special relationship with God because of his success, and because he was king, rather than remembering that it was God working through his humility that brought the success. Was his anger justified? God answered that question with leprosy.

Maybe God didn't record his justification, because it really didn't matter. Uzziah had sinned, and wouldn't listen to the priest's perspective. Sometimes years of faithfulness can be replaced with an arrogance that fuels our anger. Because of past accomplishments, we no longer see our need for further teaching or help. What's amazing is that there's no record of any repentance or return to the humility he had in the beginning. Wouldn't the leprosy have been enough?

Is My Anger Distorted?

A disrespected king...

> On the seventh day, when King Xerxes was in high spirits from wine, he commanded the seven eunuchs who served him—Mehuman, Biztha, Harbona, Bigtha, Abagtha, Zethar and Karkas—to bring before him Queen Vashti, wearing her royal crown, in order to display her beauty to the people and nobles, for she was lovely to look at. But when the attendants delivered the king's command, Queen Vashti refused to come. Then the king became furious and burned with anger. (Esther 1:10-12)

A drunken King Xerxes became furious when Queen Vashti refused to come to him during a banquet. Through the advice of his closest wise men, he had the queen removed from her position and began the search for a new queen, who became Esther. King Xerxes never asked why Queen Vashti wouldn't come. Maybe it was a legitimate reason due to illness or injury. Maybe she was simply being defiant, and had unresolved anger issues with the king. There's no record of her explaining her actions. Was his anger definitive and justified? Probably so, considering the proper royal protocol, but in any marriage there has to be good, clear communication to avoid a similar reaction when appointments are forgotten, laundry room is overflowing, or the same mistake is made for the third time in a month.

A demanding king...

> The king replied to the astrologers, "This is what I have firmly decided: If you do not tell me what my dream was and interpret it, I will have you cut into pieces and your houses turned into piles of rubble. But if you tell me the dream and explain it, you will receive from me gifts and rewards and great honor. So tell me the dream and interpret it for me." (Daniel 2:5-6)

Not only was King Nebuchadenezzar being demanding by asking his astrologers to interpret his dream, he was even expecting them to tell him the dream, too. He wasn't going to describe it in detail, but expected them to "read his mind". Of course his threat to cut them into pieces and destroy their homes would raise the stakes of his impossible request. They responded as any of us would in that situation:

> The astrologers answered the king, "There is no one on earth who can do what the king asks! No king, however great and mighty, has ever asked such a thing of any magician or enchanter or astrologer. What the king asks is too difficult. No one can reveal it to the king except the gods, and they do not live among humans."
> This made the king so angry and furious that he ordered the execution of all the wise men of Babylon. So the decree was issued to put the wise men to death, and men were sent to look for Daniel and his friends to put them to death. (Daniel 2:10-13)

Was King Nebuchadenezzar's anger definitive and justified? Husbands sometimes can relate to the astrologers when their wives react in anger about something only they, the wives, knew about. The often heard reply from the husband is, "Honey, I can't read your mind." When you ask someone to do something that they cannot possibly accomplish due to time constraints, budget, or their lack of a specific skill set, does that justify becoming angry at them? Remember when Rachel got angry with Jacob?

> When Rachel saw that she was not bearing Jacob any children, she became jealous of her sister. So she said to Jacob, "Give me children, or I'll die!" Jacob became angry with her and said, "Am I in the place of God, who has kept you from having children?" (Genesis 30:1-2)

Just like Rachel, Nebuchadnezzar had no patience or tolerance for the astrologers, because of his perception of their incompetence. How much of his intolerance came from his own frustration of not knowing what these troubling dreams meant? He was struggling with them through restless nights that left him confused. Unresolved issues can consume us and create impatience and demanding attitudes towards those people who should be helping us, or are in a position to help. Sometimes it is good to reflect on the real issue bothering us, and not the frustration with other people who aren't willing to or can't fix it.

> When Arioch, the commander of the king's guard, had gone out to put to death the wise men of Babylon, Daniel spoke to him with wisdom and tact. He asked the king's officer, "Why did the king issue such a harsh decree?" Arioch then explained the matter to Daniel. At this, Daniel went in to the king and asked for time, so that he might interpret the dream for him.
> Then Daniel returned to his house and explained the matter to his friends Hananiah, Mishael and Azariah. He urged them to plead for mercy from the God of heaven concerning this mystery, so that he and his friends might not be executed with the rest of the wise men of Babylon. During the night the mystery was revealed to Daniel in a vision. (Daniel 2:14-19a)

Even though Daniel met the king's demands through prayer, the king could easily feel justified that his angry response got him the answer, which would lead him to treat future problems the same way. It may be true that his anger worked, but is the damage to relationships and other costs worth the results? People may jump through hoops and do the seemingly impossible, but this heavy-handed method and "do it or else" threats don't build the rapport wanted in a marriage, a family, a team or a business.

A disrespected prophet…

> From there Elisha went up to Bethel. As he was walking along the road, some boys came out of the town and jeered at him. "Get out of here, baldy!"

they said. "Get out of here, baldy!" He turned around, looked at them and called down a curse on them in the name of the LORD. Then two bears came out of the woods and mauled forty-two of the boys. And he went on to Mount Carmel and from there returned to Samaria. (2 Kings 2:23-25)

Elisha had just become a prophet after God had taken Elijah in a whirlwind. Do you think Elisha's anger was definitive? Nobody likes being bullied, and these boys had no right to disrespect one of God's prophets. They had sinned against Elisha. His anger was justified, but was his response appropriate? He could have corrected them or brought fire down around them to scare them, but he didn't. With a crowd of preteen or teenage boys in the mood to make fun of people, how effective would any discussion have been? Maybe Elisha was just setting the tone to respect one of God's newly appointed prophets much like a new school teacher does to an unruly class on the first day. The passage doesn't say that any of the boys were killed, but they probably never bothered Elisha again.

As you reflect on these examples, what have you learned about your own anger? Is it often distorted? Even if it is definitive, we have to process those angry emotions in a healthy way. Authors Les Carter and Frank Minirth describe it in this way:

"There are times when anger is incorrectly associated with trivial matters. And there are times when it may be associated with legitimate concerns, but is managed irresponsibly. Balance is found when anger is linked to a reasonable issue and is communicated in a proper manner."[23]

Author Gary Chapman describes several steps that provide guidance in processing distorted anger:[24]

1. **Sharing Information**—The focus is on making the other person aware of your emotions, your thoughts and your concerns. It describes the event that provoked your feelings and not on the person. Typical statement might be something such as, "I'm feeling (frustrated, hurt, angry, disappointed, etc.) and I need your help". It's not a condemning or judgmental statement that escalates emotions and causes more damage.

2. **Gathering Information**—This step usually involves asking more questions to clarify your first impression of what happened or may be happening. Sometimes we perceive something that hurts us, but we may not have all the facts. The broken promise or emotional response may not have come from an inconsiderate heart or may not have anything to do with you at all. Additional questions help your understanding of the other person's state of mind and motive.

3. **Negotiating Understanding**—This step helps us process the negative emotions, because even if the anger is distorted and the other person did not commit a moral injustice, the hurt feelings and frustration are still there. Both people need to understand how the situation affected the other person. This requires open conversation in a nonjudgmental atmosphere. Consider the good that is in the other person as you express the details of your emotions avoiding such terms as "always" or "never."

4. **Requesting Change**—Asking the other person to change an approach or behavior is reasonable and can result in a positive effect on the relationship, as long as it's not presented in a demanding or manipulative way. This usually means reaffirming the good traits that you appreciate and love about them. Most requests made in this type of atmosphere are received positively and create a sincere response.

These steps have worked for me as a new way to process my distorted anger, both in my marriage and my parenting. It's amazing how healing it is to communicate the effect of someone's actions or response, so that they know how it affected you. The discussion doesn't have to be emotionally charged or judgmental. It actually provides better understanding and reduces the chances of repeated behavior.

Authors Carter and Minirth call this response assertiveness:

> "Communicates needs, but considers the needs and feelings of others; Guidelines (a) make sure the issue is not trivial, (b) be aware of your tone of voice and not be emotionally charged; requires self-discipline, caution and respect for the dignity of others."[25]

Remember that God designed you to have the capacity to experience anger to bring about change. How you handle your anger determines whether there is change or more damage. When your anger is definitive, usually the change needs to occur in other people. Whereas, when your anger is distorted, the change usually needs to occur in you because the other person has done nothing wrong.

CHAPTER FOUR

God's Anger

From the movie "Star Trek V: The Final Frontier", let's listen in on a conversation that Captain Kirk, Spock, Sybok (Spock's half-bother), and Dr. McCoy have with a character known as "God":

Kirk: What does God need with a starship?
McCoy: Jim, what are you doing?
Kirk: I'm asking a question.
"God": Who is this creature?
Kirk: Who am I? Don't you know? Aren't you God?
Sybok: He has his doubts.
"God": You doubt me?
Kirk: I seek proof.
McCoy: Jim! You don't ask the Almighty for his ID!
"God": Then here is the proof you seek. [Hits Kirk with lightning]
Kirk: Why is God angry?
Sybok: Why? Why have you done this to my friend?
"God": He doubts me.
Spock: You have not answered his question. What does God need with a starship?
"God": [Hits Spock with lightning; then addresses McCoy] Do you doubt me?
McCoy: I doubt any God who inflicts pain for his own pleasure.

Is this your view of God, powerful being who interacts with us mere humans only to strike us with lightning when we doubt, ask the wrong question, sin, or correct him? We all have a view of God that's shaped by our parents, family relationships, church, movies, and even the Bible.

> Should it be said, O house of Jacob: "Is the Spirit of the LORD angry? Does he do such things?" "Do not my words do good to him whose ways are upright? (Micah 2:7 NIV 1984)

Does God do such things? Yes, God gets angry, yet this Scripture reminds us that God also does good to anyone who obeys his word. He has many characteristics that we hear about all the time and that we love to think about, study, or discuss with one another: love, forgiveness, patience, forbearance, grace, helpfulness, kindness, etc. But what about his anger? You don't hear a lot about that except in the context of hell, punishment, or discipline. In the book, *Knowing God*, author J. I. Packer calls it "a right and necessary reaction to objective moral evil."[26]

In the book, *The Surprising Side of Grace—Appreciating God's Loving Anger*, author Stephen Bly describes God's anger:

> "God's anger is His just, intense indignation and displeasure caused by the injury, insult, injustice, and wickedness of mankind, both individual and corporate."[27]

It can create in us a fear or hesitancy to approach God.

> My shield is God Most High, who saves the upright in heart. God is a righteous judge, a God who displays his wrath every day. (Psalm 7:10-11)

This Psalm was written by David, who God described as a man after his own heart. David acknowledged that God displayed his wrath every day, yet could also consider him as his "shield." How could David feel the closeness and special relationship with God, yet know that he could become angry at him? More than once when David sinned, he experienced God's anger. Here's one example:

> David looked up and saw the angel of the LORD standing between heaven and earth, with a drawn sword in his hand extended over Jerusalem. Then David and the elders, clothed in sackcloth, fell facedown.
> David said to God, "Was it not I who ordered the fighting men to be counted? I am the one who has sinned and done wrong. These are but sheep. What have they done? O LORD my God, let your hand fall upon me and my family, but do not let this plague remain on your people."
> Then the angel of the LORD ordered Gad to tell David to go up and build an altar to the LORD on the threshing floor of Araunah the Jebusite...Then the LORD spoke to the angel, and he put his sword back into its sheath. At that time, when David saw that the LORD had answered him on the threshing floor of Araunah the Jebusite, he offered sacrifices there. The tabernacle of the LORD, which Moses had made in the desert, and the altar of burnt offering were at that time on the high place at Gibeon. But David could not go before it to inquire of God, because he was afraid of the sword of the angel of the LORD. (1 Chronicles 21:16-18, 27-30)

You may or may not see his wrath, but it is there. Does that mean that he is angry 24/7, or never shows any patience or love? No, of course not. When you see the evils in this world, which particular ones make you angry? When a child is abused and mistreated? When the wealthy and powerful seem to be above the law? When a husband physically abuses his wife? When a woman is raped? When a woman chooses to have an abortion? When a doctor agrees to perform an abortion? Our anger gets triggered every day and so does God's. He sees all the evil at once, which we could never handle.

Sometimes one life event can trigger our anger, but God's anger is different from ours. It is very different. I was first introduced to really thinking about and studying God's anger from Stephen Bly's book, *The Surprising Side of Grace—Appreciating God's Loving Anger*. In his book, Stephen identifies several benefits from studying God's anger:[28]

- reveals how important some things are to Him
- increases respect for his character
- provides confidence in his protection
- increases our motivation to obey Him
- provides a clearer understanding of the intensity of his love

I have found that studying his anger also helps me learn how to handle my own anger, and change the way I react to life events and people that trigger my anger. In this section, we are going to expound upon some of the characteristics Stephen Bly identified in his book[29] and add a couple from my own studies:

1. **Always Justified**—God's anger is always definitive because a moral injustice (sin) has been committed.
2. **Doesn't Show Favoritism**—When God's anger is aroused, it doesn't matter who you are or what you have done for him lately.
3. **Slow to Develop**—His anger really is slow to develop, as many Scriptures describe.
4. **Temporary**—God's anger doesn't last forever.
5. **Often Restrained**—If he didn't restrain his anger, there would be no one left to praise him or bring him glory.
6. **Neutralized by our Repentance**—God's anger subsides when we change.
7. **Remains Until its Purpose is Fulfilled**—God's anger is a tool for him to bring about change.
8. **Influenced by Prayer**—Our prayers can move God to change his anger.

This section describes the different aspects of God's anger and wrath. He felt it when he sent the flood, when he destroyed Sodom and Gomorrah, and when he allowed Assyria to take Israel away into captivity. All of the attributes and characteristics of God's anger are true, but the full weight and impact, when his anger is unleashed is best described when he allowed Babylon to take Judah and his beloved city Jerusalem into captivity. It's then that his heart and intense love are exposed, after years of sending prophet after prophet and pleading with his people to repent. God had no other option. One of the passages written during this time comes from Jeremiah, who witnessed it firsthand:

> How the Lord has covered Daughter Zion with the cloud of his anger! He has hurled down the splendor of Israel from heaven to earth; he has not remembered his footstool in the day of his anger. Without pity the Lord has swallowed up all the dwellings of Jacob; in his wrath he has torn down the strongholds of Daughter Judah. He has brought her kingdom and its princes down to the ground in dishonor. In fierce anger he has cut off every horn of Israel. He has withdrawn his right hand at the approach of the enemy. He has burned in Jacob like a flaming fire that consumes everything around it.
> Like an enemy he has strung his bow; his right hand is ready. Like a foe he has slain all who were pleasing to the eye; he has poured out his wrath like fire on the tent of Daughter Zion. The Lord is like an enemy; he has swallowed up Israel. He has swallowed up all her palaces and destroyed her strongholds. He has multiplied mourning and lamentation for Daughter Judah. He has laid waste his dwelling like a garden; he has destroyed his place of meeting. The LORD has made Zion forget her appointed festivals and her Sabbaths; in his fierce anger he has spurned both king and priest. The Lord has rejected his altar and abandoned his sanctuary. (Lamentations 2:1-7a)

From Jeremiah's perspective, God was unleashing his anger on his Daughter, his footstool, all who were pleasing to the eye, his place of meeting, even his sanctuary. Nothing was spared, not even king or priest. There was nothing that did not receive the full brunt of his rage. If there is ever a question that God could never be full of love and anger, then this was the moment that dispelled that entire myth. It's because of his intense love that his anger can be this overpowering, this overwhelming, this intimidating, and this destructive. No one with a clinched fist and an objection to what God was doing would be left standing. No one.

> "It was because of the LORD's anger that all this happened to Jerusalem and Judah, and in the end he thrust them from his presence." (Jeremiah 52:3)

By the end of the last chapter in Lamentations, even Jeremiah felt there may not be any hope left for Judah, and issued a final plea with God:

> Because of this our hearts are faint, because of these things our eyes grow dim for Mount Zion, which lies desolate, with jackals prowling over it. You, LORD, reign forever; your throne endures from generation to generation. Why do you always forget us? Why do you forsake us so long? Restore us to yourself, LORD, that we may return; renew our days as of old unless you have utterly rejected us and are angry with us beyond measure. (Lamentations 5:17-22)

God's anger is something to be remembered. Consider that the Psalms were often written as songs or spiritual hymns. Then reread Psalm 78 and consider the different attributes of God's anger described in that psalm. Songs make it easier to memorize words. The words come back when you hear a familiar tune, even if it's been years since you've heard it. Why would Asaph, a choir master and a leader of Levitical musicians under King David, write a psalm about Israel's history and God's anger? He did so because both need to be remembered. Miriam wrote about God's anger with her song in Exodus 15 after God destroyed Pharaoh and his army. Just before his death, Moses also wrote about God's anger in his song recorded in Deuteronomy 32. Notice what God tells Moses about this song:

> "Now write down this song and teach it to the Israelites and have them sing it, so that it may be a witness for me against them. When I have brought them into the land flowing with milk and honey, the land I promised on oath to their ancestors, and when they eat their fill and thrive, they will turn to other gods and worship them, rejecting me and breaking my covenant. And when many disasters and calamities come on them, this song will testify against them, because it will not be forgotten by their descendants. I know what they are disposed to do, even before I bring them into the land I promised them on oath." So Moses wrote down this song that day and taught it to the Israelites. (Deuteronomy 31:19-22)

Psalm 78 talks about God's anger being justified based on Israel's behavior, yet being merciful and sometimes restrained. God's anger is all those things and more. His anger is different from ours and it needs to be understood, placed in our songs and remembered. It is just as much a part of him as his love, but we don't discuss it as often. It's rare that God's anger is the subject of a Sunday's sermon and it's even more rare that it moves you to tears, but it should. That's because it comes from a love for you that's so intense and so jealous, that if you really understood his anger, you would want to obey everything he says, and never want to leave him or even be away from him for a moment.

But our desire to be close to him shouldn't come from a fear of retaliation or being hunted down, like an escaped prisoner by an egotistical and controlling dictator. It should come from that "wow" feeling we have after finding and falling in love with our dream person, the one who makes us feel better, even perfect, the one who makes us laugh and accepts all our flaws. Although those feelings sometimes diminish after our wedding day, it's different with God. It's the honeymoon for eternity. You've never experienced that kind of love from any human being. You've never been pursued so relentlessly and with such passion. When we continually ignore that pursuit, and stubbornly refuse to have or even want that closeness or intimacy, God's anger will eventually be aroused. This anger is not as from a jilted lover; it is not from impatience or frustration or irritation at our lack of response, but rather from a holy and just God who allows us to choose. His anger is simply a tool to bring about change, a change in you, so that all his dreams for you can come true. That's why his anger is not like ours.

As you read this section, open your heart to a different God, a God you may have never understood, especially if your only examples of angry people have left you hurt, bitter, or even angry yourself. With a healthy view of God's anger, you can learn to imitate him and handle your own anger better. It can change the way you parent your children or the way you interact with people at work or at school, and it can even heal damaged relationships that have been scarred and dysfunctional for years. It can make you more secure and confident that God loves you intensely, even when you sin…again.

CHAPTER FIVE

God's Anger—Always Justified

> *He who does not believe that God will punish sin, will not believe that he will pardon it through the blood of his Son.*
> —Charles Spurgeon (British preacher, 1860s)

Before Adam and Eve made the wrong decision, God's anger was never stirred. Until sin entered the world, God had nothing about which to be angry. Everything he had created was good. Some of it was very good. Sin arouses God's anger because it destroys everything in his design and his creation. When God's anger is stirred, it is always justified. The prophet Nahum described God's anger against the Assyrian capital, Nineveh:

> A prophecy concerning Nineveh. The book of the vision of Nahum the Elkoshite. The LORD is a jealous and avenging God; the LORD takes vengeance and is filled with wrath. The LORD takes vengeance on his foes and vents his wrath against his enemies. The LORD is slow to anger but great in power; the LORD will not leave the guilty unpunished. His way is in the whirlwind and the storm, and clouds are the dust of his feet...
> Who can withstand his indignation? Who can endure his fierce anger? his wrath is poured out like fire; the rocks are shattered before him. The LORD is good, a refuge in times of trouble. He cares for those who trust in him, but with an overwhelming flood he will make an end of Nineveh; he will pursue his foes into the realm of darkness. (Nahum 1:1-3, 6-8)

A long-time minister of Peninsula Bible Church in Palo Alto, California from 1950-1990, Ray Stedman, had a good summary of this passage:

> "God is angry, and this is no temper tantrum. There is nothing capricious about the anger of God. There is nothing selfish about it. It is a controlled but terrible rage, fearsome to behold. You can get some idea of the awfulness of this divine anger in the fact that all the Hebrew words for wrath or anger are brought together in these verses through the prophet Nahum. The words are: jealous, vengeance, wrath, anger, indignation, fierce, wrath. All of them describe the anger of God.
> Jealousy, that burning zeal for a cause felt so deeply in the heart. This is not the selfish, petty jealousy we exhibit sometimes, but God's overwhelming concern for what he loves. His vengeance, or retribution; his wrath, that towering

anger, the blackness of it, the darkness of it, is described here. The word for anger is the word that literally means 'heavy breathing', or 'hot breathing'. And the word for indignation literally means 'foaming at the mouth'! You can see how picturesque these words are. The word fierce in Hebrew literally means 'heat', and the word wrath means 'burning'. And all this to describe a God who is terrible in his wrath, moved at last to the point of pouring out his wrath upon that which has awakened it. God in a white-hot passion, burning with a terrible, blistering rage."[30]

Was it justifiable for God to feel this way about the Assyrians, even though God used them to discipline his people Israel and take Israel into captivity from 722-612 BC? They were ruthless and merciless when they conquered a nation. This was about 100 years after Jonah preached to Nineveh when the Assyrians repented. Now around 650 BC, they had returned to many of the same practices that brought God's prophet, Jonah, to their city a century before. They were proud and arrogant about their own strength, as described by the prophets Isaiah and Zephaniah:

> When the Lord has finished all his work against Mount Zion and Jerusalem, he will say, "I will punish the king of Assyria for the willful pride of his heart and the haughty look in his eyes. For he says:
> "'By the strength of my hand I have done this, and by my wisdom, because I have understanding. I removed the boundaries of nations, I plundered their treasures; like a mighty one I subdued their kings.'" (Isaiah 10:12-13)
>
> She said to herself, "I am the one! And there is none besides me." (Zephaniah 2:15a)

God's anger was justified, and the Babylonians conquered the Assyrians and captured Nineveh in 612 BC.

When your sin arouses God's anger, his anger may cause pain for you, but it produces a "harvest of righteousness and peace for those who have been trained by it", as described in Hebrews 12. When other people sin and you're affected negatively, God's anger can be your encouragement and support, as described by David when he was unjustly pursued by Saul.

> In my distress I called to the LORD; I cried to my God for help. From his temple he heard my voice; my cry came before him, into his ears.
> The earth trembled and quaked, and the foundations of the mountains shook; they trembled because he was angry. (Psalm 18:6-7)

If you take the time to consider whether God's anger is justified, it's easier to see with other people and circumstances than it is with your own life. When the evening news or your favorite news website brings you images and stories of defenseless people being abused or slaughtered, of serial killers striking again, or of blatant injustices to children, you can easily feel anger. And it's justified, because these actions are wrong. You think the appropriate punishment is deserved, and should be administered with swift consequences.

When your own actions are questioned, however, it's not so clear, because you are personally involved. Motives and history with some people cause you to react in sinful ways. Sometimes you just make bad choices, but they often come with explanations and reasons why those choices were "inevitable" or "understandable". You may not agree that the consequences are that bad, and you want grace. You may feel this way toward God at times, when he brings discipline or correction into your life, and you don't view it as justified. Because God is holy and altogether pure, his perspective is different than yours, and your objection to his discipline may simply come from your forgetting these truths.

How would you handle this command from God, and the associated consequences, if it's disobeyed?

> Do not take advantage of the widow or the fatherless. If you do and they cry out to me, I will certainly hear their cry. My anger will be aroused, and I will kill you with the sword; your wives will become widows and your children fatherless. (Exodus 22:22-24)

Is God justified to react this way, when widows or orphans are mistreated? They have no husbands or fathers to lead and protect their households. God assumes the role of protector and guardian. What if the widow or orphan is ungrateful, or commits sinful actions? We still have to trust God to deal with them as he has promised, based on their own conduct, rather than leaning on our own judgment and limited perspective.

The prophet Habakkuk preached during Jeremiah's time, when God's people were about to be conquered and exiled to Babylon. As he observed God's anger being administered through the Babylonians, he questioned God because through Habakkuk's eyes, God's people were more righteous than the enemy:

> LORD, are you not from everlasting? My God, my Holy One, you will never die. You, LORD, have appointed them to execute judgment; you, my Rock, have ordained them to punish.
> Your eyes are too pure to look on evil; you cannot tolerate wrongdoing. Why then do you tolerate the treacherous? Why are you silent while the wicked swallow up those more righteous than themselves? (Habakkuk 1:12-13)

Habakkuk made a judgment that the Babylonians were more wicked than the Israelites, and questioned why God would allow the Babylonians to "win". He didn't see or had forgotten God's history with Israel and the countless times God tried to turn his people away from their sin. Look at the following passages from Jeremiah and see if God's actions were justified:

> You have defiled the land with your prostitution and wickedness. Therefore the showers have been withheld, and no spring rains have fallen. Yet you have the brazen look of a prostitute; you refuse to blush with shame. Have you not just called to me: 'My Father, my friend from my youth, will you always be angry? Will your wrath continue forever?' This is how you talk, but you do all the evil you can. (Jeremiah 3:2b-5)
>
> So do not pray for this people nor offer any plea or petition for them; do not plead with me, for I will not listen to you. Do you not see what they are doing in the towns of Judah and in the streets of Jerusalem? The children gather wood, the fathers light the fire, and the women knead the dough and make cakes to offer to the Queen of Heaven. They pour out drink offerings to other gods to arouse my anger. But am I the one they are provoking? declares the LORD. Are they not rather harming themselves, to their own shame?
> "Therefore this is what the Sovereign LORD says: My anger and my wrath will be poured out on this place—on man and beast, on the trees of the field and on the crops of your land—and it will burn and not be quenched." (Jeremiah 7:16-20)
>
> The Babylonians who are attacking this city will come in and set it on fire; they will burn it down, along with the houses where the people aroused my anger by burning incense on the roofs to Baal and by pouring out drink offerings to other gods.
> The people of Israel and Judah have done nothing but evil in my sight from their youth; indeed, the people of Israel have done nothing but arouse my anger with what their hands have made, declares the LORD. From the day it was built until now, this city has so aroused my anger and wrath that I must remove it from my sight. The people of Israel and Judah have provoked me by all the evil they have done—they, their kings and officials, their priests and prophets, the people of Judah and those living in Jerusalem. They turned their backs to me and not their faces; though I taught them again and again, they would not listen or respond to discipline. They set up their vile images in the house that bears my Name and defiled it. They built high places for Baal in the Valley of Ben Hinnom to sacrifice their sons and daughters to Molech, though I never commanded—nor did it enter my mind—that they should do such a detestable thing and so make Judah sin. (Jeremiah 32:29-35)

These passages present a different picture now. God's patience and repeated attempts to help Israel were consistently met with resistance, stubbornness, or refusal to obey and repent. Because God's anger is slow to develop, it is more than justified when it is stirred. Of course, God reassured Habakkuk that Babylon would have its day in the future. God was aware of Babylon's sin and evil deeds, and will punish them in due time.

Even during this difficult time in Israel, there were a few people who came to Jeremiah seeking advice and God's direction, and they promised to obey:

> Then all the army officers, including Johanan son of Kareah and

God's Anger—Always Justified

> Jezaniah son of Hoshaiah, and all the people from the least to the greatest approached Jeremiah the prophet and said to him, "Please hear our petition and pray to the LORD your God for this entire remnant. For as you now see, though we were once many, now only a few are left. Pray that the LORD your God will tell us where we should go and what we should do."
>
> "I have heard you," replied Jeremiah the prophet. "I will certainly pray to the LORD your God as you have requested; I will tell you everything the LORD says and will keep nothing back from you." Then they said to Jeremiah, "May the LORD be a true and faithful witness against us if we do not act in accordance with everything the LORD your God sends you to tell us. Whether it is favorable or unfavorable, we will obey the LORD our God, to whom we are sending you, so that it will go well with us, for we will obey the LORD our God." (Jeremiah 42:1-6)

God was moved by their hearts. In his response, you can see his deep love for them, and reassuring promises to take care of them. At the same time, God laid out their choices and gave them the freedom to choose:

> Ten days later the word of the LORD came to Jeremiah. So he called together Johanan son of Kareah and all the army officers who were with him and all the people from the least to the greatest. He said to them, "This is what the LORD, the God of Israel, to whom you sent me to present your petition, says: 'If you stay in this land, I will build you up and not tear you down; I will plant you and not uproot you, for I have relented concerning the disaster I have inflicted on you. Do not be afraid of the king of Babylon, whom you now fear. Do not be afraid of him, declares the LORD, for I am with you and will save you and deliver you from his hands. I will show you compassion so that he will have compassion on you and restore you to your land.'
>
> "However, if you say, 'We will not stay in this land,' and so disobey the LORD your God, and if you say, 'No, we will go and live in Egypt, where we will not see war or hear the trumpet or be hungry for bread,' then hear the word of the LORD, you remnant of Judah. This is what the LORD Almighty, the God of Israel, says: 'If you are determined to go to Egypt and you do go to settle there, then the sword you fear will overtake you there, and the famine you dread will follow you into Egypt, and there you will die. Indeed, all who are determined to go to Egypt to settle there will die by the sword, famine and plague; not one of them will survive or escape the disaster I will bring on them.' This is what the LORD Almighty, the God of Israel, says: 'As my anger and wrath have been poured out on those who lived in Jerusalem, so will my wrath be poured out on you when you go to Egypt. You will be a curse and an object of horror, a curse and an object of reproach; you will never see this place again.'" (Jeremiah 42:7-18)

We refer to this characteristic in our relationship with God as "free will". He will not make us obey or repent. We decide whether we listen and believe his promises, or choose our own way and disobey. How did these humble, sincere Israelites respond?

> When Jeremiah had finished telling the people all the words of the LORD their God—everything the LORD had sent him to tell them—Azariah son of Hoshaiah and Johanan son of Kareah and all the arrogant men said to Jeremiah, "You are lying! The LORD our God has not sent you to say, 'You must not go to Egypt to settle there.' But Baruch son of Neriah is inciting you against us to hand us over to the Babylonians, so they may kill us or carry us into exile to Babylon." (Jeremiah 43:1-3)

Why would the Israelites respond in this way? They had just seen the destruction of Jerusalem, and God promised the same would happen to them if they went to Egypt. Why wouldn't they believe Jeremiah? They had promised to obey even if the message was "unfavorable", but when God tested their commitment, they quickly changed their minds and accused Jeremiah of lying, based on their attitudes toward Baruch, son of Neriah, who was Jeremiah's scribe. They just didn't trust that God was speaking through Jeremiah, and they had already made up their minds. God's response was justified:

> Now this is what the LORD God Almighty, the God of Israel, says: "Why bring such great disaster on yourselves by cutting off from Judah the men and women, the children and infants, and so leave yourselves without a remnant? Why arouse my anger with what your hands have made, burning incense to other gods in Egypt, where you have come to live? You will destroy yourselves and make yourselves a curse and an object of reproach among all the nations on earth." (Jeremiah 44:7-8)

> "I will punish those who live in Egypt with the sword, famine and plague, as I punished Jerusalem. None of the remnant of Judah who have gone to live in Egypt will escape or survive to return to the land of Judah, to which they long to return and live; none will return except a few fugitives."
>
> Then all the men who knew that their wives were burning incense to other gods, along with all the women who were present—a large assembly—and all the people living in Lower and Upper Egypt, said to Jeremiah, "We will not listen to the message you have spoken to us in the name of the LORD! We will certainly do everything we said we would: We will burn incense to the Queen of Heaven and will pour out drink offerings to her just as we and our ancestors, our kings and our officials did in the towns of Judah and in the streets of Jerusalem. At that time we had plenty of food and were well off and suffered no harm. But ever since we stopped burning incense to the Queen of Heaven and pouring out drink offerings to her, we have had nothing and have been perishing by sword and famine." (Jeremiah 44:13-18)

You can see how distorted their thinking had become. They associated their present day trouble with the fact that they had stopped offering sacrifices to the Queen of Heaven. Even when they viewed their lives as successful with plenty of food, well off, and suffering no harm, God's anger was building. They must have heard many of Jeremiah's messages, but never made the connection

God's Anger—Always Justified

with their Queen of Heaven worship. Maybe they just didn't believe him, because from their perspective, their lives were pretty good.

We can do the same thing by using our own wisdom and perspective rather than God's word. Just because your life seems good and you aren't suffering any hardships doesn't mean you have God's favor. His word has to continue to challenge our thinking and our priorities. Where does your confidence come from? Does it come from your lack of problems, your ability to handle everything by yourself, or that you are "making every effort" to be righteous and to know the God who created you?

God's anger can also be justified if he chooses to treat us as we have treated others. Everyone knows the Golden Rule, "Do to others as you would have them do to you" (Luke 6:31). Later in that same chapter, Jesus explained it practically:

> Do not judge, and you will not be judged. Do not condemn, and you will not be condemned. Forgive, and you will be forgiven. Give, and it will be given to you. A good measure, pressed down, shaken together and running over, will be poured into your lap. For with the measure you use, it will be measured to you. (Luke 6:37-38)

In the Old Testament, God's laws declared one thing, and Jesus applied it to the heart:

> But if there is serious injury, you are to take life for life, eye for eye, tooth for tooth, hand for hand, foot for foot, burn for burn, wound for wound, bruise for bruise. (Exodus 21:23-25)

> You have heard that it was said, 'Eye for eye, and tooth for tooth.' But I tell you, do not resist an evil person. If anyone slaps you on the right cheek, turn to them the other cheek also. (Matthew 5:38-39)

Dozens of Scriptures talk about loving one another, forgiving one another, submitting to one another, and being humble with each other. How we treat each other is important to God, and his justified anger may find its way in your life if your treatment of people is not appropriate. Consider this passage from Ezekiel just before Judah was exiled to Babylon. As a country, Edom had continual hatred toward Israel ever since Jacob and Esau went their separate ways. There were numerous conflicts throughout the centuries and God was watching:

> "'Because you have said, "These two nations and countries will be ours and we will take possession of them," even though I the LORD was there, therefore as surely as I live, declares the Sovereign LORD, I will treat you in accordance with the anger and jealousy you showed in your hatred of them and I will make myself known among them when I judge you. Then you will know

that I the LORD have heard all the contemptible things you have said against the mountains of Israel. You said, "They have been laid waste and have been given over to us to devour." You boasted against me and spoke against me without restraint, and I heard it. This is what the Sovereign LORD says: While the whole earth rejoices, I will make you desolate. Because you rejoiced when the inheritance of Israel became desolate, that is how I will treat you. You will be desolate, Mount Seir, you and all of Edom. Then they will know that I am the LORD.'" (Ezekiel 35:10-15)

Sometimes God reacts based on how we have treated or responded to him. This passage is from the prophet Zechariah, when Judah was returning from the captivity in Babylon:

And the word of the LORD came again to Zechariah: "This is what the LORD Almighty said: 'Administer true justice; show mercy and compassion to one another. Do not oppress the widow or the fatherless, the foreigner or the poor. Do not plot evil against each other.'
"But they refused to pay attention; stubbornly they turned their backs and covered their ears. They made their hearts as hard as flint and would not listen to the law or to the words that the LORD Almighty had sent by his Spirit through the earlier prophets. So the LORD Almighty was very angry. "'When I called, they did not listen; so when they called, I would not listen,' says the LORD Almighty. (Zechariah 7:8-13)

All of these examples speak about sin and God's anger in response. His reaction is justified. As you consider these things, how should you respond? Take sin more seriously than you have. Several New Testament letters make the same point:

For of this you can be sure: No immoral, impure or greedy person—such a person is an idolater—has any inheritance in the kingdom of Christ and of God. Let no one deceive you with empty words, for because of such things God's wrath comes on those who are disobedient. Therefore do not be partners with them. (Ephesians 5:5-7)

Put to death, therefore, whatever belongs to your earthly nature: sexual immorality, impurity, lust, evil desires and greed, which is idolatry. Because of these, the wrath of God is coming. You used to walk in these ways, in the life you once lived. But now you must also rid yourselves of all such things as these: anger, rage, malice, slander, and filthy language from your lips. (Colossians 3:5-8)

If we deliberately keep on sinning after we have received the knowledge of the truth, no sacrifice for sins is left, but only a fearful expectation of judgment and of raging fire that will consume the enemies of God. Anyone who rejected the law of Moses died without mercy on the testimony of two or three witnesses. How much more severely do you think someone deserves to be punished who has trampled the Son of God underfoot, who has treated as an unholy thing the blood of the covenant that sanctified them, and who has insulted the Spirit of grace? For we know him who said, "It is mine to avenge; I will repay," and again, "The Lord will judge his people." It is a dreadful thing to fall into the hands of the living God. (Hebrews 10:26-31)

Because of sin and God's holiness, his anger is always justified. If you take sin more seriously and repent when God shows it to you, then your hope will not be in your own righteousness, but rather in "Jesus, who rescues us from the coming wrath." (1 Thessalonians 1:10)

CHAPTER SIX

God's Anger—Doesn't Show Favoritism

> *Whoever imagines himself a favorite with God holds others in contempt.*
>
> —Robert Green Ingersoll

One element of God's character is that he shows no favoritism. One dictionary defines favoritism as "the practice of giving unfair preferential treatment to one person or group at the expense of another". Although God chose the Hebrew nation as "his people, his treasured possession", they weren't meant to be the only people to receive his blessings for all time. Adam and Eve did not get preferential treatment, even though they were the first humans created in God's image. All parents can relate to the special place first-borns have in our hearts. But God treated Adam and Eve the same as anyone else who sins, even if only one sin is committed.

Several New Testament writers emphasized the non-preferential part of God's character. Paul spoke about it to the church at Rome, whose people struggled with comparing Jewish heritage and Gentile ignorance:

> There will be trouble and distress for every human being who does evil: first for the Jew, then for the Gentile; but glory, honor and peace for everyone who does good: first for the Jew, then for the Gentile. For God does not show favoritism. (Romans 2:9-11)

Paul also used this character trait to help slaves live honorably:

> Anyone who does wrong will be repaid for their wrongs, and there is no favoritism. (Colossians 3:25)

And he communicated the same to their masters:

> And masters, treat your slaves in the same way. Do not threaten them, since you know that he who is both their Master and yours is in heaven, and there is no favoritism with him. (Ephesians 6:9)

Peter finally realized this truth as God showed him several years after Pentecost that Gentiles, too, could be saved:

God's Anger—Doesn't Show Favoritism

> Then Peter began to speak: "I now realize how true it is that God does not show favoritism but accepts from every nation the one who fears him and does what is right." (Acts 10:34-35)

Not only does God not show favoritism, He expects us to treat each other the same way. As expressed in this passage from Leviticus, we tend to show favoritism (or partiality) by giving less privileges to those who have less, and more privileges to those who have more. God knew that would be our tendency, and wanted to create in us hearts that treat everyone in the same manner:

> Do not pervert justice; do not show partiality to the poor or favoritism to the great, but judge your neighbor fairly. (Leviticus 19:15)

Since we are to imitate God, Paul emphasized this character trait through his letter to Timothy:

> I charge you, in the sight of God and Christ Jesus and the elect angels, to keep these instructions without partiality, and to do nothing out of favoritism. (1 Timothy 5:21)

And James addressed the same issue with his letter to all believers:
> My brothers, as believers in our glorious Lord Jesus Christ, don't show favoritism. (James 2:1)

James even exposed this sin with a specific example, when a person's financial influence dictates where a person is seated in a meeting. How do you know whether your anger is showing favoritism as you interact with people day-to-day? Sometimes asking yourself a few questions can help clarify your perspective and purify your motives:

- Would I react the same way if this person was my boss? My sister or brother? My neighbor? My daughter or son? My spouse? My mom or dad? (Sometimes our anger is more easily triggered with certain people and our history with them.)
- Am I reacting this way to gain something in return? (We can use our anger to manipulate.)
- Am I more patient and exhibit more tolerance when it's a person I like (such as a friend, versus a stranger or someone with a certain personality type that's similar to mine)?

Your anger should be based on an injustice or wrong that has been committed to you or someone else. If it's based on anything else, then you may be showing prejudice, favoritism or ulterior motives.

Given God's character to show no favoritism, how does he respond when we sin? If God's anger is aroused because of something you've done or continue to do, he will respond the same way and allow the natural consequences to play out, regardless of who you are or what you have done for him. Consider the men sent out to explore the land of Canaan:

> The LORD said to Moses, "Send some men to explore the land of Canaan, which I am giving to the Israelites. From each ancestral tribe send one of its leaders."...At the end of forty days they returned from exploring the land.
> They came back to Moses and Aaron and the whole Israelite community at Kadesh in the Desert of Paran. There they reported to them and to the whole assembly and showed them the fruit of the land. They gave Moses this account: "We went into the land to which you sent us, and it does flow with milk and honey! Here is its fruit. But the people who live there are powerful, and the cities are fortified and very large. We even saw descendants of Anak there. The Amalekites live in the Negev; the Hittites, Jebusites and Amorites live in the hill country; and the Canaanites live near the sea and along the Jordan."
> Then Caleb silenced the people before Moses and said, "We should go up and take possession of the land, for we can certainly do it."
> But the men who had gone up with him said, "We can't attack those people; they are stronger than we are." And they spread among the Israelites a bad report about the land they had explored. They said, "The land we explored devours those living in it. All the people we saw there are of great size. We saw the Nephilim there (the descendants of Anak come from the Nephilim). We seemed like grasshoppers in our own eyes, and we looked the same to them." (Numbers 13:1-2, 25-33)

These men were leaders from each tribe. They had built a reputation and provided leadership over time to establish themselves as reliable and capable people. Yet when they became fearful, and did not trust in God's providence and character as Caleb and Joshua did, God's anger was targeted equally among them, as well as to the people they influenced. God did not show favoritism to these leaders even though they had made sacrifices in serving his people over the last 40 days. He didn't excuse their reaction to fatigue or exhaustion. He also didn't treat the Israelites differently, considering they had not seen the Promised Land, but merely believed the report they heard:

> That night all the members of the community raised their voices and wept aloud. All the Israelites grumbled against Moses and Aaron, and the whole assembly said to them, "If only we had died in Egypt! Or in this wilderness! Why is the LORD bringing us to this land only to let us fall by the sword? Our wives and children will be taken as plunder. Wouldn't it be better for us to go back to Egypt?" And they said to each other, "We should choose a leader and go back to Egypt." (Numbers 14:1-4)

From God's perspective, the people were all guilty of showing contempt to him and he responded accordingly:

> The LORD replied, "I have forgiven them, as you asked. Nevertheless, as surely as I live and as surely as the glory of the LORD fills the whole earth, not one of those who saw my glory and the signs I performed in Egypt and in the wilderness but who disobeyed me and tested me ten times—not one of them will ever see the land I promised on oath to their ancestors. No one who has treated me with contempt will ever see it." (Numbers 14:20-23)

God's anger was aroused when Aaron and Miriam questioned their brother Moses' leadership:

> Miriam and Aaron began to talk against Moses because of his Cushite wife, for he had married a Cushite. "Has the LORD spoken only through Moses?" they asked. "Hasn't he also spoken through us?" And the LORD heard this.
> (Now Moses was a very humble man, more humble than anyone else on the face of the earth.)
> At once the LORD said to Moses, Aaron and Miriam, "Come out to the tent of meeting, all three of you." So the three of them went out. Then the LORD came down in a pillar of cloud; he stood at the entrance to the tent and summoned Aaron and Miriam. When the two of them stepped forward, he said, "Listen to my words:
> "When there is a prophet among you, I, the LORD, reveal myself to them in visions, I speak to them in dreams. But this is not true of my servant Moses; he is faithful in all my house. With him I speak face to face, clearly and not in riddles; he sees the form of the LORD. Why then were you not afraid to speak against my servant Moses?"
> The anger of the LORD burned against them, and he left them.
> When the cloud lifted from above the tent, Miriam's skin was leprous—it became as white as snow. Aaron turned toward her and saw that she had a defiling skin disease, and he said to Moses, "Please, my lord, I ask you not to hold against us the sin we have so foolishly committed. (Numbers 12:1-11)

God didn't treat them differently because Miriam was a prophet (Exodus 15:20), or because Aaron provided leadership during the exodus from Egypt. Even though they played a significant role in Israel's history, and they were Moses' brother and sister, God did not show favoritism when their sin aroused his anger.

When God punished Moses by not allowing him to enter the Promised Land, he could have considered all that Moses had been through, and how much he had provided for God's people. God described Moses as a very humble man, more humble than anyone else on the face of the earth. Yet, when Moses showed contempt toward God, as he struck the rock instead of speaking to it, God delivered his just punishment. Moses discussed it with God:

> At that time I pleaded with the LORD: "Sovereign LORD, you have begun to show to your servant your greatness and your strong hand. For what god is there in heaven or on earth who can do the deeds and mighty works you do? Let me go over and see the good land beyond the Jordan—that fine hill country and Lebanon."
> But because of you the LORD was angry with me and would not listen to me. "That is enough," the LORD said. "Do not speak to me anymore about this matter. Go up to the top of Pisgah and look west and north and south and east. Look at the land with your own eyes, since you are not going to cross this Jordan. (Deuteronomy 3:23-27)

Moses had such a close friendship with God that on several occasions, he persuaded God to change his angry reaction to the Israelites' continual grumbling or complaining. Moses couldn't persuade God this time, concerning his own punishment, even though he continued to discuss it to a point where God had to say, "That is enough!" Sometimes my heart is softened toward my own children based on their reasoning, and I change their punishment. I re-evaluate my reaction as, "maybe I was too harsh" or, "I've been a little irritable lately." Even if your logic is appropriate, once you do it, that child will remember and they will pursue the next persuasive talk with even more determination. God is not like that. Of course, he doesn't have the sinful nature to consider as we do, but he did not let Moses talk him out of his discipline. He must have entertained the discussion for a time based on his friendship and relationship with Moses, but at some point, it was over. He showed no favoritism, even with Moses.

When God used the Assyrians to administer discipline to the Israelites and carry them into exile, He became angry with the King of Assyria and handled him directly:

> Who is it you have ridiculed and blasphemed? Against whom have you raised your voice and lifted your eyes in pride? Against the Holy One of Israel!...
> Have you not heard? Long ago I ordained it. In days of old I planned it; now I have brought it to pass, that you have turned fortified cities into piles of stone...
> But I know where you are and when you come and go and how you rage against me. Because you rage against me and because your insolence has reached my ears, I will put my hook in your nose and my bit in your mouth, and I will make you return by the way you came...
> Therefore this is what the LORD says concerning the king of Assyria: "'He will not enter this city or shoot an arrow here. He will not come before it with shield or build a siege ramp against it. By the way that he came he will return; he will not enter this city, declares the LORD. I will defend this city and save it, for my sake and for the sake of David my servant.'"
> That night the angel of the LORD went out and put to death a hundred and eighty-five thousand in the Assyrian camp. When the people got up the next morning—there were all the dead bodies! So Sennacherib king of Assyria broke

God's Anger—Doesn't Show Favoritism

camp and withdrew. He returned to Nineveh and stayed there. (2 Kings 19:22, 25, 27-28, 32-36)

> "Woe to the Assyrian, the rod of my anger, in whose hand is the club of my wrath! I send him against a godless nation, I dispatch him against a people who anger me, to seize loot and snatch plunder, and to trample them down like mud in the streets. But this is not what he intends, this is not what he has in mind; his purpose is to destroy, to put an end to many nations...
>
> "When the Lord has finished all his work against Mount Zion and Jerusalem, he will say, "I will punish the king of Assyria for the willful pride of his heart and the haughty look in his eyes. For he says: "'By the strength of my hand I have done this, and by my wisdom, because I have understanding. I removed the boundaries of nations, I plundered their treasures; like a mighty one I subdued their kings.'" (Isaiah 10:5-7, 12-13)

God did not show favoritism to the Assyrians, even though they helped God achieve his purposes. It didn't matter. No one is exempt from the natural consequences of his own sin.

The same thing happened when God used Babylon to bring discipline to Judah:

> "Sit in silence, go into darkness, queen city of the Babylonians; no more will you be called queen of kingdoms. I was angry with my people and desecrated my inheritance; I gave them into your hand, and you showed them no mercy. Even on the aged you laid a very heavy yoke. You said, 'I am forever—the eternal queen!' But you did not consider these things or reflect on what might happen.
>
> "Now then, listen, you lover of pleasure, lounging in your security and saying to yourself, 'I am, and there is none besides me. I will never be a widow or suffer the loss of children.' Both of these will overtake you in a moment, on a single day: loss of children and widowhood. They will come upon you in full measure, in spite of your many sorceries and all your potent spells." (Isaiah 47:5-9)

Maybe God will use you to help with someone else's sin, but if you're harsh or unloving in the process, he will deal with you as well. God doesn't get overwhelmed as we do. He doesn't get fatigued in handling issue after issue as we do. If his purposes expose more sin, he will deal with it all...person by person, whether with a leader or a greeter. God's anger does not show favoritism when it comes to our sin, even within the church.

A similar incident occurred when King Ahaz of Judah committed evil in the Lord's eyes. God delivered Ahaz into the hands of King Resin of Aram and King Pekah of Israel. But when Israel viciously slaughtered these men from Judah, the Lord took note that they killed 120,000 soldiers in a single day and took captive 200,000 women and children back to Samaria.

> But a prophet of the LORD named Oded was there, and he went out to

meet the army when it returned to Samaria. He said to them, "Because the LORD, the God of your ancestors, was angry with Judah, he gave them into your hand. But you have slaughtered them in a rage that reaches to heaven. And now you intend to make the men and women of Judah and Jerusalem your slaves. But aren't you also guilty of sins against the LORD your God? Now listen to me! Send back your fellow Israelites you have taken as prisoners, for the LORD's fierce anger rests on you." (2 Chronicles 28:9-11)

From the Old Testament to the New Testament, God's character is the same. He will reward or discipline according to what we deserve:

One thing God has spoken, two things I have heard: "Power belongs to you, God, and with you, Lord, is unfailing love"; and, "You reward everyone according to what they have done." (Psalms 62:11-12)

"I the LORD search the heart and examine the mind, to reward each person according to their conduct, according to what their deeds deserve." (Jeremiah 17:10)

For we must all appear before the judgment seat of Christ, so that each of us may receive what is due us for the things done while in the body, whether good or bad. (2 Corinthians 5:10)

When you don't see God's blessings based on your expectations and evaluations of your life, you may think, "I am not receiving what I deserve!" Or if God decides that some discipline is in order to help you mature and change, you may think, "God is not being fair!" or "I don't deserve this!". Only the mature person is able to accept reproof and correction without resentment. God is not a referee who makes bad calls; he is not moody or having a bad day. Be careful when you think God is not being fair to you. Do you really want to receive all that you deserve?

Paul understood this concept, and tried to help the Christians in the church at Rome understand it, too. It was such a difficult idea for the Jews to grasp, the concept that Gentiles could be saved, even though they didn't have the heritage or history or the law. But then God had to turn right around and help the Gentiles remain humble and grateful, because they started to get the "entitlement" mindset. Paul wrote the following to communicate the existence of the same character trait in God, that he does not show favoritism:

I am talking to you Gentiles. Inasmuch as I am the apostle to the Gentiles, I take pride in my ministry in the hope that I may somehow arouse my own people to envy and save some of them...

If some of the branches have been broken off, and you, though a wild olive shoot, have been grafted in among the others and now share in the nourishing sap from the olive root, do not consider yourself to be superior to those other

God's Anger—Doesn't Show Favoritism

branches. If you do, consider this: You do not support the root, but the root supports you. You will say then, "Branches were broken off so that I could be grafted in." Granted. But they were broken off because of unbelief, and you stand by faith. Do not be arrogant, but tremble. For if God did not spare the natural branches, he will not spare you either.

Consider therefore the kindness and sternness of God: sternness to those who fell, but kindness to you, provided that you continue in his kindness. Otherwise, you also will be cut off. (Romans 11:13-14, 17-22)

This arrogance can be just as tempting for us as the years go by. Being a disciple in God's church is such an honor, a privilege, and a blessing. After 10, 20 or 30 years as disciples, we can forget what it was like to be a "Gentile." We can become dull to our own sin and begin thinking that God will treat us differently, because of all the money we've given, hours sacrificed, people converted, character changed, or even our increased knowledge of the Bible. Just remember, God's anger may be slow to develop, but when it is aroused, he will not show favoritism to anyone.

CHAPTER SEVEN

God's Anger–Slow to Develop

Beware of him that is slow to anger; for when it is long coming, it is the stronger when it comes, and the longer kept.
—Francis Quarles

Many of the Psalmists characterized God's anger as slow to develop:

But you, Lord, are a compassionate and gracious God, slow to anger, abounding in love and faithfulness. (Psalm 86:15)

The LORD is compassionate and gracious, slow to anger, abounding in love. He will not always accuse, nor will he harbor his anger forever; he does not treat us as our sins deserve or repay us according to our iniquities. (Psalm 103:8-10)

The LORD is gracious and compassionate, slow to anger and rich in love. The LORD is good to all; he has compassion on all he has made. (Psalm 145:8-9)

Several of the prophets also saw God that way:

He prayed to the LORD, "Isn't this what I said, LORD, when I was still at home? That is what I tried to forestall by fleeing to Tarshish. I knew that you are a gracious and compassionate God, slow to anger and abounding in love, a God who relents from sending calamity. (Jonah 4:2)

Rend your heart and not your garments. Return to the LORD your God, for he is gracious and compassionate, slow to anger and abounding in love, and he relents from sending calamity. (Joel 2:13)

The LORD is slow to anger but great in power; the LORD will not leave the guilty unpunished. His way is in the whirlwind and the storm, and clouds are the dust of his feet. (Nahum 1:3)

Where did all of these poets and prophets learn about this attribute of God's character? They learned about it from God himself, as he told Moses after the "golden calf" incident:

God's Anger—Slow to Develop

> So Moses chiseled out two stone tablets like the first ones and went up Mount Sinai early in the morning, as the LORD had commanded him; and he carried the two stone tablets in his hands. Then the LORD came down in the cloud and stood there with him and proclaimed his name, the LORD. And he passed in front of Moses, proclaiming, "The LORD, the LORD, the compassionate and gracious God, slow to anger, abounding in love and faithfulness, maintaining love to thousands, and forgiving wickedness, rebellion and sin. Yet he does not leave the guilty unpunished; he punishes the children and their children for the sin of the parents to the third and fourth generation." (Exodus 34:4-7)

The Lord reminded Moses that even though he is slow to anger, he will still allow or bring the natural consequences of our sin into our lives. Just because you may be experiencing some of God's discipline in your life right now, don't interpret it automatically as God's anger. Our view of God and his anger can be shaped by our parents, our environment, and our own insecurities, when we doubt that God believes in us anymore or loves us unconditionally. When you consider what transpired prior to God talking to Moses about his own character, you can begin to appreciate just how much it really takes to stir his anger.

Before and during the Exodus, God displayed his love and ability to take care of the Israelites:

- Led them out of Egypt with powerful miracles, several times sparing the Israelites Egypt's pain and suffering (Exodus 7-12)
- Led them with a pillar of cloud by day and a pillar of fire by night that never left them as a reminder of God's presence and help them know when and where to move (Exodus 13)
- Split the Red Sea allowing them to cross on dry land and completely destroyed Pharaoh and the Egyptian army (Exodus 14)

There are two timeframes regarding God's relationship with the Israelites when they came out of Egypt. The first timeframe is the first year in the desert, when Moses received the Ten Commandments and the rest of the laws at Mt. Sinai. If the Israelites would have focused on remembering the events from the Exodus, their hearts could have remained grateful when they expressed their needs while in the desert. They didn't recall those incidents, of course, so they began to complain and grumble about many of their circumstances, which challenged God's patience, his love, and eventually his anger. It all came to a head when they made the golden calf while Moses was on the mountain receiving the Ten Commandments. God wanted to destroy them, but Moses interceded. In response, God allowed the Levites to kill 3000 people and he sent a plague among them.

The second timeframe was the second year in the desert when they reached Canaan, also called the Promised Land. After the twelve chosen leaders explored the land and ten of them didn't believe that God would help them defeat the inhabitants, God's anger was aroused again.

> The LORD said to Moses, "How long will these people treat me with contempt? How long will they refuse to believe in me, in spite of all the signs I have performed among them? I will strike them down with a plague and destroy them, but I will make you into a nation greater and stronger than they." (Numbers 14:11-12)

Moses intervened again and God agreed not to destroy the people immediately, but he decided that they would die in the wilderness over the next 40 years. Ten of the twelve scouts died immediately from a plague. God had reached his limit:

> The LORD replied, "I have forgiven them, as you asked. Nevertheless, as surely as I live and as surely as the glory of the LORD fills the whole earth, not one of those who saw my glory and the signs I performed in Egypt and in the wilderness but who disobeyed me and tested me ten times—not one of them will ever see the land I promised on oath to their ancestors. No one who has treated me with contempt will ever see it. (Numbers 14:20-23)

> The LORD said to Moses and Aaron: "How long will this wicked community grumble against me? I have heard the complaints of these grumbling Israelites. So tell them, 'As surely as I live, declares the LORD, I will do to you the very thing I heard you say: In this wilderness your bodies will fall—every one of you twenty years old or more who was counted in the census and who has grumbled against me. Not one of you will enter the land I swore with uplifted hand to make your home, except Caleb son of Jephunneh and Joshua son of Nun.
> As for your children that you said would be taken as plunder, I will bring them in to enjoy the land you have rejected. But as for you, your bodies will fall in this wilderness. Your children will be shepherds here for forty years, suffering for your unfaithfulness, until the last of your bodies lies in the wilderness. For forty years—one year for each of the forty days you explored the land—you will suffer for your sins and know what it is like to have me against you.' I, the LORD, have spoken, and I will surely do these things to this whole wicked community, which has banded together against me. They will meet their end in this wilderness; here they will die." (Numbers 14:26-35)

God's anger was aroused and his punishment was just and final. It was not negotiable. Did you notice that God told Moses that the Israelites "had disobeyed me and tested me ten times"? God kept track and didn't forget any of the moments when the Israelites complained and grumbled. As an engineer, I wondered whether it was really ten times, or if God just picked a number greater than three to make a point. Let's look back on those moments and see if God's anger was slow to develop and if it really was ten times:

God's Anger—Slow to Develop

FIRST TIMEFRAME—Israelites left Egypt and were hanging out around Mt. Sinai for about a year:

Incident #1—Israelites complained about no water, so God turned the bitter water sweet, then brought them to a desert oasis (Exodus 15).

> So the people grumbled against Moses, saying, "What are we to drink?" (Exodus 15:24)

Incident #2—Israelites complained about no food, so God brought quail and daily manna (Ex 16), but the way they expressed their hunger would hurt God because they were accusing him of starving them to death!

> The Israelites said to them, "If only we had died by the LORD's hand in Egypt! There we sat around pots of meat and ate all the food we wanted, but you have brought us out into this desert to starve this entire assembly to death." (Exodus 16:3)

Incident #3—Israelites disobeyed God and kept some of the manna until morning, which made Moses angry (Exodus 16).

Incident #4—Israelites disobeyed God and looked for manna on the Sabbath. (Exodus 16)

> Then the LORD said to Moses, "How long will you refuse to keep my commands and my instructions?" (Exodus 16:28)

Incident #5—Israelites complained about no water, so God brought water from a rock as Moses struck it (Exodus 17).

> So they quarreled with Moses and said, "Give us water to drink." Moses replied, "Why do you quarrel with me? Why do you put the LORD to the test?" But the people were thirsty for water there, and they grumbled against Moses. They said, "Why did you bring us up out of Egypt to make us and our children and livestock die of thirst?"...
> And he called the place Massah and Meribah because the Israelites quarreled and because they tested the LORD saying, "Is the LORD among us or not?" (Exodus 17:2-3, 7)

God began questioning their hearts and their commitment to him, but he hadn't really become angry yet. Would you have shown this amount of patience? Would your anger be stirred when they complained and grumbled several times, or questioned your motive and love for them? What would you have done when they just refused to obey concerning the manna? It's one thing to express a need, but to do it with an ungrateful spirit and demanding attitude tests my patience and love for someone. As parents, we are tempted in this way by our children, and leaders can be tempted by the members of their congregation or small group. We all have our "hot buttons" that normally only need to be pressed once or twice to arouse our anger. We have even less patience when we are tired or stressed about other things.

At this point, the relationship was a bit strained, but God was still providing for them and meeting their needs. As God communicated his commands and laws to Moses, the people agreed to listen and obey:

> So Moses went back and summoned the elders of the people and set before them all the words the LORD had commanded him to speak. The people all responded together, "We will do everything the LORD has said." So Moses brought their answer back to the LORD. (Exodus 19:7-8)

> When Moses went and told the people all the LORD's words and laws, they responded with one voice, "Everything the LORD has said we will do." (Exodus 24:3)

> Then he took the Book of the Covenant and read it to the people. They responded, "We will do everything the LORD has said; we will obey." (Exodus 24:7)

Does your patience increase when people or children are cooperative or sincere for a time? When my children say "I'm sorry," and really mean it, my heart changes towards them and my patience increases. When my children respond quickly, "Oh, sorry," but it's not sincere or heartfelt, then I tend to view them with a wary eye. I can tell when they just say it because they are supposed to say it, or because they are trying to avoid a higher degree of punishment. Which way was it for the Israelites? I don't know and sometimes I'm not sure as a parent, but one thing I've learned with my children is that their hearts are revealed in the next few hours, or in the next few days. If their apology or commitment is sincere, they have a more cooperative spirit and show less irritation. If their apology is not real, they show their true colors very quickly, usually the same day.

Incident #6—Moses went up on the mountain for 40 days and 40 nights, and the people became impatient, creating the golden calf in Exodus 32. God wanted to destroy them all and start over with Moses, but Moses interceded and God relented:

> The LORD replied to Moses, "Whoever has sinned against me I will blot out of my book. Now go, lead the people to the place I spoke of, and my angel will go before you. However, when the time comes for me to punish, I will punish them for their sin." And the LORD struck the people with a plague because of what they did with the calf Aaron had made. (Exodus 32:33-35)

God's Anger—Slow to Develop

By declaring this statement about the golden calf, "These are your gods, Israel, who brought you up out of Egypt," the Israelites had pushed God's "hot button." If you are a parent, and your children found someone or something else and declared, "This is my real family; they have provided for me and helped me through the last several years," you may experience a little of what God felt and the pain it caused. God's reaction was fueled by hurt and anger towards his people:

> Then the LORD said to Moses, "Leave this place, you and the people you brought up out of Egypt, and go up to the land I promised on oath to Abraham, Isaac and Jacob, saying, 'I will give it to your descendants.' I will send an angel before you and drive out the Canaanites, Amorites, Hittites, Perizzites, Hivites and Jebusites. Go up to the land flowing with milk and honey. But I will not go with you, because you are a stiff-necked people and I might destroy you on the way."
> When the people heard these distressing words, they began to mourn and no one put on any ornaments. For the LORD had said to Moses, "Tell the Israelites, 'You are a stiff-necked people. If I were to go with you even for a moment, I might destroy you. Now take off your ornaments and I will decide what to do with you.'" So the Israelites stripped off their ornaments at Mount Horeb. (Exodus 33:1-6)

Maybe even God recognized a moment where he needed some time to cool off and reconsider how to proceed with his people. God's anger can be aroused, but it is not dependent on his fatigue or stress as ours is. His love motivates him to overlook so much and to continue to believe in us when we don't listen, and we complain or grumble, while continuing to promise to obey him. For the next few months, the Israelites completed the Tabernacle, Moses got a new set of laws, and they set up the priesthood. There weren't a lot of conflicts between the Israelites and God. After just over a year since leaving Egypt, the Israelites had another opportunity to show their faithfulness and commitment to what they said to Moses about obedience to God.

SECOND TIMEFRAME—Israelites left Mt. Sinai and traveled to the Promised Land:

Incident #7—Leaving Sinai, the people complained about their hardships. God's anger was aroused, and fire consumed some of the outskirts of camp (Numbers 11).

Incident #8—The rabble with them began to crave other food and Israelites complained about having only manna to eat. The Lord became exceedingly angry and gave them quail for a month because they rejected the Lord and said, "Why did we ever leave Egypt?" He also sent a plague among them that killed those who craved other food (Numbers 11).

Incident #9—Aaron and Miriam opposed Moses and "the anger of the Lord burned against them" as Miriam had leprosy for 7 days (Numbers 12).

Incident #10—The people explored the Promised Land, but grumbled against Moses and Aaron, afraid their children would be taken as plunder. They wanted to choose a leader and go back to Egypt. They talked about stoning Moses and Aaron (Numbers 14).

God was correct. The Israelites "had disobeyed me and tested me ten times" and he responded with a punishment that would last 40 years. His anger was slow to develop, considering everything he had endured, from their ungrateful and demanding spirits, to their insincere promises and commitments. Most of us would have probably brought the punishment sooner or may not have listened to Moses...twice.

When God did bring punishment, it was appropriate and just. It does seem that God had less patience once they reached the Promised Land, but considering their history from Mt. Sinai, it was the loving thing to do to give them another chance, but at the same time "turn up the heat" when their hearts didn't change. This is not the only such case study in Israel's history. God's anger was slow to develop with other people, too.

When Jonah disobeyed God and ran away, God brought a storm and made the storm rougher as time went on. When the crew threw Jonah overboard, God provided a large fish, then waited three days and three nights for Jonah's heart to change. As Jonah repented, and promised "what I have vowed I will make good", the large fish vomited him onto dry land and God repeated his command. God may have waited more than three days if Jonah wasn't ready to repent. Even as God continued to teach Jonah through a vine and Jonah's own anger, he was patient and loving toward him.

When it comes to other people, we are as Jonah was, wanting God's anger to be instant and his retribution to be swift. Of course, we want his patience and mercy when it comes to ourselves. Considering our own sin and the mercy we have already received is a great place to start to show this same love to other people as we deal with their weaknesses and sin. Paul understood this as he wrote to Timothy:

> I thank Christ Jesus our Lord, who has given me strength, that he considered me trustworthy, appointing me to his service. Even though I was once a blasphemer and a persecutor and a violent man, I was shown mercy because I acted in ignorance and unbelief. The grace of our Lord was poured out on me abundantly, along with the faith and love that are in Christ Jesus.
>
> Here is a trustworthy saying that deserves full acceptance: Christ Jesus came into the world to save sinners—of whom I am the worst. But for that very reason I was shown mercy so that in me, the worst of sinners, Christ Jesus might display his immense patience as an example for those who would believe in him and receive eternal life. (1 Timothy 1:12-16)

Then when Paul wrote to the Corinthians of their multitude of sinful issues (immorality, improper Lord's Supper, lawsuits, arguing, division about leaders, boasting about gifts, etc), he could sincerely write about love and anger based on his own relationship with God:

> Love is patient, love is kind. It does not envy, it does not boast, it is not proud. It does not dishonor others, it is not self-seeking, it is not easily angered, it keeps no record of wrongs. (1 Corinthians 13:4-5)

After Moses died, God worked through Joshua to conquer the Promised Land, then started to lead his people through judges, then kings (although that's not what he wanted):

> But when they said, "Give us a king to lead us," this displeased Samuel; so he prayed to the LORD. And the LORD told him: "Listen to all that the people are saying to you; it is not you they have rejected, but they have rejected me as their king. As they have done from the day I brought them up out of Egypt until this day, forsaking me and serving other gods, so they are doing to you...
> When that day comes, you will cry out for relief from the king you have chosen, but the LORD will not answer you in that day."
> But the people refused to listen to Samuel. "No!" they said. "We want a king over us. Then we will be like all the other nations, with a king to lead us and to go out before us and fight our battles."
> When Samuel heard all that the people said, he repeated it before the LORD. The LORD answered, "Listen to them and give them a king." (1 Samuel 8:6-8, 18-22a)

> You are destroyed, Israel, because you are against me, against your helper. Where is your king, that he may save you? Where are your rulers in all your towns, of whom you said, 'Give me a king and princes'? So in my anger I gave you a king, and in my wrath I took him away. (Hosea 13:9-11)

God continued to reach out to his people through prophets, but the people's hearts didn't really change for any sustained period of time. Approximately 500 years after the Exodus, the kingdom was divided into the northern kingdom, Israel, and the southern kingdom, Judah, because of unrepentant sin.

God's anger was eventually aroused to a point where he disciplined both kingdoms, as he sent Israel into captivity by Assyria about 200 years later:

> All this took place because the Israelites had sinned against the LORD their God, who had brought them up out of Egypt from under the power of Pharaoh king of Egypt. They worshiped other gods and followed the practices of the nations the LORD had driven out before them, as well as the practices that the kings of Israel had introduced. The Israelites secretly did things against the LORD their God that were not right. From watchtower to fortified city they built themselves high places in all their towns. They set up sacred stones and

Asherah poles on every high hill and under every spreading tree. At every high place they burned incense, as the nations whom the LORD had driven out before them had done. They did wicked things that aroused the LORD's anger. They worshiped idols, though the LORD had said, "You shall not do this."

The LORD warned Israel and Judah through all his prophets and seers: "Turn from your evil ways. Observe my commands and decrees, in accordance with the entire Law that I commanded your ancestors to obey and that I delivered to you through my servants the prophets."

But they would not listen and were as stiff-necked as their ancestors, who did not trust in the LORD their God. They rejected his decrees and the covenant he had made with their ancestors and the statutes he had warned them to keep. They followed worthless idols and themselves became worthless. They imitated the nations around them although the LORD had ordered them, "Do not do as they do."

They forsook all the commands of the LORD their God and made for themselves two idols cast in the shape of calves, and an Asherah pole. They bowed down to all the starry hosts, and they worshiped Baal. They sacrificed their sons and daughters in the fire. They practiced divination and sought omens and sold themselves to do evil in the eyes of the LORD, arousing his anger.

So the LORD was very angry with Israel and removed them from his presence. Only the tribe of Judah was left, and even Judah did not keep the commands of the LORD their God. They followed the practices Israel had introduced. Therefore the LORD rejected all the people of Israel; he afflicted them and gave them into the hands of plunderers, until he thrust them from his presence.

When he tore Israel away from the house of David, they made Jeroboam son of Nebat their king. Jeroboam enticed Israel away from following the LORD and caused them to commit a great sin. The Israelites persisted in all the sins of Jeroboam and did not turn away from them until the LORD removed them from his presence, as he had warned through all his servants the prophets. So the people of Israel were taken from their homeland into exile in Assyria, and they are still there. (2 Kings 17:7-23)

And he sent Judah into captivity by Babylon about 100 years after that:

And though the LORD has sent all his servants the prophets to you again and again, you have not listened or paid any attention. They said, "Turn now, each of you, from your evil ways and your evil practices, and you can stay in the land the LORD gave to you and your ancestors for ever and ever. Do not follow other gods to serve and worship them; do not arouse my anger with what your hands have made. Then I will not harm you."

"But you did not listen to me," declares the LORD, "and you have aroused my anger with what your hands have made, and you have brought harm to yourselves." (Jeremiah 25:4-7)

If it took hundreds of years for him to thrust them from his presence, then one could view God's anger as being very slow to develop. How do these examples affect you? I can tell you how they have affected me:

God's Anger—Slow to Develop

- Since God counted and remembered all ten of the Israelites' complaints and grumblings, I have become more cautious about how I pray about my needs and share my emotions day-to-day. I don't hesitate to express the needs with the emotions; I just make sure I remember the blessings and what God has already done for me and my family.
- I am more grateful for the blood of Jesus that allows me to have forgiveness, second chances, and time to change.
- I am motivated to really repent and not just flippantly say, "Oh, sorry about that."

The Hebrews writer shared the same lesson as he reflected on God's anger toward Israel's sin:

> That is why I was angry with that generation; I said, 'Their hearts are always going astray, and they have not known my ways.'
> So I declared on oath in my anger, 'They shall never enter my rest.'
> See to it, brothers and sisters, that none of you has a sinful, unbelieving heart that turns away from the living God. But encourage one another daily, as long as it is called "Today," so that none of you may be hardened by sin's deceitfulness. (Hebrews 3:10-13)

Paul said it best in his letter to the church at Rome:

> Now we know that God's judgment against those who do such things is based on truth. So when you, a mere human being, pass judgment on them and yet do the same things, do you think you will escape God's judgment? Or do you show contempt for the riches of his kindness, forbearance and patience, not realizing that God's kindness is intended to lead you to repentance? (Romans 2:2-4)

Peter also understood this concept when writing his second letter:

> But do not forget this one thing, dear friends: With the Lord a day is like a thousand years, and a thousand years are like a day. The Lord is not slow in keeping his promise, as some understand slowness. Instead he is patient with you, not wanting anyone to perish, but everyone to come to repentance. (2 Peter 3:8-9)

God's anger is meant to bring about change, and that usually means change in us or repentance. God's anger is slow to develop, and hopefully his patience will motivate you to truly repent when God disciplines you or shows you a sin in your life. Otherwise, his wrath will eventually be revealed.

CHAPTER EIGHT

God's Anger–Temporary

Don't take life too seriously. It's only a temporary condition.
—Bill Knapp

Although Bill Knapp's quote shouldn't be a guide for viewing God and his commands, life on earth is temporary. Everything associated with this life is temporary, from animal and plant life, to buildings and nations. Since I'm writing this chapter during tax season, I will mention here that even the Internal Revenue Service (IRS) won't be around forever. That's a bad thing if you get a big tax refund every year. The good and the bad about this life will all be gone one day. That end can bring rejoicing and relief as well as heartache and tears.

When you consider angry emotions, though, I'm not sure that they will be gone forever. Whenever Jesus spoke about the final judgment, he mentioned six times in the book of Matthew that there "will be weeping and gnashing of teeth". The particular phrase "gnashing of teeth" means angry complaining or a show of anger or dismay. Your anger or tears may last forever, depending on where you stand on Judgment Day. God's punishment can be viewed as temporary in this life, but eternal in the next life. But what about God's anger?

> Sing the praises of the LORD, you his faithful people; praise his holy name. For his anger lasts only a moment, but his favor lasts a lifetime; weeping may stay for the night, but rejoicing comes in the morning. (Psalm 30:4-5)

> The LORD is compassionate and gracious, slow to anger, abounding in love. He will not always accuse, nor will he harbor his anger forever; he does not treat us as our sins deserve or repay us according to our iniquities. (Psalm 103:8-10)

In order to answer the question, we need to keep in mind God's view of time:

> But do not forget this one thing, dear friends: With the Lord a day is like a thousand years, and a thousand years are like a day. (2 Peter 3:8)

Think about the times when God displayed his anger:

- During the 40-day rainstorm that flooded the earth, Noah was in the ark just over a year.
- Israel's wandering in the desert lasted 40 years.
- Israel's exile to Assyria lasted 110 years.
- Judah's exile to Babylon lasted 70 years.

None of these events lasted forever. Consider David when he sinned against God and God let him choose his own punishment:

> Satan rose up against Israel and incited David to take a census of Israel. So David said to Joab and the commanders of the troops, "Go and count the Israelites from Beersheba to Dan. Then report back to me so that I may know how many there are."
> But Joab replied, "May the LORD multiply his troops a hundred times over. My lord the king, are they not all my lord's subjects? Why does my lord want to do this? Why should he bring guilt on Israel?"
> The king's word, however, overruled Joab; so Joab left and went throughout Israel and then came back to Jerusalem. Joab reported the number of the fighting men to David: In all Israel there were one million one hundred thousand men who could handle a sword, including four hundred and seventy thousand in Judah.
> But Joab did not include Levi and Benjamin in the numbering, because the king's command was repulsive to him. This command was also evil in the sight of God; so he punished Israel.
> Then David said to God, "I have sinned greatly by doing this. Now, I beg you, take away the guilt of your servant. I have done a very foolish thing."
> The LORD said to Gad, David's seer, "Go and tell David, 'This is what the LORD says: I am giving you three options. Choose one of them for me to carry out against you.'"
> So Gad went to David and said to him, "This is what the LORD says: 'Take your choice: three years of famine, three months of being swept away before your enemies, with their swords overtaking you, or three days of the sword of the LORD—days of plague in the land, with the angel of the LORD ravaging every part of Israel.' Now then, decide how I should answer the one who sent me."
> David said to Gad, "I am in deep distress. Let me fall into the hands of the LORD, for his mercy is very great; but do not let me fall into human hands." (1 Chronicles 21:1-13)

David chose the option with the shortest time frame—three days. He thought about it and chose the sword of the Lord, remembering God's mercy. Sometimes we have the same mindset as David when we have to endure a negative consequence in our life by thinking, "just get it over with". This mindset can apply to a simple medicine shot, a costly repair bill that will fix an item once and for all rather than having it be a constant nickel-and-dime drain on the budget, or a difficult talk with someone that you know will be painful and challenging. It is sometimes easier to endure something painful when you know the pain isn't going to last.

A satiric view of this mindset comes from one of the demotivational posters at Despair.com, which is called "Regret". It shows a snowboarder going over a high, snow-covered cliff, giving the impression that it's going to be a painful landing. The caption reads, "It hurts to admit when you've made mistakes—but when they're big enough, the pain only lasts a second." When a child disobeys and a spanking is inevitable, it is hard for the child to understand that the pain will only last a moment, but they need to learn this concept. As a parent, I looked forward to the prayer, forgiveness, and reconciliation afterwards.

The Hebrews writer seems to imply that this perspective allowed Jesus to work through his emotions in the Garden of Gethsemane, and embrace the cross:

> And let us run with perseverance the race marked out for us, fixing our eyes on Jesus, the pioneer and perfecter of faith. For the joy set before him he endured the cross, scorning its shame, and sat down at the right hand of the throne of God. Consider him who endured such opposition from sinners, so that you will not grow weary and lose heart. (Hebrews 12:1b-3)

Sometimes it's discouraging to go through God's discipline, because the change is hard or difficult. But imitating Jesus' perspective provides inspiration and motivation to endure, persevere, and embrace the change, no matter how long it takes. Jesus saw the joy we would have if he went through with his sacrifice for us, the joy of pleasing his Father, and the joy he and the Father would share together with their extended family for all eternity. The sacrifice was worth it to him, and God's discipline will be worth it to you, because there will be other people you'll be able to help along the way. Being more mature will allow you to avoid similar problems in the future. Besides, it is pleasing to God to see you grow and allow his discipline to change you.

God tried to help his people learn this concept when they would not repent of their sin, and he disciplined them through the Assyrians:

> So the LORD was very angry with Israel and removed them from his presence. Only the tribe of Judah was left, and even Judah did not keep the commands of the LORD their God. They followed the practices Israel had introduced. Therefore the LORD rejected all the people of Israel; he afflicted them and gave them into the hands of plunderers, until he thrust them from his presence. (2 Kings 17:18-20)

> Therefore this is what the Lord, the LORD Almighty, says: "My people who live in Zion, do not be afraid of the Assyrians, who beat you with a rod and lift up a club against you, as Egypt did. Very soon my anger against you will end and my wrath will be directed to their destruction." (Isaiah 10:24-25)

God's Anger—Temporary

Even when God disciplines us, many times the reason God's anger is temporary is because his love for us is so great. During the Assyrian captivity, beginning in 722 BC through 612 BC (when the Babylonians captured Nineveh, the capital of Assyria), Isaiah and Micah described it well:

> "For a brief moment I abandoned you, but with deep compassion I will bring you back. In a surge of anger I hid my face from you for a moment, but with everlasting kindness I will have compassion on you," says the LORD your Redeemer. "To me this is like the days of Noah, when I swore that the waters of Noah would never again cover the earth. So now I have sworn not to be angry with you, never to rebuke you again. Though the mountains be shaken and the hills be removed, yet my unfailing love for you will not be shaken nor my covenant of peace be removed, says the LORD, who has compassion on you. (Isaiah 54:7-10)

> Foreigners will rebuild your walls, and their kings will serve you. Though in anger I struck you, in favor I will show you compassion. (Isaiah 60:10)

> Do not gloat over me, my enemy! Though I have fallen, I will rise. Though I sit in darkness, the LORD will be my light. Because I have sinned against him, I will bear the LORD's wrath, until he pleads my case and upholds my cause. He will bring me out into the light; I will see his righteousness. Then my enemy will see it and will be covered with shame, she who said to me, "Where is the LORD your God?" My eyes will see her downfall; even now she will be trampled underfoot like mire in the streets. (Micah 7:8-10)

> Who is a God like you, who pardons sin and forgives the transgression of the remnant of his inheritance? You do not stay angry forever but delight to show mercy. You will again have compassion on us; you will tread our sins underfoot and hurl all our iniquities into the depths of the sea. You will be faithful to Jacob, and show love to Abraham, as you pledged on oath to our ancestors in days long ago. (Micah 7:18-20)

Yes, God was angry with Israel, and he allowed Assyria to take Israel captive for about 110 years, but in Isaiah 54, God called it "a brief moment". God handled Judah's 70-year exile into Babylon in a similar way:

> "The days are coming," declares the LORD, "when I will make a new covenant with the people of Israel and with the people of Judah. It will not be like the covenant I made with their ancestors when I took them by the hand to lead them out of Egypt, because they broke my covenant, though I was a husband to them," declares the LORD. "This is the covenant I will make with the people of Israel after that time," declares the LORD. "I will put my law in their minds and write it on their hearts. I will be their God, and they will be my people." (Jeremiah 31:31-33)

> Then the angel of the LORD said, "LORD Almighty, how long will you withhold mercy from Jerusalem and from the towns of Judah, which you have been

angry with these seventy years?" So the LORD spoke kind and comforting words to the angel who talked with me.

Then the angel who was speaking to me said, "Proclaim this word: This is what the LORD Almighty says: 'I am very jealous for Jerusalem and Zion, and I am very angry with the nations that feel secure. I was only a little angry, but they went too far with the punishment.'

"Therefore this is what the LORD says: 'I will return to Jerusalem with mercy, and there my house will be rebuilt. And the measuring line will be stretched out over Jerusalem,' declares the LORD Almighty." (Zechariah 1:12-16)

> This is what the LORD Almighty says: "Just as I had determined to bring disaster on you and showed no pity when your ancestors angered me," says the LORD Almighty, "so now I have determined to do good again to Jerusalem and Judah. Do not be afraid. These are the things you are to do: Speak the truth to each other, and render true and sound judgment in your courts; do not plot evil against each other, and do not love to swear falsely. I hate all this," declares the LORD. (Zechariah 8:14-17)

When Zechariah reminded God that his people had been in this Babylonian captivity for 70 years, the Lord "spoke kind and comforting words to the angel", who then gave that reassuring message to Zechariah. God's anger is temporary, and it should bring some comfort to you, even if you're undergoing God's discipline at this time in your life. It isn't going to last forever. God still loves you, and he longs to show you compassion and mercy. Hopefully, you're learning the lesson quickly, because God is willing to view years as a "brief moment."

CHAPTER NINE

God's Anger—Often Restrained

> *Anger, if not restrained, is frequently more hurtful to us than the injury that provokes it.*
> —Lucius Annaeus Seneca (Roman philosopher, 1st Century AD)

Even though God's anger is justified, we can be comforted knowing that it is restrained from time to time. As the Psalmist in Psalm 78 considered Israel's history, and the repeated cycle of sin-God's discipline-repentance-sin, he took note that God didn't destroy them completely:

> In spite of all this, they kept on sinning; in spite of his wonders, they did not believe. So he ended their days in futility and their years in terror. Whenever God slew them, they would seek him; they eagerly turned to him again. They remembered that God was their Rock, that God Most High was their Redeemer. But then they would flatter him with their mouths, lying to him with their tongues; their hearts were not loyal to him, they were not faithful to his covenant. Yet he was merciful; he forgave their iniquities and did not destroy them. Time after time he restrained his anger and did not stir up his full wrath. He remembered that they were but flesh, a passing breeze that does not return. (Psalm 78:32-39)

From his perspective, God had ample opportunity and justifiable cause to eliminate the Israelites and start over. He had done this before through Noah and the flood, and he was being tempted again in the desert. This time, however, God was swayed by Moses' prayer and intervention, as described in Exodus 32, after the golden calf incident. Why would God relent and restrain his anger when they deserved it?

Throughout their history, the Israelites had plagues, pestilence, military defeat, and exiles, but they were never completely wiped out. When Jesus saw the condition of the temple and the market atmosphere, he waited to make a whip by hand out of cords in John 2. And in a separate incident in Mark 11, Jesus slept on it overnight before "clearing the temple". Other chapters within this book explore God changing his mind, based on our repentance or prayers. At other times, however, God delayed or even relented, and completely changed his mind concerning his response to the anger stirred within him, brought about by different motives:

For Himself...

> For my own name's sake I delay my wrath; for the sake of my praise I hold it back from you, so as not to destroy you completely. See, I have refined you, though not as silver; I have tested you in the furnace of affliction. For my own sake, for my own sake, I do this. How can I let myself be defamed? I will not yield my glory to another. (Isaiah 48:9-11)

To defame means "to attack the good name or reputation of". How would destroying us bring defamation to God, or cause him to yield his glory to another? Think about what would be left if God gave full vent to his anger, based on the things that we do day after day. As author Stephen Bly said, "If He didn't restrain his anger, there would be no one left to praise Him or bring Him glory."[31] We were created to bring glory to God. If we were all gone, there would be only the angels and other heavenly beings to praise him and worship at his throne. When we are saved, our rejoicing brings glory to God as we thank him, praise him, and obey him with whole hearts. Isaiah said it best:

> Since you are precious and honored in my sight, and because I love you, I will give people in exchange for you, nations in exchange for your life. Do not be afraid, for I am with you; I will bring your children from the east and gather you from the west. I will say to the north, 'Give them up!' and to the south, 'Do not hold them back.' Bring my sons from afar and my daughters from the ends of the earth—everyone who is called by my name, whom I created for my glory, whom I formed and made. (Isaiah 43:4-7)

Jesus received glory and honor directly from God on the mountain of transfiguration, as Peter recalled:

> He received honor and glory from God the Father when the voice came to him from the Majestic Glory, saying, "This is my Son, whom I love; with him I am well pleased." (2 Peter 1:17)

We also receive that same honor and glory when we make our decision to follow Jesus and are baptized (Acts 2:38). At that moment, when our sins are forgiven (Act 22:16) and we are made perfect in his eyes (Hebrews 10:14), God says the same thing to us, "This is my son or daughter..."

We can be perfect in God's eyes, even as we continue to grow and change through the Holy Spirit. This is my favorite passage in the entire Bible:

> For by one sacrifice he has made perfect forever those who are being made holy. (Hebrews 10:14)

As God brings discipline into our life, we become more and more holy, but we are still perfect, as we are covered by the blood of Christ. This

God's Anger—Often Restrained

transformation also brings glory to God, as we live this life and continue to change to become more and more like Jesus:

> Now the Lord is the Spirit, and where the Spirit of the Lord is, there is freedom. And we all, who with unveiled faces contemplate the Lord's glory, are being transformed into his image *with ever-increasing glory*, which comes from the Lord, who is the Spirit. (2 Corinthians 3:17-18)

The entire process brings glory to God in both the present life and the life to come:

> In him we were also chosen, having been predestined according to the plan of him who works out everything in conformity with the purpose of his will, in order that we, who were the first to put our hope in Christ, might be for *the praise of his glory*. And you also were included in Christ when you heard the message of truth, the gospel of your salvation. When you believed, you were marked in him with a seal, the promised Holy Spirit, who is a deposit guaranteeing our inheritance until the redemption of those who are God's possession—*to the praise of his glory*. (Ephesians 1:11-14)

Paul summed it up in his letter to the Romans:

> What if God, although choosing to show his wrath and make his power known, bore with great patience the objects of his wrath—prepared for destruction? What if he did this to make the riches of his glory known to the objects of his mercy, whom he prepared in advance for glory— even us, whom he also called, not only from the Jews but also from the Gentiles? (Romans 9:22-24)

Sometimes God isn't willing to give that glory to anyone else or to any other purpose, even when He's angry.

> A person's wisdom yields patience; it is to one's glory to overlook an offense. (Proverbs 19:11)

Consider the following example with Jehoahaz king of Israel:

> In the twenty-third year of Joash son of Ahaziah king of Judah, Jehoahaz son of Jehu became king of Israel in Samaria, and he reigned seventeen years. He did evil in the eyes of the LORD by following the sins of Jeroboam son of Nebat, which he had caused Israel to commit, and he did not turn away from them. So the LORD's anger burned against Israel, and for a long time he kept them under the power of Hazael king of Aram and Ben-Hadad his son. Then Jehoahaz sought the LORD's favor, and the LORD listened to him, for he saw how severely the king of Aram was oppressing Israel. The LORD provided a deliverer for Israel, and they escaped from the power of Aram. So the Israelites lived in their own homes as they had before. But they did not turn away from the sins of

> the house of Jeroboam, which he had caused Israel to commit; they continued in them. Also, the Asherah pole remained standing in Samaria.
> Hazael king of Aram oppressed Israel throughout the reign of Jehoahaz. But the LORD was gracious to them and had compassion and showed concern for them because of his covenant with Abraham, Isaac and Jacob. To this day he has been unwilling to destroy them or banish them from his presence. (2 Kings 13:1-6, 22-23)

They weren't really repenting, but God remembered his covenant and showed compassion for their suffering and consequences from their sin.

Another example is with King Solomon:

> King Solomon, however, loved many foreign women besides Pharaoh's daughter—Moabites, Ammonites, Edomites, Sidonians and Hittites. They were from nations about which the LORD had told the Israelites, "You must not intermarry with them, because they will surely turn your hearts after their gods." Nevertheless, Solomon held fast to them in love. He had seven hundred wives of royal birth and three hundred concubines, and his wives led him astray. As Solomon grew old, his wives turned his heart after other gods, and his heart was not fully devoted to the LORD his God, as the heart of David his father had been. He followed Ashtoreth the goddess of the Sidonians, and Molech the detestable god of the Ammonites. So Solomon did evil in the eyes of the LORD; he did not follow the LORD completely, as David his father had done.
> On a hill east of Jerusalem, Solomon built a high place for Chemosh the detestable god of Moab, and for Molech the detestable god of the Ammonites. He did the same for all his foreign wives, who burned incense and offered sacrifices to their gods. The LORD became angry with Solomon because his heart had turned away from the LORD, the God of Israel, who had appeared to him twice. Although he had forbidden Solomon to follow other gods, Solomon did not keep the LORD's command. So the LORD said to Solomon, "Since this is your attitude and you have not kept my covenant and my decrees, which I commanded you, I will most certainly tear the kingdom away from you and give it to one of your subordinates. Nevertheless, for the sake of David your father, I will not do it during your lifetime. I will tear it out of the hand of your son. Yet I will not tear the whole kingdom from him, but will give him one tribe for the sake of David my servant and for the sake of Jerusalem, which I have chosen." (1 Kings 11:1-13)

Considering Solomon's choices and his lack of response to his sin later in life, God was justified to completely abandon his people, Israel. Instead he chose to delay his wrath and even scale it back, by dividing his kingdom into Israel and one tribe, Judah, all for the sake of Solomon's father, David, and God's city, Jerusalem. God still wanted the dream of having a people totally devoted to him and worshiping at the Temple Solomon had built in Jerusalem.

Here is another motive for God restraining his anger:

God's Anger—Often Restrained

For us...

> If in spite of this you still do not listen to me but continue to be hostile toward me, then in my anger I will be hostile toward you, and I myself will punish you for your sins seven times over...
>
> Yet in spite of this, when they are in the land of their enemies, I will not reject them or abhor them so as to destroy them completely, breaking my covenant with them. I am the LORD their God. But for their sake I will remember the covenant with their ancestors whom I brought out of Egypt in the sight of the nations to be their God. I am the LORD. (Leviticus 26:27-28, 44-45)

> They did not destroy the peoples as the LORD had commanded them, but they mingled with the nations and adopted their customs. They worshiped their idols, which became a snare to them...Many times he delivered them, but they were bent on rebellion and they wasted away in their sin. Yet he took note of their distress when he heard their cry; for their sake he remembered his covenant and out of his great love he relented. He caused all who held them captive to show them mercy. (Psalm 106:34-36, 43-46)

When the Psalmist mentioned that God delivered them many times, he was probably referring to the time of the Judges:

> Then the LORD raised up judges, who saved them out of the hands of these raiders. Yet they would not listen to their judges but prostituted themselves to other gods and worshiped them. They quickly turned from the ways of their ancestors, who had been obedient to the LORD's commands. Whenever the LORD raised up a judge for them, he was with the judge and saved them out of the hands of their enemies as long as the judge lived; for the LORD relented because of their groaning under those who oppressed and afflicted them. But when the judge died, the people returned to ways even more corrupt than those of their ancestors, following other gods and serving and worshiping them. They refused to give up their evil practices and stubborn ways. Therefore the LORD was very angry with Israel... (Judges 2:16-20)

God relented and raised up a judge to save Israel, motivated by Israel's suffering and "groaning". It's not easy for God to watch our suffering, even if it is due to our own sin and the subsequent natural consequences.

Another example of God's restraint is the story of Jehoshaphat, king of Judah. He married the daughter of Ahab, the King of Israel, and helped him fight against Ramoth Gilead. King Ahab was an evil king in God's eyes.

> When Jehoshaphat king of Judah returned safely to his palace in Jerusalem, Jehu the seer, the son of Hanani, went out to meet him and said to the king, "Should you help the wicked and love those who hate the LORD? Because of this, the wrath of the LORD is on you. There is, however, some good in you, for you have rid the land of the Asherah poles and have set your heart on seeking God." (2 Chronicles 19:1-3)

After a powerful victory over "a vast army", won by faith and dependence on God..., Jehoshaphat made a similar mistake with Ahab's son:

> Later, Jehoshaphat king of Judah made an alliance with Ahaziah king of Israel, whose ways were wicked. He agreed with him to construct a fleet of trading ships. After these were built at Ezion Geber, Eliezer son of Dodavahu of Mareshah prophesied against Jehoshaphat, saying, "Because you have made an alliance with Ahaziah, the LORD will destroy what you have made." The ships were wrecked and were not able to set sail to trade. (2 Chronicles 20:35-37)

God could have displayed more anger toward Jehoshaphat with his unspiritual choices and alliances, but he chose to restrain the punishment. Think about what happened with the first couple God created. Adam and Eve's curse was true and they did die, just not immediately. They had plenty of time to think about their punishment and what caused the natural consequences of not being with God in the Garden of Eden.

Another example of his restraint was when Ezra led God's people to repent of marrying foreign women. He recognized that God had spared a remnant:

> What has happened to us is a result of our evil deeds and our great guilt, and yet, our God, you have punished us less than our sins deserved and have given us a remnant like this. Shall we then break your commands again and intermarry with the peoples who commit such detestable practices? Would you not be angry enough with us to destroy us, leaving us no remnant or survivor? LORD, the God of Israel, you are righteous! We are left this day as a remnant. Here we are before you in our guilt, though because of it not one of us can stand in your presence. (Ezra 9:13-15)

God's restraint gave Ezra motivation to help the Israelites not continue in their sin. We should be motivated in the same way.

When the flood didn't change the problem with sinful people, God promised not to the push the "reset button" and start over by destroying the earth through water. It's great to be able to restart a computer when it's not cooperating, or if it's doing weird things, but this method doesn't work as well with people, as we learn through watching the Israelites in the desert. Even as Jerusalem was being captured and burned, God wanted to find another way to handle its sinfulness:

> "I looked for someone among them who would build up the wall and stand before me in the gap on behalf of the land so I would not have to destroy it, but I found no one. So I will pour out my wrath on them and consume them with my fiery anger, bringing down on their own heads all they have done, declares the Sovereign LORD." (Ezekiel 22:30-31)

Jesus brought the eternal solution, but what about the days left until his

God's Anger—Often Restrained

return? As he describes that day, Peter focused on God's love for us as the reason God restrains his anger:

> But do not forget this one thing, dear friends: With the Lord a day is like a thousand years, and a thousand years are like a day. The Lord is not slow in keeping his promise, as some understand slowness. Instead he is patient with you, not wanting anyone to perish, but everyone to come to repentance. (2 Peter 3:8-9)

During one of the darkest times in Israel's history, Hosea captured the heart of God, torn between his righteous anger towards his people, and his deep love for them:

> When Israel was a child, I loved him, and out of Egypt I called my son. But the more they were called, the more they went away from me. They sacrificed to the Baals and they burned incense to images. It was I who taught Ephraim to walk, taking them by the arms; but they did not realize it was I who healed them. I led them with cords of human kindness, with ties of love. To them I was like one who lifts a little child to the cheek, and I bent down to feed them.
> Will they not return to Egypt and will not Assyria rule over them because they refuse to repent? A sword will flash in their cities; it will devour their false prophets and put an end to their plans. My people are determined to turn from me. Even though they call me God Most High, I will by no means exalt them.
> How can I give you up, Ephraim? How can I hand you over, Israel? How can I treat you like Admah? How can I make you like Zeboyim? My heart is changed within me; all my compassion is aroused. I will not carry out my fierce anger, nor will I devastate Ephraim again. For I am God, and not a man—the Holy One among you. I will not come against their cities. (Hosea 11:1-9)

As Nehemiah reflected upon Israel's history during the golden calf incident and the 40 years wandering in the desert, he was impacted by God's restraint and saw the good that God did, even though he punished Israel:

> But they, our ancestors, became arrogant and stiff-necked, and they did not obey your commands. They refused to listen and failed to remember the miracles you performed among them. They became stiff-necked and in their rebellion appointed a leader in order to return to their slavery. But you are a forgiving God, gracious and compassionate, slow to anger and abounding in love. Therefore you did not desert them, even when they cast for themselves an image of a calf and said, 'This is your god, who brought you up out of Egypt,' or when they committed awful blasphemies.
> Because of your great compassion you did not abandon them in the wilderness. By day the pillar of cloud did not fail to guide them on their path, nor the pillar of fire by night to shine on the way they were to take. You gave your good Spirit to instruct them. You did not withhold your manna from their mouths, and you gave them water for their thirst. For forty years you sustained them in the wilderness;

they lacked nothing, their clothes did not wear out nor did their feet become swollen...For many years you were patient with them. By your Spirit you warned them through your prophets. Yet they paid no attention, so you gave them into the hands of the neighboring peoples. But in your great mercy you did not put an end to them or abandon them, for you are a gracious and merciful God. (Nehemiah 9:16-21, 30-31)

Even while the Israelites were "being punished" by wandering in the desert for 40 years, God allowed them to have military victories over the Canaanite king of Arad, Sihon the Amorite king of Heshbon, and Og king of Bashan, as described in Numbers 21. Sometimes God's love for us is the main reason he restrains his anger. Consider that God's anger is often aroused because of his deep, passionate love for us, and yet it is then restrained because of that same love. It's not like a sentimental mom who isn't willing to discipline her children and bring pain or suffering into their lives. It's a crazy love that knows no bounds or limits as to how it is displayed. To not receive all that we deserve can be the greatest gift and the greatest motivation.

CHAPTER TEN

God's Anger—Neutralized by Repentance

Anger begins in folly, and ends in repentance.
—Pythagoras (Greek mathematician and philosopher, –500 BC)

God's anger is always justified, but it can be removed or altered with repentance. He expressed this through Jeremiah during a time when Judah was being destroyed:

> Go, proclaim this message toward the north: 'Return, faithless Israel,' declares the LORD, 'I will frown on you no longer, for I am faithful,' declares the LORD, 'I will not be angry forever. Only acknowledge your guilt—you have rebelled against the LORD your God, you have scattered your favors to foreign gods under every spreading tree, and have not obeyed me,' declares the LORD. (Jeremiah 3:11-13)

Long before Jeremiah, Solomon prayed at the dedication of the temple. He pleaded with God for just such a moment:

> When they sin against you—for there is no one who does not sin—and you become angry with them and give them over to their enemies, who take them captive to their own land, far away or near; and if they have a change of heart in the land where they are held captive, and repent and plead with you in the land of their captors and say, 'We have sinned, we have done wrong, we have acted wickedly'; and if they turn back to you with all their heart and soul in the land of their enemies who took them captive, and pray to you toward the land you gave their ancestors, toward the city you have chosen and the temple I have built for your Name; then from heaven, your dwelling place, hear their prayer and their plea, and uphold their cause. And forgive your people, who have sinned against you; forgive all the offenses they have committed against you, and cause their captors to show them mercy; for they are your people and your inheritance, whom you brought out of Egypt, out of that iron-smelting furnace. (1 Kings 8:46-51)

There are several examples in the Scriptures where this is evident:

Example #1

When the Israelite men were sexually immoral with Moabite women and worshiped their god, Baal of Peor, Aaron's grandson Phinehas drove a spear through both a man and a Moabite woman while they were sinning. Then God said:

> Phinehas son of Eleazar, the son of Aaron, the priest, has turned my anger away from the Israelites. Since he was as zealous for my honor among them as I am, I did not put an end to them in my zeal. Therefore tell him I am making my covenant of peace with him. (Numbers 25:11-12)

God sent a plague that killed 24,000 people, which didn't stop until Phinehas responded to the Israelite man who brought a Moabite woman into his tent in full view of Moses and the whole assembly. Phinehas would not tolerate that type of blatant, sinful contempt for God's commands. His conviction and wholehearted repentance brought a quick change to God's anger.

Example #2

Before the Israelites battled with the city of Jericho, God specifically told them not to take any of the plunder. When Achan stole some of the plunder, God's anger was aroused:

> But the Israelites were unfaithful in regard to the devoted things; Achan son of Karmi, the son of Zimri, the son of Zerah, of the tribe of Judah, took some of them. So the LORD's anger burned against Israel...
> Then Joshua, together with all Israel, took Achan son of Zerah, the silver, the robe, the gold bar, his sons and daughters, his cattle, donkeys and sheep, his tent and all that he had, to the Valley of Achor. Joshua said, "Why have you brought this trouble on us? The LORD will bring trouble on you today."
> Then all Israel stoned him, and after they had stoned the rest, they burned them. Over Achan they heaped up a large pile of rocks, which remains to this day. Then the LORD turned from his fierce anger. Therefore that place has been called the Valley of Achor ever since. (Joshua 7:1, 24-26)

Only when the entire Israelite community responded did God relent and turn away from his anger.

Example #3

God gave the Israelites direction on how to deal with their own people who began serving foreign gods:

> If you hear it said about one of the towns the LORD your God is giving you to live in that troublemakers have arisen among you and have led the people of their town astray, saying, "Let us go and worship other gods" (gods you have not known), then you must inquire, probe and investigate it thoroughly. And if it is

God's Anger—Neutralized by Repentance

true and it has been proved that this detestable thing has been done among you, you must certainly put to the sword all who live in that town. You must destroy it completely, both its people and its livestock. You are to gather all the plunder of the town into the middle of the public square and completely burn the town and all its plunder as a whole burnt offering to the LORD your God. That town is to remain a ruin forever, never to be rebuilt, and none of the condemned things are to be found in your hands. Then the LORD will turn from his fierce anger, will show you mercy, and will have compassion on you. He will increase your numbers, as he promised on oath to your ancestors—because you obey the LORD your God by keeping all his commands that I am giving you today and doing what is right in his eyes. (Deuteronomy 13:12-18)

Although it may seem harsh to destroy everything in the town, even children and people who may not have started the problem, keep in mind that the people of the town allowed themselves to be led astray. Had there been a Phinehas in that town to take a stand, God would probably not have destroyed everyone. A spiritual view of God's direction realizes his hatred for sin and how the Israelites needed to repent – completely and thoroughly. This radical view is similar to Jesus' direction for us:

If your right eye causes you to stumble, gouge it out and throw it away. It is better for you to lose one part of your body than for your whole body to be thrown into hell. (Matthew 5:29)

Example #4

When the Israelites served foreign gods, God allowed them to be conquered by their enemies:

Again the Israelites did evil in the eyes of the LORD. They served the Baals and the Ashtoreths, and the gods of Aram, the gods of Sidon, the gods of Moab, the gods of the Ammonites and the gods of the Philistines. And because the Israelites forsook the LORD and no longer served him, he became angry with them. He sold them into the hands of the Philistines and the Ammonites, who that year shattered and crushed them. For eighteen years they oppressed all the Israelites on the east side of the Jordan in Gilead, the land of the Amorites. The Ammonites also crossed the Jordan to fight against Judah, Benjamin and Ephraim; Israel was in great distress. Then the Israelites cried out to the LORD, "We have sinned against you, forsaking our God and serving the Baals."

The LORD replied, "When the Egyptians, the Amorites, the Ammonites, the Philistines, the Sidonians, the Amalekites and the Maonites oppressed you and you cried to me for help, did I not save you from their hands? But you have forsaken me and served other gods, so I will no longer save you. Go and cry out to the gods you have chosen. Let them save you when you are in trouble!"

But the Israelites said to the LORD, "We have sinned. Do with us whatever you think best, but please rescue us now." Then they got rid of the foreign gods among them and served the LORD. And he could bear Israel's misery no longer. (Judges 10:6-16)

God didn't rescue them right away, but wanted to see a change in heart and action. Jephthah led the Israelites to victory in their next battle with the Ammonites.

Example #5

When Ahab couldn't gain possession of Naboth's vineyard and responded with sulking and anger, his wife, Jezebel, orchestrated false charges against Naboth, and had him stoned to death. Then Ahab went to take possession of the vineyard:

> Then the word of the LORD came to Elijah the Tishbite: "Go down to meet Ahab king of Israel, who rules in Samaria. He is now in Naboth's vineyard, where he has gone to take possession of it. Say to him, 'This is what the LORD says: Have you not murdered a man and seized his property?' Then say to him, 'This is what the LORD says: In the place where dogs licked up Naboth's blood, dogs will lick up your blood—yes, yours!'"
> Ahab said to Elijah, "So you have found me, my enemy!"
> "I have found you," he answered, "because you have sold yourself to do evil in the eyes of the LORD. He says, 'I am going to bring disaster on you. I will wipe out your descendants and cut off from Ahab every last male in Israel—slave or free. I will make your house like that of Jeroboam son of Nebat and that of Baasha son of Ahijah, because you have provoked me to anger and have caused Israel to sin.'...
> (There was never a man like Ahab, who sold himself to do evil in the eyes of the LORD, urged on by Jezebel his wife. He behaved in the vilest manner by going after idols, like the Amorites the LORD drove out before Israel.)
> When Ahab heard these words, he tore his clothes, put on sackcloth and fasted. He lay in sackcloth and went around meekly.
> Then the word of the LORD came to Elijah the Tishbite: "Have you noticed how Ahab has humbled himself before me? Because he has humbled himself, I will not bring this disaster in his day, but I will bring it on his house in the days of his son." (1 Kings 21:17-22, 25-28)

Ahab's life deserved God's discipline and anger, yet God was moved by Ahab's response. He delayed the punishment until after Ahab's death. God's response is even more amazing considering how God viewed Ahab's life:

> Ahab son of Omri did more evil in the eyes of the LORD than any of those before him. He not only considered it trivial to commit the sins of Jeroboam son of Nebat, but he also married Jezebel daughter of Ethbaal king of the Sidonians, and began to serve Baal and worship him. He set up an altar for Baal in the temple of Baal that he built in Samaria. Ahab also made an Asherah pole and did more to arouse the anger of the LORD, the God of Israel, than did all the kings of Israel before him. (1 Kings 16:30-33)

God's Anger—Neutralized by Repentance

Example #6

David's grandson, Rehoboam, became king, but he didn't have the same heart toward God:

> After Rehoboam's position as king was established and he had become strong, he and all Israel with him abandoned the law of the LORD. Because they had been unfaithful to the LORD, Shishak king of Egypt attacked Jerusalem in the fifth year of King Rehoboam. With twelve hundred chariots and sixty thousand horsemen and the innumerable troops of Libyans, Sukkites and Cushites that came with him from Egypt, he captured the fortified cities of Judah and came as far as Jerusalem.
>
> Then the prophet Shemaiah came to Rehoboam and to the leaders of Judah who had assembled in Jerusalem for fear of Shishak, and he said to them, "This is what the LORD says, 'You have abandoned me; therefore, I now abandon you to Shishak.'"
>
> The leaders of Israel and the king humbled themselves and said, "The LORD is just."
>
> When the LORD saw that they humbled themselves, this word of the LORD came to Shemaiah: "Since they have humbled themselves, I will not destroy them but will soon give them deliverance. My wrath will not be poured out on Jerusalem through Shishak. They will, however, become subject to him, so that they may learn the difference between serving me and serving the kings of other lands."
>
> When Shishak king of Egypt attacked Jerusalem, he carried off the treasures of the temple of the LORD and the treasures of the royal palace. He took everything, including the gold shields Solomon had made. So King Rehoboam made bronze shields to replace them and assigned these to the commanders of the guard on duty at the entrance to the royal palace. Whenever the king went to the LORD's temple, the guards went with him, bearing the shields, and afterward they returned them to the guardroom. Because Rehoboam humbled himself, the LORD's anger turned from him, and he was not totally destroyed. Indeed, there was some good in Judah...He did evil because he had not set his heart on seeking the LORD. (2 Chronicles 12:1-12, 14)

Even though Rehoboam "abandoned the law of the Lord", he did humble himself and God noticed. Rehoboam still had David's spiritual seed in him, but it wasn't growing and producing good fruit in his life. The last verse sums up why that wasn't happening: "He had not set his heart on seeking the LORD". If your heart isn't set and determined to "seek first his kingdom and his righteousness" (Matt 6:33), it's just a matter a time before you become unfaithful and abandon the Lord just as Rehoboam did.

Example #7

When Ahaz's son Hezekiah became King of Judah, he worked to turn God's wrath away:

> In the first month of the first year of his reign, he opened the doors of the temple of the LORD and repaired them. He brought in the priests and the Levites, assembled them in the square on the east side and said: "Listen to me, Levites! Consecrate yourselves now and consecrate the temple of the LORD, the God of your ancestors. Remove all defilement from the sanctuary. Our parents were unfaithful; they did evil in the eyes of the LORD our God and forsook him. They turned their faces away from the LORD's dwelling place and turned their backs on him. They also shut the doors of the portico and put out the lamps. They did not burn incense or present any burnt offerings at the sanctuary to the God of Israel. Therefore, the anger of the LORD has fallen on Judah and Jerusalem; he has made them an object of dread and horror and scorn, as you can see with your own eyes. This is why our fathers have fallen by the sword and why our sons and daughters and our wives are in captivity. Now I intend to make a covenant with the LORD, the God of Israel, so that his fierce anger will turn away from us." (2 Chronicles 29:3-10)

Hezekiah encouraged the Israelites to do the same:

> At the king's command, couriers went throughout Israel and Judah with letters from the king and from his officials, which read:
> "People of Israel, return to the LORD, the God of Abraham, Isaac and Israel, that he may return to you who are left, who have escaped from the hand of the kings of Assyria. Do not be like your parents and your fellow Israelites, who were unfaithful to the LORD, the God of their ancestors, so that he made them an object of horror, as you see. Do not be stiff-necked, as your ancestors were; submit to the LORD. Come to his sanctuary, which he has consecrated forever. Serve the LORD your God, so that his fierce anger will turn away from you. If you return to the LORD, then your fellow Israelites and your children will be shown compassion by their captors and will return to this land, for the LORD your God is gracious and compassionate. He will not turn his face from you if you return to him." (2 Chronicles 30:6-9)

Hezekiah's efforts did bring relief, as his prayer with the prophet Isaiah moved God to destroy the Assyrian army attacking Jerusalem with 185,000 enemy soldiers being struck down in a single night! (2 Kings 19). Later on, however, Hezekiah lost his humility:

> In those days Hezekiah became ill and was at the point of death. He prayed to the LORD, who answered him and gave him a miraculous sign. But Hezekiah's heart was proud and he did not respond to the kindness shown him; therefore the LORD's wrath was on him and on Judah and Jerusalem. Then Hezekiah repented of the pride of his heart, as did the people of Jerusalem; therefore the LORD's wrath did not come on them during the days of Hezekiah. (2 Chronicles 32:24-26)

Again, God delayed his wrath until Hezekiah died. According to 2 Kings

God's Anger—Neutralized by Repentance

21:9, Hezekiah's son, Manasseh, "led them astray, so that they did more evil than the nations the LORD had destroyed before the Israelites". This happened near the end of the southern kingdom Judah, and the people were eventually taken into captivity by the Babylonians.

Example #8

Manasseh became king as a preteen. If you are a parent with a preteen, imagine what it would be like if he or she became the leader of your local congregation.

> Manasseh was twelve years old when he became king, and he reigned in Jerusalem fifty-five years. He did evil in the eyes of the LORD, following the detestable practices of the nations the LORD had driven out before the Israelites. He rebuilt the high places his father Hezekiah had demolished; he also erected altars to the Baals and made Asherah poles. He bowed down to all the starry hosts and worshiped them. He built altars in the temple of the LORD, of which the LORD had said, "My Name will remain in Jerusalem forever." In both courts of the temple of the LORD, he built altars to all the starry hosts. He sacrificed his children in the fire in the Valley of Ben Hinnom, practiced divination and witchcraft, sought omens, and consulted mediums and spiritists. He did much evil in the eyes of the LORD, arousing his anger.
>
> He took the image he had made and put it in God's temple, of which God had said to David and to his son Solomon, "In this temple and in Jerusalem, which I have chosen out of all the tribes of Israel, I will put my Name forever. I will not again make the feet of the Israelites leave the land I assigned to your ancestors, if only they will be careful to do everything I commanded them concerning all the laws, decrees and regulations given through Moses." But Manasseh led Judah and the people of Jerusalem astray, so that they did more evil than the nations the LORD had destroyed before the Israelites. (2 Chronicles 33:1-9)

Considering all the evil Manasseh had committed, even sacrificing his own children to these foreign gods, God's response was justified and appropriate:

> The LORD said through his servants the prophets: "Manasseh king of Judah has committed these detestable sins. He has done more evil than the Amorites who preceded him and has led Judah into sin with his idols. Therefore this is what the LORD, the God of Israel, says: I am going to bring such disaster on Jerusalem and Judah that the ears of everyone who hears of it will tingle. I will stretch out over Jerusalem the measuring line used against Samaria and the plumb line used against the house of Ahab. I will wipe out Jerusalem as one wipes a dish, wiping it and turning it upside down. I will forsake the remnant of my inheritance and give them into the hands of enemies. They will be looted and plundered by all their enemies; they have done evil in my eyes and have aroused my anger from the day their ancestors came out of Egypt until this day." (2 Kings 21:10-15)

However, just as his father Hezekiah did, Manasseh responded to God's discipline and God delayed his wrath again:

> The LORD spoke to Manasseh and his people, but they paid no attention. So the LORD brought against them the army commanders of the king of Assyria, who took Manasseh prisoner, put a hook in his nose, bound him with bronze shackles and took him to Babylon. In his distress he sought the favor of the LORD his God and humbled himself greatly before the God of his ancestors. And when he prayed to him, the LORD was moved by his entreaty and listened to his plea; so he brought him back to Jerusalem and to his kingdom. Then Manasseh knew that the LORD is God.
>
> Afterward he rebuilt the outer wall of the City of David, west of the Gihon spring in the valley, as far as the entrance of the Fish Gate and encircling the hill of Ophel; he also made it much higher. He stationed military commanders in all the fortified cities in Judah.
>
> He got rid of the foreign gods and removed the image from the temple of the LORD, as well as all the altars he had built on the temple hill and in Jerusalem; and he threw them out of the city. Then he restored the altar of the LORD and sacrificed fellowship offerings and thank offerings on it, and told Judah to serve the LORD, the God of Israel. The people, however, continued to sacrifice at the high places, but only to the LORD their God. (2 Chronicles 33:10-17)

Manasseh's son, Amon, was King of Judah for only two years, but he didn't continue with the repentance. Amon's son, Josiah, however, did show the same heart even as an eight-year-old king.

Example #9

King Josiah led many reforms throughout Judah, and God delayed his wrath because of his repentance. Josiah became King of Judah at eight years old. He began to seek God at 16 years of age, and began to purge Judah and Jerusalem of high places, Asherah poles, carved idols, and cast images when he was 20. He did this "purging" throughout Judah, then went back to Jerusalem. He began repairing the Temple at the age of 26, when he found the Book of the Law:

> When the king heard the words of the Book of the Law, he tore his robes. He gave these orders to Hilkiah the priest, Ahikam son of Shaphan, Akbor son of Micaiah, Shaphan the secretary and Asaiah the king's attendant: "Go and inquire of the LORD for me and for the people and for all Judah about what is written in this book that has been found. Great is the LORD's anger that burns against us because those who have gone before us have not obeyed the words of this book; they have not acted in accordance with all that is written there concerning us."
>
> Hilkiah the priest, Ahikam, Akbor, Shaphan and Asaiah went to speak to the prophet Huldah, who was the wife of Shallum son of Tikvah, the son of Harhas, keeper of the wardrobe. She lived in Jerusalem, in the New Quarter.

God's Anger—Neutralized by Repentance

> She said to them, "This is what the LORD, the God of Israel, says: Tell the man who sent you to me, 'This is what the LORD says: I am going to bring disaster on this place and its people, according to everything written in the book the king of Judah has read. Because they have forsaken me and burned incense to other gods and aroused my anger by all the idols their hands have made, my anger will burn against this place and will not be quenched.' Tell the king of Judah, who sent you to inquire of the LORD, 'This is what the LORD, the God of Israel, says concerning the words you heard: Because your heart was responsive and you humbled yourself before the LORD when you heard what I have spoken against this place and its people—that they would become a curse and be laid waste—and because you tore your robes and wept in my presence, I also have heard you, declares the LORD. Therefore I will gather you to your ancestors, and you will be buried in peace. Your eyes will not see all the disaster I am going to bring on this place.'" (2 Kings 22:11-20)

Josiah proceeded to clean up everything in Jerusalem, the temple, and high places throughout Judah, but this time he made sure the people pledged to keep the covenant themselves. So for the next 13 years, the people of Judah followed the Lord. When Josiah was killed in battle at 39 years old, his sons quickly went back to the same evil practices that Josiah had abolished. Shortly afterward, God brought Babylon to destroy Judah, and they were exiled for the next 70 years.

> Neither before nor after Josiah was there a king like him who turned to the LORD as he did—with all his heart and with all his soul and with all his strength, in accordance with all the Law of Moses.
> Nevertheless, the LORD did not turn away from the heat of his fierce anger, which burned against Judah because of all that Manasseh had done to arouse his anger. So the LORD said, "I will remove Judah also from my presence as I removed Israel, and I will reject Jerusalem, the city I chose, and this temple, about which I said, 'My Name shall be there.'" (2 Kings 23:25-27)

Even though Josiah repented and showed his commitment to turn Judah back to the Lord, the people did not have the same resolve. The Lord's anger was delayed because of Josiah's actions. Before the exile, the prophet Jeremiah pleaded with Judah to repent:

> Circumcise yourselves to the LORD, circumcise your hearts, you people of Judah and inhabitants of Jerusalem, or my wrath will flare up and burn like fire because of the evil you have done—burn with no one to quench it...
> So put on sackcloth, lament and wail, for the fierce anger of the LORD has not turned away from us...
> I looked, and the fruitful land was a desert; all its towns lay in ruins before the LORD, before his fierce anger. (Jeremiah 4:4, 8, 26)

Sometimes God's wrath will remain, waiting for us to truly repent. Before the Babylonians took the Israelites captive, several of God's prophets reminded them that if they would just repent, God would change his anger into compassion:

> Return, Israel, to the LORD your God. Your sins have been your downfall! Take words with you and return to the LORD. Say to him: "Forgive all our sins and receive us graciously, that we may offer the fruit of our lips. Assyria cannot save us; we will not mount warhorses. We will never again say 'Our gods' to what our own hands have made, for in you the fatherless find compassion."
> "I will heal their waywardness and love them freely, for my anger has turned away from them." (Hosea 14:1-4)
>
> Gather together, gather yourselves together, you shameful nation, before the decree takes effect and that day passes like windblown chaff, before the LORD's fierce anger comes upon you, before the day of the LORD's wrath comes upon you. Seek the LORD, all you humble of the land, you who do what he commands. Seek righteousness, seek humility; perhaps you will be sheltered on the day of the LORD's anger. (Zephaniah 2:1-3)

Although God gave them many opportunities and showed his patience through the prophets' messages, time eventually ran out:

> "The LORD was very angry with your ancestors. Therefore tell the people: This is what the LORD Almighty says: 'Return to me,' declares the LORD Almighty, 'and I will return to you,' says the LORD Almighty. Do not be like your ancestors, to whom the earlier prophets proclaimed: This is what the LORD Almighty says: 'Turn from your evil ways and your evil practices.' But they would not listen or pay attention to me, declares the LORD. Where are your ancestors now? And the prophets, do they live forever? But did not my words and my decrees, which I commanded my servants the prophets, overtake your ancestors?
> "Then they repented and said, 'The LORD Almighty has done to us what our ways and practices deserve, just as he determined to do.'" (Zechariah 1:2-6)

King Hezekiah, his son Manasseh, then his great-grandson Josiah, all brought a temporary delay of God's wrath because they repented. Their examples did not create a permanent change in the Israelites, so God's wrath eventually was displayed and directed towards Israel. When you consider how much evil Manasseh carried out for years, and how much damage he caused by leading Israel down that path, it's amazing that God still responded to his change of heart. This attribute of God's anger encourages me, because as long as I keep a humble, responsive heart toward God's discipline, I can remain faithful my entire life and lead my family to be faithful as well.

We really don't have any choice because if we don't repent, God's anger will eventually be displayed in our lives as well:

But because of your stubbornness and your unrepentant heart, you are storing up wrath against yourself for the day of God's wrath, when his righteous judgment will be revealed. God "will repay each person according to what they have done." To those who by persistence in doing good seek glory, honor and immortality, he will give eternal life. But for those who are self-seeking and who reject the truth and follow evil, there will be wrath and anger. (Romans 2:5-8)

CHAPTER ELEVEN

God's Anger—Has a Purpose

The purpose of anger is to let us know that something in our life needs changing and to provide the energy to make a change.
—Garrison Wynn

Since God designed anger to bring about change, his own anger does the same. His anger often remains until that purpose is fulfilled. When the Israelites were punished for not believing that God could deliver them to defeat the inhabitants of the Promised Land in Canaan, his anger lasted 40 years, until that entire generation had died.

> Do not harden your hearts as you did at Meribah, as you did that day at Massah in the wilderness, where your ancestors tested me; they tried me, though they had seen what I did. For forty years I was angry with that generation; I said, 'They are a people whose hearts go astray, and they have not known my ways.' So I declared on oath in my anger, 'They shall never enter my rest.' (Psalm 95:8-11)

Once his purpose was accomplished, God took the Israelites into Canaan. When they were exiled to Babylon, their banishment lasted 70 years, based on a change in power from the Babylonians to the Persians:

> The LORD, the God of their ancestors, sent word to them through his messengers again and again, because he had pity on his people and on his dwelling place. But they mocked God's messengers, despised his words and scoffed at his prophets until the wrath of the LORD was aroused against his people and there was no remedy. He brought up against them the king of the Babylonians, who killed their young men with the sword in the sanctuary, and did not spare young men or young women, the elderly or the infirm. God gave them all into the hands of Nebuchadnezzar.
>
> He carried to Babylon all the articles from the temple of God, both large and small, and the treasures of the LORD's temple and the treasures of the king and his officials. They set fire to God's temple and broke down the wall of Jerusalem; they burned all the palaces and destroyed everything of value there. He carried into exile to Babylon the remnant, who escaped from the sword, and

God's Anger—Has a Purpose

they became servants to him and his successors until the kingdom of Persia came to power. The land enjoyed its Sabbath rests; all the time of its desolation it rested, until the seventy years were completed in fulfillment of the word of the LORD spoken by Jeremiah. (2 Chronicles 36:15-21)

God's anger is not the final state. It has a function or a purpose. It's a tool for him to bring about change. God is not a moody, temperamental being that will change his mind if we give him enough time. If a problem needs to be corrected, his anger is not diminished until the problem is rectified. Jeremiah spoke about this before the exile to Babylon:

See, the storm of the LORD will burst out in wrath, a whirlwind swirling down on the heads of the wicked. The anger of the LORD will not turn back until he fully accomplishes the purposes of his heart. In days to come you will understand it clearly. (Jeremiah 23:19-20)

Think of Jonah's three days living inside the large fish, or Paul's three days fasting and praying, after he was blinded while traveling to Damascus. God was looking to bring about change in their hearts. In both cases, the three-day duration was probably not arbitrary. They both repented, but each had a different perspective on his life and God's intervention. What if their hearts needed more than three days to change? Do you think God would have waited an extra day—an extra week? God would have continued the course until the desired change was accomplished.

Consider when the prophet Nathan confronted David about his sin of adultery with Bathsheba:

Then David said to Nathan, "I have sinned against the LORD."
Nathan replied, "The LORD has taken away your sin. You are not going to die. But because by doing this you have shown utter contempt for the LORD, the son born to you will die." (2 Samuel 12:13-14)

God's response to David's sin was firm, immediate, and controlled, and it had natural consequences. After seven days, the son died, even though David had fasted in an attempt to change God's mind. But when Bathsheba gave birth to another son, Solomon, the Bible tells a different story:

Then David comforted his wife Bathsheba, and he went to her and made love to her. She gave birth to a son, and they named him Solomon. The LORD loved him; and because the LORD loved him, he sent word through Nathan the prophet to name him Jedidiah. (which means loved by the Lord) (2 Samuel 12:24-25)

God didn't continue to kill other children that David had with Bathsheba. The Lord loved Solomon and his anger had already been resolved. There were other consequences to David's sin that still occurred, such as his son, Absalom, sleeping with David's wives, and the sword claiming the life of his sons, Amnon and Absalom.

At another time, David sinned by counting his men and not trusting in God to give him military victories. As his punishment, David chose three days of the sword of the Lord:

> So the LORD sent a plague on Israel from that morning until the end of the time designated, and seventy thousand of the people from Dan to Beersheba died. When the angel stretched out his hand to destroy Jerusalem, the LORD relented concerning the disaster and said to the angel who was afflicting the people, "Enough! Withdraw your hand." The angel of the LORD was then at the threshing floor of Araunah the Jebusite. (2 Samuel 24:15-16)

The plague was sent from that morning "until the end of the time designated", which was three days. When God relented, did he do so out of his compassion for Jerusalem, or was it at the end of the 72nd hour? We may not know the answer to that question, but God had to have been moved by David's response:

> When David saw the angel who was striking down the people, he said to the LORD, "I have sinned; I, the shepherd, have done wrong. These are but sheep. What have they done? Let your hand fall on me and my family."...
> David built an altar to the LORD there and sacrificed burnt offerings and fellowship offerings. Then the LORD answered his prayer in behalf of the land, and the plague on Israel was stopped. (2 Samuel 24:17, 25)

David truly repented, but the story ends differently when we don't repent. Before the Assyrian captivity, the Israelites would not repent and return to God, so he continued with the discipline fueled by his anger:

> Arameans from the east and Philistines from the west have devoured Israel with open mouth. Yet for all this, his anger is not turned away, his hand is still upraised. But the people have not returned to him who struck them, nor have they sought the LORD Almighty. (Isaiah 9:12-13)

> Who handed Jacob over to become loot, and Israel to the plunderers? Was it not the LORD, against whom we have sinned? For they would not follow his ways; they did not obey his law. So he poured out on them his burning anger, the violence of war. It enveloped them in flames, yet they did not understand; it consumed them, but they did not take it to heart. (Isaiah 42:24-25)

About 60 years before the Assyrian captivity, the prophet Amos captured the main purpose for God's discipline:

> "Burn leavened bread as a thank offering and brag about your freewill

God's Anger—Has a Purpose

offerings— boast about them, you Israelites, for this is what you love to do," declares the Sovereign LORD.

"I gave you empty stomachs in every city and lack of bread in every town, yet you have not returned to me," declares the LORD.

"I also withheld rain from you when the harvest was still three months away. I sent rain on one town, but withheld it from another. One field had rain; another had none and dried up. People staggered from town to town for water but did not get enough to drink, yet you have not returned to me," declares the LORD.

"Many times I struck your gardens and vineyards, destroying them with blight and mildew. Locusts devoured your fig and olive trees, yet you have not returned to me," declares the LORD.

"I sent plagues among you as I did to Egypt. I killed your young men with the sword, along with your captured horses. I filled your nostrils with the stench of your camps, yet you have not returned to me," declares the LORD.

"I overthrew some of you as I overthrew Sodom and Gomorrah. You were like a burning stick snatched from the fire, yet you have not returned to me," declares the LORD.

"Therefore this is what I will do to you, Israel, and because I will do this to you, Israel, prepare to meet your God." (Amos 4:5-12)

Before the Babylonian captivity, Ezekiel also captured this purpose:

Therefore as surely as I live, declares the Sovereign LORD, because you have defiled my sanctuary with all your vile images and detestable practices, I myself will shave you; I will not look on you with pity or spare you. A third of your people will die of the plague or perish by famine inside you; a third will fall by the sword outside your walls; and a third I will scatter to the winds and pursue with drawn sword.

Then my anger will cease and my wrath against them will subside, and I will be avenged. And when I have spent my wrath on them, they will know that I the LORD have spoken in my zeal.

I will make you a ruin and a reproach among the nations around you, in the sight of all who pass by. You will be a reproach and a taunt, a warning and an object of horror to the nations around you when I inflict punishment on you in anger and in wrath and with stinging rebuke. I the LORD have spoken. (Ezekiel 5:11-15)

Then my wrath against you will subside and my jealous anger will turn away from you; I will be calm and no longer angry.

Because you did not remember the days of your youth but enraged me with all these things, I will surely bring down on your head what you have done, declares the Sovereign LORD. Did you not add lewdness to all your other detestable practices? (Ezekiel 16:42-43)

Now your impurity is lewdness. Because I tried to cleanse you but you would not be cleansed from your impurity, you will not be clean again until my wrath against you has subsided.

> I the LORD have spoken. The time has come for me to act. I will not hold back; I will not have pity, nor will I relent. You will be judged according to your conduct and your actions, declares the Sovereign LORD. (Ezekiel 24:13-14)

Since God doesn't speak to us directly or use "enemies" to conquer us as he did in the Old Testament, has he changed and become "more loving" in the New Testament? God is the same, and his anger still has a purpose. He may choose to accomplish the change through other means:

> Let everyone be subject to the governing authorities, for there is no authority except that which God has established. The authorities that exist have been established by God...
> For the one in authority is God's servant for your good. But if you do wrong, be afraid, for rulers do not bear the sword for no reason. They are God's servants, agents of wrath to bring punishment on the wrongdoer. (Romans 13:1, 4)

How should all of this affect your view of God? His deep love for you and his desire to bring about change motivates God to continue the discipline until we see it and repent. Asaph describes this aspect of God's anger in Psalm 76:

> At your rebuke, God of Jacob, both horse and chariot lie still. It is you alone who are to be feared. Who can stand before you when you are angry? From heaven you pronounced judgment, and the land feared and was quiet—when you, God, rose up to judge, to save all the afflicted of the land. Surely your wrath against mankind brings you praise, and the survivors of your wrath are restrained. (Psalm 76:6-10)

His anger should produce a fear of God, and praise for God. And it should restrain you from a similar situation in the future. Is that how you view God's discipline and his anger? Is that how you typically respond?

How should all of this affect your own anger? When your anger is triggered, as you process how to respond, you should ask yourself what is the purpose of your response? What change do you want to see? Can you influence that change? If your anger doesn't have a purpose, then maybe you're just venting your own frustration or irritation. God's anger is never like that. His focus is clear. And when his anger occurs, it has a purpose, and the anger doesn't stop until that purpose is fulfilled. Our anger should be the same as God's in this respect.

CHAPTER TWELVE

God's Anger–Influenced by Prayer

Prayer does not change the purpose of God. But prayer does change the action of God.

—Chuck Smith

Have you ever been able to persuade someone to change his anger? It's not easy when the person is emotionally charged, and especially if you're the target of that anger. We've probably all had success at some point in our lives to help someone else calm down and reconsider what they want to do. Sometimes you offer a different perspective or additional facts that clarify what happened or what motive was involved. It's encouraging to see the change in the other person, and it provides us with a good feeling that we've helped someone else and possibly saved the relationship from further damage.

Considering that God's anger is always justified and definitive, how can we influence and even change his reaction coming from his anger? Why would God listen to mere humans about his decision? He is always right. If we can influence God's anger through prayer, then how do we approach God? What heart do we need to get God's attention without questioning his judgment, or appearing that we know better?

To answer these questions, we need to examine the Scriptures and learn from real prayers that did move God.

Response to Sodom and Gomorrah:

> Then the LORD said, "The outcry against Sodom and Gomorrah is so great and their sin so grievous that I will go down and see if what they have done is as bad as the outcry that has reached me. If not, I will know."
> The men turned away and went toward Sodom, but Abraham remained standing before the LORD. Then Abraham approached him and said: "Will you sweep away the righteous with the wicked? What if there are fifty righteous people in the city? Will you really sweep it away and not spare the place for the sake of the fifty righteous people in it? Far be it from you to do such a thing—to kill the righteous with the wicked, treating the righteous and the wicked alike. Far be it from you! Will not the Judge of all the earth do right?"
> The LORD said, "If I find fifty righteous people in the city of Sodom, I will spare the whole place for their sake."

> Then Abraham spoke up again: "Now that I have been so bold as to speak to the Lord, though I am nothing but dust and ashes, what if the number of the righteous is five less than fifty? Will you destroy the whole city for lack of five people?"
> "If I find forty-five there," he said, "I will not destroy it."
> Once again he spoke to him, "What if only forty are found there?"
> He said, "For the sake of forty, I will not do it."
> Then he said, "May the Lord not be angry, but let me speak. What if only thirty can be found there?" He answered, "I will not do it if I find thirty there."
> Abraham said, "Now that I have been so bold as to speak to the Lord, what if only twenty can be found there?"
> He said, "For the sake of twenty, I will not destroy it."
> Then he said, "May the Lord not be angry, but let me speak just once more. What if only ten can be found there?"
> He answered, "For the sake of ten, I will not destroy it."
> When the LORD had finished speaking with Abraham, he left, and Abraham returned home. (Genesis 18:20-33)

Abraham questioned God's character, based on what he knew about God. It took courage and confidence for Abraham to say, "Will not the Judge of all the earth do right?" It's hard for me to think that I could say something like that to God. Abraham was making a judgment that God was not doing the right thing. Abraham then admitted that it was bold to speak that way, but quickly added that he was nothing but "dust and ashes." It's interesting that Abraham asks God not to be angry…twice. Have you ever approached someone who is angry and tried to challenge his thinking? It's a situation where you could easily become the object of the anger. Abraham is respectful and tactful.

But Abraham didn't flinch, and he didn't hesitate to approach God. Once he was convinced that God would do the right thing, consistent with the character Abraham had known for a long time, acknowledging he would spare the city if ten righteous people were found, Abraham stopped. Maybe Abraham was only thinking of his nephew, Lot, and assumed that Lot would be saved from the pending destruction. He didn't try to convince God to not destroy Sodom and Gomorrah, or to reduce the number to five. He was satisfied with God's response and his change of heart.

Even though God was still going to destroy the cities, he had been influenced by Abraham's questions. God didn't shut down the discussion or threaten Abraham, or respond with, "You have a lot of nerve asking me about my intentions" or "How dare you question my authority!" Even when God is angry, he welcomes the interaction, and considers our perspective and opinion, when our hearts are humble and righteous. Isn't that amazing?

Here is his response to a proud king:

> By the word of the LORD a man of God came from Judah to Bethel, as Jeroboam was standing by the altar to make an offering. By the word of the

God's Anger—Influenced by Prayer

LORD he cried out against the altar: "Altar, altar! This is what the LORD says: 'A son named Josiah will be born to the house of David. On you he will sacrifice the priests of the high places who make offerings here, and human bones will be burned on you.'" That same day the man of God gave a sign: "This is the sign the LORD has declared: The altar will be split apart and the ashes on it will be poured out."

When King Jeroboam heard what the man of God cried out against the altar at Bethel, he stretched out his hand from the altar and said, "Seize him!" But the hand he stretched out toward the man shriveled up, so that he could not pull it back. Also, the altar was split apart and its ashes poured out according to the sign given by the man of God by the word of the LORD.

Then the king said to the man of God, "Intercede with the LORD your God and pray for me that my hand may be restored." So the man of God interceded with the LORD, and the king's hand was restored and became as it was before...

Even after this, Jeroboam did not change his evil ways, but once more appointed priests for the high places from all sorts of people. Anyone who wanted to become a priest he consecrated for the high places. This was the sin of the house of Jeroboam that led to its downfall and to its destruction from the face of the earth. (1 Kings 13:1-6, 33-34)

Jeroboam led Israel to commit many sins that eventually led to their Assyrian captivity. In this incident, his pride lashed out against the prophet, but God corrected Jeroboam by causing his hand to shrivel immediately. Even with the prophet's words coming true, with the altar splitting, and with God responding to Jeroboam's request for healing, Jeroboam didn't turn back to God. How many times does God forgive, heal, and answer our prayers, only to see our hearts return to the very things that brought the discipline into our lives? If God's anger can be softened to turn away and heal an evil king like Jeroboam, what if we truly repent and pray?

Contemplate his response to the "golden calf" incident:

Then the LORD said to Moses, "Go down, because your people, whom you brought up out of Egypt, have become corrupt. They have been quick to turn away from what I commanded them and have made themselves an idol cast in the shape of a calf. They have bowed down to it and sacrificed to it and have said, 'These are your gods, Israel, who brought you up out of Egypt.'

"I have seen these people," the LORD said to Moses, "and they are a stiff-necked people. Now leave me alone so that my anger may burn against them and that I may destroy them. Then I will make you into a great nation."

But Moses sought the favor of the LORD his God. "LORD," he said, "why should your anger burn against your people, whom you brought out of Egypt with great power and a mighty hand? Why should the Egyptians say, 'It was with evil intent that he brought them out, to kill them in the mountains and to wipe them off the face of the earth'? Turn from your fierce anger; relent and do not bring disaster on your people. Remember your servants Abraham, Isaac and Israel, to whom you swore by your own self: 'I will make your descendants as numerous as the stars in the sky and I will give your descendants all this land I promised them, and it will be their inheritance forever.'" Then the LORD relented and did not bring on his people the disaster he had threatened. (Exodus 32:7-14)

> The next day Moses said to the people, "You have committed a great sin. But now I will go up to the LORD; perhaps I can make atonement for your sin."
> So Moses went back to the LORD and said, "Oh, what a great sin these people have committed! They have made themselves gods of gold. But now, please forgive their sin—but if not, then blot me out of the book you have written."
> The LORD replied to Moses, "Whoever has sinned against me I will blot out of my book. Now go, lead the people to the place I spoke of, and my angel will go before you. However, when the time comes for me to punish, I will punish them for their sin."
> And the LORD struck the people with a plague because of what they did with the calf Aaron had made. (Exodus 32:30-35)

God listened to Moses and did not destroy the Israelites, although he did punish them with a plague. Moses reasoned with God, praised him for the good he had brought Israel, and reminded him of his promises. Moses was not afraid to directly plead with God to turn from his anger and relent. His friendship with God allowed Moses the freedom to approach him, and he felt comfortable enough to share what he really thought about God's decision. Do you have that intimacy in your relationship to God? Or do you hesitate thinking, "God is always right" or "What right do I have to question God?" God didn't question Moses for being so bold or arrogant. He welcomed Moses' thoughts as a friend. Even a psalmist took note that Moses had interceded:

> At Horeb they made a calf and worshiped an idol cast from metal. They exchanged their glorious God for an image of a bull, which eats grass. They forgot the God who saved them, who had done great things in Egypt, miracles in the land of Ham and awesome deeds by the Red Sea. So he said he would destroy them—had not Moses, his chosen one, stood in the breach before him to keep his wrath from destroying them. (Psalm 106:19-23)

Moses interceded again, when ten of the twelve spies didn't believe God would help them defeat the inhabitants of the Promised Land:

> The LORD said to Moses, "How long will these people treat me with contempt? How long will they refuse to believe in me, in spite of all the signs I have performed among them? I will strike them down with a plague and destroy them, but I will make you into a nation greater and stronger than they."
> Moses said to the LORD, "Then the Egyptians will hear about it! By your power you brought these people up from among them. And they will tell the inhabitants of this land about it. They have already heard that you, LORD, are with these people and that you, LORD, have been seen face to face, that your cloud stays over them, and that you go before them in a pillar of cloud by day and a

God's Anger—Influenced by Prayer

> pillar of fire by night. If you put all these people to death, leaving none alive, the nations who have heard this report about you will say, 'The LORD was not able to bring these people into the land he promised them on oath, so he slaughtered them in the wilderness.'
> "Now may the Lord's strength be displayed, just as you have declared: 'The LORD is slow to anger, abounding in love and forgiving sin and rebellion. Yet he does not leave the guilty unpunished; he punishes the children for the sin of the parents to the third and fourth generation.' In accordance with your great love, forgive the sin of these people, just as you have pardoned them from the time they left Egypt until now."
> The LORD replied, "I have forgiven them, as you asked. Nevertheless, as surely as I live and as surely as the glory of the LORD fills the whole earth, not one of those who saw my glory and the signs I performed in Egypt and in the wilderness but who disobeyed me and tested me ten times—not one of them will ever see the land I promised on oath to their ancestors. No one who has treated me with contempt will ever see it. (Numbers 14:11-23)

Moses praised God for his power in bringing the Israelites out of Egypt. He reasoned with God about the Lord's reputation and reminded him of his character that he himself expressed to Moses in Exodus 34. God listened to Moses again and did not destroy the Israelites, although he did punish them by not allowing them to enter the Promised Land, sentencing them to die in the desert over the next 40 years.

Sometimes we don't receive what we deserve for our sins because of God's love for us. Sometimes it's because other people love us, too. Moses intervened twice and spared the Israelites from God's wrath through his prayers. He intervened a third time through his brother, Aaron. Shortly afterwards, there was an incident when Korah, Dathan and Abiram challenged Moses' leadership:

> The LORD said to Moses and Aaron, "Separate yourselves from this assembly so I can put an end to them at once."
> But Moses and Aaron fell facedown and cried out, "O God, the God who gives breath to all living things, will you be angry with the entire assembly when only one man sins?"
> Then the LORD said to Moses, "Say to the assembly, 'Move away from the tents of Korah, Dathan and Abiram.'" (Numbers 16:20-24)

The earth opened up and swallowed these men and their families as an earthquake would, and fire consumed all 250 of their followers. The next day, the rest of the Israelites took exception to God's reaction, and started blaming Moses and Aaron. The only thing that restrained God's angry response was Moses and Aaron's love for the people:

> "The next day the whole Israelite community grumbled against Moses and Aaron. "You have killed the LORD's people," they said.
> But when the assembly gathered in opposition to Moses and Aaron and

> turned toward the tent of meeting, suddenly the cloud covered it and the glory of the LORD appeared. Then Moses and Aaron went to the front of the tent of meeting, and the LORD said to Moses, "Get away from this assembly so I can put an end to them at once." And they fell facedown.
> Then Moses said to Aaron, "Take your censer and put incense in it, along with burning coals from the altar, and hurry to the assembly to make atonement for them. Wrath has come out from the LORD; the plague has started." So Aaron did as Moses said, and ran into the midst of the assembly. The plague had already started among the people, but Aaron offered the incense and made atonement for them. He stood between the living and the dead, and the plague stopped. But 14,700 people died from the plague, in addition to those who had died because of Korah. Then Aaron returned to Moses at the entrance to the tent of meeting, for the plague had stopped." (Numbers 16:41-50)

This time Moses didn't pray and reason with God. He probably knew his people's only hope was to have Aaron make atonement for them in a way that God would accept. Who knows how many more people would have died if Moses hadn't acted on their behalf. We can accomplish the same response through our prayers for other people struggling with sin.

Here is God's response when Israel's 70-year captivity in Babylon was completed:

> In the first year of Darius son of Xerxes (a Mede by descent), who was made ruler over the Babylonian kingdom—in the first year of his reign, I, Daniel, understood from the Scriptures, according to the word of the LORD given to Jeremiah the prophet, that the desolation of Jerusalem would last seventy years. So I turned to the Lord God and pleaded with him in prayer and petition, in fasting, and in sackcloth and ashes. I prayed to the LORD my God and confessed...
> "Now, Lord our God, who brought your people out of Egypt with a mighty hand and who made for yourself a name that endures to this day, we have sinned, we have done wrong. Lord, in keeping with all your righteous acts, turn away your anger and your wrath from Jerusalem, your city, your holy hill. Our sins and the iniquities of our ancestors have made Jerusalem and your people an object of scorn to all those around us. (Daniel 9:1-4a, 15-16)

Just as Moses did, Daniel allowed the Scriptures and God's promises to be the basis for his approach to God. You can see his humility and his plea for God to turn away from his anger. God did allow the Israelites to leave Babylon's captivity and return to the Promised Land. Would God have done that anyway, based on his promise that the captivity would end after 70 years? Probably, but Daniel's desire to see Israel's restoration according to God's promise did not keep him from praying and pleading. Remember, a relationship with God and a friendship can move God through your prayers, even prayers based on a promise just about to be fulfilled. How much more should we pray and plead for situations where there's no promised time or established date?

Consider how several of the psalmists had this heart:

God's Anger—Influenced by Prayer

LORD, do not rebuke me in your anger or discipline me in your wrath. Have mercy on me, LORD, for I am faint; heal me, LORD, for my bones are in agony. My soul is in deep anguish. How long, LORD, how long? Turn, LORD, and deliver me; save me because of your unfailing love. (Psalm 6:1-4)

Hear my voice when I call, LORD; be merciful to me and answer me. My heart says of you, "Seek his face!" Your face, LORD, I will seek. Do not hide your face from me, do not turn your servant away in anger; you have been my helper. Do not reject me or forsake me, God my Savior. (Psalm 27:7-9)

You have rejected us, God, and burst upon us; you have been angry—now restore us! (Psalm 60:1)

How long, LORD? Will you be angry forever? How long will your jealousy burn like fire? Pour out your wrath on the nations that do not acknowledge you, on the kingdoms that do not call on your name; for they have devoured Jacob and devastated his homeland.
Do not hold against us the sins of past generations; may your mercy come quickly to meet us, for we are in desperate need. Help us, God our Savior, for the glory of your name; deliver us and forgive our sins for your name's sake. Why should the nations say, "Where is their God?" (Psalm 79:5-10a)

Restore us, O God; make your face shine on us, that we may be saved. How long, LORD God Almighty, will your anger smolder against the prayers of your people? (Psalm 80:3-4)

You, LORD, showed favor to your land; you restored the fortunes of Jacob. You forgave the iniquity of your people and covered all their sins. You set aside all your wrath and turned from your fierce anger.
Restore us again, God our Savior, and put away your displeasure toward us. Will you be angry with us forever? Will you prolong your anger through all generations? Will you not revive us again, that your people may rejoice in you? (Psalm 85:1-6)

But you have rejected, you have spurned, you have been very angry with your anointed one. You have renounced the covenant with your servant and have defiled his crown in the dust...
How long, LORD? Will you hide yourself forever? How long will your wrath burn like fire? (Psalm 89:38-39, 46)

We are consumed by your anger and terrified by your indignation. You have set our iniquities before you, our secret sins in the light of your presence. All our days pass away under your wrath; we finish our years with a moan. Our days may come to seventy years, or eighty, if our strength endures; yet the best of them are but trouble and sorrow, for they quickly pass, and we fly away. If only we knew the power of your anger! Your wrath is as great as the fear that is your due. Teach us to number our days, that we may gain a heart of wisdom.

> Relent, LORD! How long will it be? Have compassion on your servants. Satisfy us in the morning with your unfailing love, that we may sing for joy and be glad all our days. Make us glad for as many days as you have afflicted us, for as many years as we have seen trouble. (Psalm 90:7-15)

It is altogether right to plead with God, and to follow these examples in our prayers. Even the prophet, Isaiah, felt a need to pray for God to relent. He praised God, confessed sin, and pleaded for mercy, while acknowledging God's wrath and anger:

> Since ancient times no one has heard, no ear has perceived, no eye has seen any God besides you, who acts on behalf of those who wait for him. You come to the help of those who gladly do right, who remember your ways. But when we continued to sin against them, you were angry. How then can we be saved? All of us have become like one who is unclean, and all our righteous acts are like filthy rags; we all shrivel up like a leaf, and like the wind our sins sweep us away. No one calls on your name or strives to lay hold of you; for you have hidden your face from us and have given us over to our sins.
> Yet you, LORD, are our Father. We are the clay, you are the potter; we are all the work of your hand. Do not be angry beyond measure, LORD; do not remember our sins forever. Oh, look on us, we pray, for we are all your people. Your sacred cities have become a wasteland; even Zion is a wasteland, Jerusalem a desolation. Our holy and glorious temple, where our ancestors praised you, has been burned with fire, and all that we treasured lies in ruins. After all this, LORD, will you hold yourself back? Will you keep silent and punish us beyond measure? (Isaiah 64:4-12)

Imagine yourself witnessing the destruction of God's Temple, or the devastation of his beloved city, Jerusalem. If you were in touch with the shattered dream in God's heart, and how far Israel's heart had fallen, God's discipline would seem altogether right and deserved. Months or even years later, however, would you begin to wonder when it would turn around? Maybe there were a few faithful people left, a remnant that still cared about God's righteousness and wanted to obey the Scriptures. Maybe then you would begin praying as Isaiah did.

But we are not in Jerusalem, and the Temple, as a building, is no longer where God dwells. What would ever compel you to pray in this way? You would pray as Isaiah did only if you sensed that God was angry with you, or your family, or your church, because of unrepented sin or worship of the American "thorns";

> The seed that fell among thorns stands for those who hear, but as they go on their way they are choked by life's worries, riches and pleasures, and they do not mature. (Luke 8:14)

God's Anger—Influenced by Prayer

Can you truly say, at this point in your life, that your desire for God and his Kingdom is greater than it's ever been? The challenges of school, work or losing a job, marriage and parenting, financial stress, aging parents, or your own health issues can all distract and create "life's worries". Living in America can easily provide "riches and pleasures" that are not only thorns, but vines that entangle, or hinder our building something for God that will last.

As Jeremiah witnessed the destruction of Jerusalem, he prayed often about God's anger because he had seen it firsthand. This memory kept him humble and provided the right perspective on life:

> But the LORD is the true God; he is the living God, the eternal King. When he is angry, the earth trembles; the nations cannot endure his wrath...
> LORD, I know that people's lives are not their own; it is not for them to direct their steps. Discipline me, LORD, but only in due measure—not in your anger, or you will reduce me to nothing. Pour out your wrath on the nations that do not acknowledge you, on the peoples who do not call on your name. For they have devoured Jacob; they have devoured him completely and destroyed his homeland. (Jeremiah 10:10, 23-25)

Is God angry with you? I don't know. You have to answer that question based on what you now know about God's anger. It is slow to develop, temporary and often restrained. You may not see it now, but if you are not living according to the Scriptures, then eventually God's anger will be made known. Remember that his anger is simply a tool to bring about change...a change in you. Maybe you have a clear conscience, but remember what Paul said:

> My conscience is clear, but that does not make me innocent. It is the Lord who judges me. Therefore judge nothing before the appointed time; wait until the Lord comes. He will bring to light what is hidden in darkness and will expose the motives of the heart. At that time each will receive their praise from God. (1 Corinthians 4:4-5)

If you have a desire to see God work in your life as he has in the past or even in greater ways, then pray and cry out the way Habakkuk did:

> LORD, I have heard of your fame; I stand in awe of your deeds, LORD. Repeat them in our day, in our time make them known; in wrath remember mercy. (Habakkuk 3:2)

CHAPTER THIRTEEN

Jesus—God's Anger Walked on the Earth

> *The Son is the radiance of God's glory and the exact representation of his being, sustaining all things by his powerful word.*
> —Hebrews 1:3 (NIV 2011)

Since Jesus is the exact representation of God's being, then his anger should also be the exact representation of God's anger. This is an area of Jesus' character that isn't often discussed. He did experience anger many times. As we examine the different situations, let's consider how he responded, so that we can imitate him when we see the same thing in people around us. And we can understand what upset him, so that we can avoid the same mistakes in our hearts.

(1) Clearing the Temple

Early in his ministry, Jesus cleared the temple and clearly displayed anger about what was happening there:

> When it was almost time for the Jewish Passover, Jesus went up to Jerusalem. In the temple courts he found people selling cattle, sheep and doves, and others sitting at tables exchanging money. So he made a whip out of cords, and drove all from the temple courts, both sheep and cattle; he scattered the coins of the money changers and overturned their tables. To those who sold doves he said, "Get these out of here! Stop turning my Father's house into a market!" His disciples remembered that it is written: "Zeal for your house will consume me." (John 2:13-17)

What were the disciples thinking? The man they had only known for a short time had become unhinged and violent. He was yelling, overturning furniture, and throwing money everywhere. His whip scattered animals and objects alike. Did the disciples just stand there and observe the chaos, or did they run and hide, afraid of the backlash to come from the Pharisees and Sanhedrin? What would they have said that evening at dinner? Would anyone ask Jesus about it? Or would they just look at the ground in silence? Maybe Jesus was quoting Psalm 69 as he made the whip. Maybe Jesus openly discussed the situation that night. Scriptures do not elaborate on the fallout, except for some Jews who objected to his response. The disciples did remember a passage from that Psalm:

> For I endure scorn for your sake, and shame covers my face. I am a foreigner to my own family, a stranger to my own mother's children; for zeal for your house consumes me, and the insults of those who insult you fall on me. (Psalm 69:7-9)

According to the Jewish historian, Josephus,[32] construction on the temple began in 20 BC under Herod the Great, and was completed by Herod Agrippa around AD 63. For the Jewish people, the temple represented more than just a building. It included bustling commercial activity, crowds of worshippers, nationalist aspirations, political identity, historical memory, architectural splendor, and religious affiliation. The temple constituted the essence of Jewish faith, in both a literal and symbolic sense.

For the festivals that took place in Jerusalem, many of the attending Jews traveled long distances to participate. It may not have been convenient or practical for them to bring the necessary animals and supplies to perform the sacrifices and offerings required at these festivals. Some of them would purchase what they needed in Jerusalem to be able to fully participate in all aspects of the festival. There would also be "money changers" to convert their currency into local currency, and many of these money changers took advantage of the pilgrims with dishonest currency exchanges. Over time, these transactions became commonplace and probably migrated from outside the temple courts (or court of the Gentiles), to inside the temple courts. Was it the extortion by the currency exchange or "money changers" that upset Jesus, or the location of the transactions? Maybe it was both.

As Jesus evaluated the scene, he didn't fly into a rage or threaten anyone. Instead, he took time to make a whip out of cords and consider how he should proceed. He showed self-control and the patience to think through his options, the corresponding consequences, and the tradeoffs. By the time the whip was made, he knew exactly what he should do and how he should do it. This is a great example for us as we wrestle with our own anger. Instead of reacting as soon as our anger is triggered, we should take the time to reflect on the situation before we respond. Often this extra time will bring clarity, other perspectives, and the opportunity to consider alternative responses to accomplish the same purpose and bring about change.

Near the end of his three-year ministry, the transactions had begun infiltrating the temple area again. Maybe they returned long before this time:

> Jesus entered Jerusalem and went into the temple courts. He looked around at everything, but since it was already late, he went out to Bethany with the Twelve. The next day as they were leaving Bethany, Jesus was hungry...

> On reaching Jerusalem, Jesus entered the temple courts and began driving out those who were buying and selling there. He overturned the tables of the money changers and the benches of those selling doves, and would not allow anyone to carry merchandise through the temple courts. And as he taught them, he said, "Is it not written: 'My house will be called a house of prayer for all nations'? But you have made it 'a den of robbers.'" (Mark 11:11-12a, 15-17)

This temple cleansing was different. Jesus didn't make a whip again, but chose to sleep on it before reacting. This is another example of self-control and thinking through how to respond. The next day, not only did he overturn furniture again and scatter their money everywhere, he also would not allow anyone to carry merchandise through the temple courts. Did he physically stop anyone and take him by the arm, and lead him into another area? Did he simply block the entrance, as in a 1960's protest? However he did it, he started preaching to the crowd and quoting passages from Isaiah and Jeremiah:

> And foreigners who bind themselves to the LORD to minister to him, to love the name of the LORD, and to be his servants, all who keep the Sabbath without desecrating it and who hold fast to my covenant—these I will bring to my holy mountain and give them joy in my house of prayer. Their burnt offerings and sacrifices will be accepted on my altar; for my house will be called a house of prayer for all nations." (Isaiah 56:6-7)

> Will you steal and murder, commit adultery and perjury, burn incense to Baal and follow other gods you have not known, and then come and stand before me in this house, which bears my Name, and say, "We are safe"—safe to do all these detestable things? Has this house, which bears my Name, become a den of robbers to you? But I have been watching! declares the LORD. (Jeremiah 7:9-11)

His angry response was controlled, and it had a purpose. His radical reaction definitely got the people's attention and protests. Since the temple is no longer a part of our worship experience, do we have similar situations in our lives today? It makes me consider my heart and my thoughts during worship or prayer. Worship and prayer should be a focused and uninterrupted time with God. Distractions and other duties or priorities should be minimized. The money changers weren't focused on worship or God. Their greed and extortion probably didn't help the worshipers' mindset or emotions, either.

(2) Cursing a fig tree

Before Jesus cleared the temple a second time, he encountered a fig tree on his way to Jerusalem. His response seems rather selfish and quick-tempered, as if Jesus was a little irritated that day:

> The next day as they were leaving Bethany, Jesus was hungry. Seeing in the distance a fig tree in leaf, he went to find out if it had any fruit. When he

reached it, he found nothing but leaves, because it was not the season for figs. Then he said to the tree, "May no one ever eat fruit from you again." And his disciples heard him say it...

When evening came, Jesus and his disciples went out of the city. In the morning, as they went along, they saw the fig tree withered from the roots. Peter remembered and said to Jesus, "Rabbi, look! The fig tree you cursed has withered!" (Mark 11:12-14, 19-21)

When Jesus spoke to the fig tree, his emotions and tone of voice must have conveyed seriousness, because Peter remembered the moment as the fig tree being "cursed". It especially seems out of place since it wasn't the season for figs. This situation would be like you or I getting upset with an apple tree at a time when none of the apple trees were bearing fruit. Why would Jesus expect any figs to be on the tree in the first place? There's more to it than that, however, as described below:

The Barren Fig Tree, was published many years ago by W. M. Christie, a Church of Scotland minister in Palestine under the British mandatory regime. First, he pointed out the time of year at which the incident is said to have occurred (first few days of April). Christie wrote, "Now, the facts connected with the fig tree are these: Toward the end of March the leaves begin to appear, and in about a week the foliage coating is complete. Coincident with this, and sometimes even before, there appears quite a crop of small knobs, not the real figs, but a kind of early forerunner. They grow to the size of green almonds, in which condition they are eaten by peasants and others when hungry. When they come to their own indefinite maturity, they drop off." These precursors of the true fig are called taqsh in Palestinian Arabic. Their appearance is a harbinger of the fully formed appearance of the true fig some six weeks later. So, as the book of Mark says, the time for figs had not yet come. But if the leaves appear without any taqsh, that is a sign that there will be no figs. Since Jesus found "nothing but leaves"—leaves without any *taqsh*—he knew that "it was an absolutely hopeless, fruitless fig tree" and said as much.[33]

Considering that Jesus had been thinking about the Temple area the night before and knew what he planned to do once he got there, he could have intended this fig tree incident to mean more than just not having a snack that day. Jesus addressed Peter's astonishment with a lesson on faith and prayer, because Peter was amazed that the fig tree withered so quickly during their visit to Jerusalem that day. When you consider the money changers in the Temple area, and the following passage from Jeremiah, maybe Jesus was applying this Scripture to their hearts:

> Are they ashamed of their detestable conduct? No, they have no shame at all; they do not even know how to blush. So they will fall among the fallen; they will

be brought down when they are punished, says the LORD. "'I will take away their harvest, declares the LORD. There will be no grapes on the vine. There will be no figs on the tree, and their leaves will wither. What I have given them will be taken from them.'" (Jeremiah 8:12-13)

If this speculation is true, then Jesus' anger displayed toward a helpless fig tree was really justified anger toward what was happening in the Temple area. It probably fueled what took place in the Temple area a few minutes later.

(3) Healing a shriveled hand

> Another time Jesus went into the synagogue, and a man with a shriveled hand was there. Some of them were looking for a reason to accuse Jesus, so they watched him closely to see if he would heal him on the Sabbath. Jesus said to the man with the shriveled hand, "Stand up in front of everyone."
> Then Jesus asked them, "Which is lawful on the Sabbath: to do good or to do evil, to save life or to kill?" But they remained silent. He looked around at them in anger and, deeply distressed at their stubborn hearts, said to the man, "Stretch out your hand." He stretched it out, and his hand was completely restored. Then the Pharisees went out and began to plot with the Herodians how they might kill Jesus. (Mark 3:1-6)

This was the first of many heated discussions with the Pharisees and teachers of the law. Jesus didn't get upset and angry with anyone who had a question about the kingdom of God or his teaching. This particular group frequently tested Jesus with questions in order to trap him, accuse him, or somehow find a way to discredit him and his teaching. They were critical of his fasting, his healing, his forgiveness, his disregard for tradition, his teaching, and his disciples. They aggressively pursued Jesus, made plans to kill him, and even argued about him among themselves. What was in their hearts made Jesus angry, as shown in Matthew 23, where he called them blind guides, hypocrites, and a brood of vipers. Jesus reasoned with them, challenged them, and even turned away and left them at times. Several times Jesus escaped their desire to stone him to death. A few of them believed, and Jesus continued to have hope for the Pharisees by often accepting invitations to eat in their homes. We all struggle with character weaknesses, emotions, and sins, but if your heart wants to do the right thing and be righteous, you should feel comfortable and confident to approach Jesus with any question or clarification:

> For we do not have a high priest who is unable to empathize with our weaknesses, but we have one who has been tempted in every way, just as we are—yet he did not sin. Let us then approach God's throne of grace with confidence, so that we may receive mercy and find grace to help us in our time of need. (Hebrews 4:15-16)

Jesus—God's Anger Walked on the Earth

(4) Parables

Many of Jesus' parables had hidden meanings. Some of them were directed at the Pharisees and the teachers of the law and they knew it, which infuriated them. It's interesting to me that several of the parables have an element where the master becomes angry. Jesus wasn't shy about teaching about God's anger. He even told a parable where "the older son" became angry as a lesson to the Jews who were angry at Jesus. Following are some other examples of this anger in parables:

Unmerciful Servant—Master angry at unforgiving servant who had been forgiven. (Matthew 18:21-35)

Talents—Master angry at the response of the man with one talent. (Matthew 25:14-30)

Wedding Banquet—Host angry at invited people who killed his servants. (Matthew 22:1-14)

Great Banquet—Host angry at invited guests who made excuses why they couldn't come. (Luke 14:16-24)

Lost Son—Older son angry that his father threw party for younger son (Luke 15:11-32)

Anger provides the opportunity for many lessons, and Jesus used it throughout his parables. His doing so makes me think that more of our sermons and lessons should include the same element, refreshing our hearts and minds to know that God has anger and displays it every day (Psalm 7:11).

(5) Rebukes

Jesus rebuked evil spirits and the forces of nature. Below is a dictionary definition for rebuke:

> Rebuke—A harsh criticism; to reprove; censure severely or angrily

It's probably difficult or impossible, based on these definitions, to deliver a rebuke without feeling angry. Here are a few examples in Jesus' life:

> In the synagogue there was a man possessed by a demon, an impure spirit. He cried out at the top of his voice, "Go away! What do you want with us, Jesus of Nazareth? Have you come to destroy us? I know who you are—the Holy One of God!"
> "Be quiet!" Jesus said sternly. "Come out of him!" Then the demon threw the man down before them all and came out without injuring him.
> All the people were amazed and said to each other, "What words these are! With authority and power he gives orders to impure spirits and they come out!" And the news about him spread throughout the surrounding area.

> Jesus left the synagogue and went to the home of Simon. Now Simon's mother-in-law was suffering from a high fever, and they asked Jesus to help her. So he bent over her and rebuked the fever, and it left her. She got up at once and began to wait on them. At sunset, the people brought to Jesus all who had various kinds of sickness, and laying his hands on each one, he healed them. Moreover, demons came out of many people, shouting, "You are the Son of God!" But he rebuked them and would not allow them to speak, because they knew he was the Messiah. (Luke 4:33-41)
>
> That day when evening came, he said to his disciples, "Let us go over to the other side." Leaving the crowd behind, they took him along, just as he was, in the boat. There were also other boats with him. A furious squall came up, and the waves broke over the boat, so that it was nearly swamped. Jesus was in the stern, sleeping on a cushion. The disciples woke him and said to him, "Teacher, don't you care if we drown?"
> He got up, rebuked the wind and said to the waves, "Quiet! Be still!" Then the wind died down and it was completely calm.
> He said to his disciples, "Why are you so afraid? Do you still have no faith?"
> They were terrified and asked each other, "Who is this? Even the wind and the waves obey him!" (Mark 4:35-41)
>
> A man in the crowd called out, "Teacher, I beg you to look at my son, for he is my only child. A spirit seizes him and he suddenly screams; it throws him into convulsions so that he foams at the mouth. It scarcely ever leaves him and is destroying him. I begged your disciples to drive it out, but they could not."
> "You unbelieving and perverse generation," Jesus replied, "how long shall I stay with you and put up with you? Bring your son here."
> Even while the boy was coming, the demon threw him to the ground in a convulsion. But Jesus rebuked the impure spirit, healed the boy and gave him back to his father. And they were all amazed at the greatness of God. (Luke 9:38-43a)

Jesus occasionally rebuked his disciples. It was part of their training and Jesus didn't shy away from it:

> He then began to teach them that the Son of Man must suffer many things and be rejected by the elders, the chief priests and the teachers of the law, and that he must be killed and after three days rise again. He spoke plainly about this, and Peter took him aside and began to rebuke him.
> But when Jesus turned and looked at his disciples, he rebuked Peter. "Get behind me, Satan!" he said. "You do not have in mind the concerns of God, but merely human concerns." (Mark 8:31-33)
>
> As the time approached for him to be taken up to heaven, Jesus resolutely set out for Jerusalem. And he sent messengers on ahead, who went into a Samaritan village to get things ready for him; but the people there did not welcome him, because he was heading for Jerusalem. When the disciples James and John saw this, they

Jesus—God's Anger Walked on the Earth

asked, "Lord, do you want us to call fire down from heaven to destroy them?" But Jesus turned and rebuked them. Then he and his disciples went to another village. (Luke 9:51-56)

People were bringing little children to Jesus for him to place his hands on them, but the disciples rebuked them. When Jesus saw this, he was indignant. He said to them, "Let the little children come to me, and do not hinder them, for the kingdom of God belongs to such as these. Truly I tell you, anyone who will not receive the kingdom of God like a little child will never enter it." And he took the children in his arms, placed his hands on them and blessed them. (Mark 10:13-16)

Later Jesus appeared to the Eleven as they were eating; he rebuked them for their lack of faith and their stubborn refusal to believe those who had seen him after he had risen. (Mark 16:14)

In fact, Jesus taught them that there would be situations where they would need to rebuke one another:

Jesus said to his disciples: "Things that cause people to stumble are bound to come, but woe to anyone through whom they come. It would be better for them to be thrown into the sea with a millstone tied around their neck than to cause one of these little ones to stumble. So watch yourselves.
If your brother or sister sins against you, rebuke them; and if they repent, forgive them. Even if they sin against you seven times in a day and seven times come back to you saying 'I repent,' you must forgive them."
The apostles said to the Lord, "Increase our faith!" (Luke 17:1-5)

Jesus' tendency to rebuke must have been so commonplace that even the Pharisees discerned a situation that they thought merited a rebuke from Jesus:

When he came near the place where the road goes down the Mount of Olives, the whole crowd of disciples began joyfully to praise God in loud voices for all the miracles they had seen:
"Blessed is the king who comes in the name of the Lord!" "Peace in heaven and glory in the highest!"
Some of the Pharisees in the crowd said to Jesus, "Teacher, rebuke your disciples!"
"I tell you," he replied, "if they keep quiet, the stones will cry out." (Luke 19:37-40)

Of course, this part of Jesus' character does not give you license to rebuke someone every time he irritates you, or to rebuke a child every time she disobeys you. It should play a role as you disciple and train each other to be more like Jesus. Just remember that you are not Jesus, and anytime your anger is stirred, be careful how you respond so that you don't add more sin to the situation.

All of these examples communicate that Jesus did get angry at the same things that anger God. His responses imitated many of God's characteristics, such as Slow to Anger, Temporary, Restrained, Purposeful, etc. As we follow Jesus, let's teach about God's anger and be encouraged to imitate his self-control and patience when our anger is stirred. At the same time, let us not shy away from a rebuke if it's needed.

Angry Men of God

The title of this section may seem like an oxymoron, but some of the most powerful men in the Bible had anger issues. The world may view an angry leader as having passion, zeal, or even the ability to bring about change, but not without permanent, collateral damage, even if the goals are achieved.

> *How much more grievous are the consequences of anger than the causes of it.*
> —Marcus Aurelius

This section looks at different men of the Bible and evaluates what caused their anger, how they responded, and what we can learn from them. Anger may have made them more human and fallible, but they were still chosen by God to lead people. If we really listen to the Holy Spirit through these examples, we, too, can learn to handle and manage our anger while leading others powerfully.

CHAPTER FOURTEEN

Angry Men of God: Naaman—My Way

Many people are familiar with the song "My Way" written by Paul Anka and performed by Frank Sinatra, Elvis Presley and others. One stanza stands out to me as we consider the story of Naaman:

> "Regrets, I've had a few
> But then again, too few to mention
> I did what I had to do and saw it through without exemption
> I planned each charted course, each careful step along the byway
> And more, much more than this, I did it my way."

Naaman was a successful man. He had become the commander of Aram's army. Maybe the words to this song could describe how he achieved so much. Confidence and passion in accomplishing your goals bring satisfaction, sense of purpose, and even self-esteem. You expect things to happen and you'll do whatever is necessary to see it through. Along the way there are obstacles, people who may not agree or like your goals, and circumstances beyond your control that hinder progress or make it more difficult. These are the moments where you may be tempted to become angry or respond with frustrated emotions. Here's a great example of how a man responded to his anger in his own way and in a godly way:

> Now Naaman was commander of the army of the king of Aram. He was a great man in the sight of his master and highly regarded, because through him the LORD had given victory to Aram. He was a valiant soldier, but he had leprosy.
> Now bands of raiders from Aram had gone out and had taken captive a young girl from Israel, and she served Naaman's wife. She said to her mistress, "If only my master would see the prophet who is in Samaria! He would cure him of his leprosy." (2 Kings 5:1-3)

So Naaman got permission from the king of Aram and set out to find this healing prophet. As commander of the entire army, Naaman was probably a man of conviction, action, and resolve. As he remembered the effects that leprosy had on his life, Naaman grew more and more excited about the prospect of being healed forever. It was bad enough having leprosy and not being able to develop normal, close friendships for fear that the leprosy would be transmitted, but he was also the commander, a position which carries with it a normal separation from the regular soldiers. Maybe his leprosy was a well-kept secret.

As the commander, Naaman probably experienced better provisions for himself and his family than the regular soldiers experienced. He grew accustomed to having the best of everything, so it's no surprise that his expectations for his encounter with Elisha would be high. Either through stories about Elisha or his own imagination, Naaman thought about all the details during his long trip. Sometimes you may be that way regarding how a holiday party should go, how you will ask for that promotion or raise, how you expect to be treated by other family members, how this business should handle your complaint as a loyal customer, or how reliable your computer or internet connection should be, etc. It's okay to have expectations based on your preferences, your experience, or what you perceive as fair and just; however, when those expectations are not met, it can trigger an emotion that easily turns to anger.

> So Naaman went with his horses and chariots and stopped at the door of Elisha's house. Elisha sent a messenger to say to him, "Go, wash yourself seven times in the Jordan, and your flesh will be restored and you will be cleansed."
>
> But Naaman went away angry and said, "I thought that he would surely come out to me and stand and call on the name of the LORD his God, wave his hand over the spot and cure me of my leprosy. Are not Abana and Pharpar, the rivers of Damascus, better than all the waters of Israel? Couldn't I wash in them and be cleansed?" So he turned and went off in a rage. (2 Kings 5:9-12)

Naaman's expectations were not fulfilled that day. It wasn't even close. He expected to be greeted by Elisha himself and not some servant, which probably made him feel disrespected. He expected Elisha to visibly call on God and perform his healing directly on the infected spot. Not only did these expectations not occur, but Naaman was told to wash in the Jordan River, in which he probably couldn't see himself playing as a kid, let alone bathing as an adult! Maybe he could have wrestled with and come to terms with the first two affronts, since Elisha might have been a very popular prophet with a steady stream of healing-seeking followers. But to use the Jordan River to heal a man of his stature was unacceptable, insulting, and disrespectful. The longer he thought about it, the more he burned inwardly. That would not be the moment for a soldier to ask for a better weapon or more provisions, or to ask, "When are we moving out?" It would not be a time to talk to Naaman about anything.

Was Naaman's anger definitive or distorted? If it was definitive, then what wrong did Elisha commit against Naaman? Maybe he could have shown more respect to his guest, but Elisha may not have known he was coming. The situation is similar to someone coming to your house unexpectedly and unannounced, expecting you to drop everything and wait on them. Considering Naaman had a need to be healed and Elisha gave him the advice on how to get healed, I think Naaman's needs were met. There doesn't seem to be any wrongdoing committed by Elisha. Naaman's anger was distorted. He perceived that he had been insulted and disrespected, but that was because of his preconceived expectations of how a commander should be healed. He lost perspective, but fortunately Naaman had people around him willing to speak to him about his angry response.

> Naaman's servants went to him and said, "My father, if the prophet had told you to do some great thing, would you not have done it? How much more, then, when he tells you, 'Wash and be cleansed'!" (2 Kings 5:13)

Thank God for people in our lives to help us when we need it. The people present helped clarify the proper interpretation of Elisha's directions, and re-evaluate the significance of not giving the instructions in the way Naaman expected. They helped Naaman remember the real reason for coming to Elisha, to get healed. Did it really matter how that healing occurred? You may feel the same when the wedding doesn't go perfectly, but you remember who you're marrying; or when someone in customer service takes longer than the time we have available because of the company's process for handling complaints, but you remember that you, too, have a job that isn't always time-efficient; or when the internet connection slows way down just when you only have 10 minutes to finish a task, but you remember that this technology isn't perfectly reliable 24/7.

> So he went down and dipped himself in the Jordan seven times, as the man of God had told him, and his flesh was restored and became clean like that of a young boy.
> Then Naaman and all his attendants went back to the man of God. He stood before him and said, "Now I know that there is no God in all the world except in Israel. So please accept a gift from your servant." The prophet answered, "As surely as the LORD lives, whom I serve, I will not accept a thing." And even though Naaman urged him, he refused. (2 Kings 5:14-16)

So, what the prophet Elisha told Naaman was correct, and no wrong had been committed. Naaman regained his perspective by considering the servants' advice. They were right that Naaman would have done anything to be healed. That was the purpose for him visiting Elisha, but Naaman had lost sight of that. If Naaman had not changed, how eager would Elisha have been to help him the next time he came calling? Once he had the right perspective, Naaman embraced the prophet's words and was immediately healed. It's not enough to just calm down; true healing only occurs when your perspective changes and you realize your anger is distorted, causing an inappropriate reaction. Only with

Angry Men of God

this realization can you become humble enough to be reconciled with those involved and be healed. Consider this excerpt from Gary Chapman's book:

> "The person who has not learned the difference between definitive anger and distorted anger will assume that his anger is always legitimate and the other person's actions always wrong. Such an assumption does not allow anger to be resolved and this rigid insistence on being right will, in fact, stimulate an angry response from the other person."[34]

What about your anger? Is it usually distorted? Are you simply reacting to a perceived wrongdoing? Sometimes our anger is definitive, but how we respond to it will determine whether true healing occurs in the situation, or whether more damage is done.

CHAPTER FIFTEEN

Angry Men of God: Moses–Double-Edge Sword

> *When I am angry I can write, pray, and preach well, for then my whole temperament is quickened, my understanding sharpened, and all mundane vexations and temptations gone.*
>
> —Martin Luther

As God searched for a leader to take his people out of Egypt, what type of person would he need? What would his character need to be? Sensitive? Humble? Authoritative? Self-starting? The job was only leading two million people who were learning about how to trust God and let him lead them to a land and lifestyle that they've never experienced before. There should have been plenty of people from which to choose. Maybe God should have posted a job application online through Monster or CareerBuilder websites, then have a recruiting company filter through the thousands of online applications, and narrow the field to just a few for interviews. Actually, God knew exactly who he wanted and it was Moses. What did God see in Moses? Initially Moses had a concern for his fellow Hebrews and the injustice they suffered at the hands of the Egyptians, some of whom Moses may have known growing up in Pharaoh's house:

> One day, after Moses had grown up, he went out to where his own people were and watched them at their hard labor. He saw an Egyptian beating a Hebrew, one of his own people. Looking this way and that and seeing no one, he killed the Egyptian and hid him in the sand. The next day he went out and saw two Hebrews fighting. He asked the one in the wrong, "Why are you hitting your fellow Hebrew?"
>
> The man said, "Who made you ruler and judge over us? Are you thinking of killing me as you killed the Egyptian?" Then Moses was afraid and thought, "What I did must have become known."
>
> When Pharaoh heard of this, he tried to kill Moses, but Moses fled from Pharaoh and went to live in Midian, where he sat down by a well. Now a priest of Midian had seven daughters, and they came to draw water and fill the troughs to water their father's flock. Some shepherds came along and drove them away, but Moses got up and came to their rescue and watered their flock." (Exodus 2:11-17)

Even as he tried to correct the injustice, he didn't inquire of God but acted on his own wisdom. Even though fear drove him to run, he still took action to aid the women by the well. The shepherds were wrong for excluding the women, and Moses saw to it that the women had the same opportunity. Moses wasn't apathetic to the world around him. He had definitive anger toward injustice and toward people who couldn't defend themselves. He must have felt some inner calling to save his people, a calling put there by God. He was rough around the edges, but God saw something special. With time, hard work, and training, God saw the potential within Moses. Moses already had the foundation that we lack at times, a foundation of caring about the world and loving the people around us. We should be moved in our spirit when there is an injustice and someone is unfairly treated instead of just thinking, "Oh well, that's just the way life goes sometimes."

The same thinking applies in the corporate world. Who are the people that get recognized early in their careers and placed on the "fast track" to be groomed by management to lead for the future? Aren't they those who have passion for making things better? They have ideas, vision, and the willingness to take action. They are self-starters who would rather ask for forgiveness than get permission to get through the corporate bureaucracy. Moses had those qualities, too, but there was a difference in Moses compared to the other young men in Pharaoh's house. He had a heart for God's people and a moral conscience about right and wrong. He was just the kind of man God needed to lead two million people.

Although killing the Egyptian was not the best way to handle his definitive anger, Moses at least had anger about the harsh and brutal conditions the Hebrews endured in slavery. Let's take a look at how Moses reacted to God's training, with special emphasis on how Moses handled his anger. God used it for the good of leading his people; however, it also caused Moses some heartache. His anger could be viewed as a double-edge sword.

Forty years had passed with Moses making a life as a shepherd with the Midianite priest, whose daughters Moses had rescued at the well. We don't know anything about how Moses handled his anger during that time, but I'm sure there were adversities such as weather, illness, predators and other shepherds fighting over the same resources in the land. For some reason, God waited. Maybe the shepherding lifestyle would better prepare Moses to lead than the schools within Pharaoh's household. Maybe God was waiting for time to heal the damage done by Moses' impertinence.

When God finally approached him about going back to Egypt, the same fears that caused Moses to run 40 years earlier came back as fresh as the day he left. When Moses left Egypt, he was afraid of Pharaoh's attempt to kill him, and he was not confident that the Israelites would trust him to lead them, based on their reaction to him killing the Egyptian.

> Moses answered, "What if they do not believe me or listen to me and say, 'The LORD did not appear to you'?" (Exodus 4:1)

> Now the LORD had said to Moses in Midian, "Go back to Egypt, for all those who wanted to kill you are dead." (Exodus 4:19)

After working through Moses' excuses and addressing his real fears about going back to Egypt, God had his man. God knew the real fear inside Moses' heart and addressed it. Sometimes when we respond to definitive anger and we handle it wrong or if things seem to get worse, we have doubts and start to second guess ourselves. In response, we avoid conflict or situations where there will likely be angry emotions. If that's happened to you, it could be that your approach could be better and you just need more training, or it could be that the situation just needed more patience, perseverance, and self-control. Sometimes a situation escalates because the other person is not handling his anger righteously and it may not have anything to do with your approach. If your anger is truly definitive and you are responding to an injustice, or someone has sinned against you or someone else, your confidence has to be in God to work through you, and not in your ability to handle it correctly. Remember that Moses had performed wrongly, yet God called him to go back.

One of the ways Moses learned to handle his anger differently was to be open with God. Take for example, his first approach to Pharaoh, who responded by making the Israelites make bricks without straw. This command from Pharaoh made their task even more difficult and they let Moses know:

> When they left Pharaoh, they found Moses and Aaron waiting to meet them, and they said, "May the LORD look on you and judge you! You have made us obnoxious to Pharaoh and his officials and have put a sword in their hand to kill us."
> Moses returned to the LORD and said, "Why, Lord, why have you brought trouble on this people? Is this why you sent me? Ever since I went to Pharaoh to speak in your name, he has brought trouble on this people, and you have not rescued your people at all." (Exodus 5:20-23)

Now the people were angry with Moses, which made him angry, and he went to God with all of it, even though his anger was directed at God not rescuing his people (i.e., it's your fault, God, that they are angry with me). God was fine with that. He didn't rebuke Moses for feeling that way, but gave him direction and reminded him of his promises and plan.

> Then the LORD said to Moses, "Go, tell Pharaoh king of Egypt to let the Israelites go out of his country." But Moses said to the LORD, "If the Israelites will not listen to me, why would Pharaoh listen to me, since I speak with faltering lips?" (Exodus 6:10-12)

Here again, Moses was blaming himself and doubting that the situation would work out, because of the past and how this first encounter seemingly made things worse. When Moses brought it up again, God gave him a specific plan to deal with his fears:

> Now when the LORD spoke to Moses in Egypt, he said to him, "I am the LORD. Tell Pharaoh king of Egypt everything I tell you."
> But Moses said to the LORD, "Since I speak with faltering lips, why would Pharaoh listen to me?"...
> Then the LORD said to Moses, "See, I have made you like God to Pharaoh, and your brother Aaron will be your prophet. You are to say everything I command you, and your brother Aaron is to tell Pharaoh to let the Israelites go out of his country. (Exodus 6:28-30, Exodus 7:1-2)

With each plague and as specific prayers were answered, Moses' confidence grew and so did his handling of his own anger, as shown with the last plague:

> So Moses said, "This is what the LORD says: 'About midnight I will go throughout Egypt. Every firstborn son in Egypt will die, from the firstborn son of Pharaoh, who sits on the throne, to the firstborn son of the female slave, who is at her hand mill, and all the firstborn of the cattle as well. There will be loud wailing throughout Egypt—worse than there has ever been or ever will be again. But among the Israelites not a dog will bark at any person or animal.' Then you will know that the LORD makes a distinction between Egypt and Israel. All these officials of yours will come to me, bowing down before me and saying, 'Go, you and all the people who follow you!' After that I will leave." Then Moses, hot with anger, left Pharaoh. (Exodus 11:4-8)

After Moses and the Israelites left Egypt, God spoke about his relationship to Moses, which was a significant factor in Moses learning to deal with his own anger:

> The LORD would speak to Moses face to face, as one speaks to a friend. (Exodus 33:11a)

> Moses said to the LORD, "You have been telling me, 'Lead these people,' but you have not let me know whom you will send with me. You have said, 'I know you by name and you have found favor with me.' If you are pleased with me, teach me your ways so I may know you and continue to find favor with you. Remember that this nation is your people."
> The LORD replied, "My Presence will go with you, and I will give you rest."
> Then Moses said to him, "If your Presence does not go with us, do not send us up from here. How will anyone know that you are pleased with me and with your people unless you go with us? What else will distinguish me and your people from all the other people on the face of the earth?"
> And the LORD said to Moses, "I will do the very thing you have asked, because I am pleased with you and I know you by name. (Exodus 33:12-17)

The openness and honesty that characterized Moses' relationship and friendship with God allowed Moses to handle his anger in a positive, healthy way. You can have the same results in your own relationship to God and in your relationships within the body of Christ. Without someone to express and share the emotions, encouraging us to understand their perspective, we are left to our own patterns of dealing with intense situations and escalating emotions.

Even as Moses' confidence grew, his anger and frustration was still triggered by these two million people after they left Egypt. Let's look at several situations and how Moses responded:

When they complained about not having any food...

> So Moses and Aaron said to all the Israelites, "In the evening you will know that it was the LORD who brought you out of Egypt, and in the morning you will see the glory of the LORD, because he has heard your grumbling against him. Who are we, that you should grumble against us?" Moses also said, "You will know that it was the LORD when he gives you meat to eat in the evening and all the bread you want in the morning, because he has heard your grumbling against him. Who are we? You are not grumbling against us, but against the LORD." (Exodus 16:6-8)

When they disobeyed and kept some of the manna until morning...

> The Israelites did as they were told; some gathered much, some little. And when they measured it by the omer, the one who gathered much did not have too much, and the one who gathered little did not have too little. Everyone had gathered just as much as they needed.
>
> Then Moses said to them, "No one is to keep any of it until morning."
>
> However, some of them paid no attention to Moses; they kept part of it until morning, but it was full of maggots and began to smell. So Moses was angry with them. (Exodus 16:17-20)

When they complained about having no water...

> The whole Israelite community set out from the Desert of Sin, traveling from place to place as the LORD commanded. They camped at Rephidim, but there was no water for the people to drink. So they quarreled with Moses and said, "Give us water to drink."
>
> Moses replied, "Why do you quarrel with me? Why do you put the LORD to the test?"
>
> But the people were thirsty for water there, and they grumbled against Moses. They said, "Why did you bring us up out of Egypt to make us and our children and livestock die of thirst?"
>
> Then Moses cried out to the LORD, "What am I to do with these people? They are almost ready to stone me." (Exodus 17:1-4)

Moses' anger was definitive, and he correctly processed their attitudes and complaining as being against the Lord, and not him. He didn't take it personally as he had when the Israelites were forced to make bricks without straw. He did have to vent some emotions with God privately. Thinking that you are about to be stoned would be reason enough to ask God for a few minutes. Even as a Psalmist reflected on this incident, he commented about how the people's attitude affected Moses' anger:

> By the waters of Meribah they angered the LORD, and trouble came to Moses because of them; for they rebelled against the Spirit of God, and rash words came from Moses' lips. (Psalm 106:32-33)

When Aaron's sons didn't offer the sin offering correctly...

> When Moses inquired about the goat of the sin offering and found that it had been burned up, he was angry with Eleazar and Ithamar, Aaron's remaining sons, and asked, "Why didn't you eat the sin offering in the sanctuary area? It is most holy; it was given to you to take away the guilt of the community by making atonement for them before the LORD. Since its blood was not taken into the Holy Place, you should have eaten the goat in the sanctuary area, as I commanded."
>
> Aaron replied to Moses, "Today they sacrificed their sin offering and their burnt offering before the LORD, but such things as this have happened to me. Would the LORD have been pleased if I had eaten the sin offering today?" When Moses heard this, he was satisfied. (Leviticus 10:16-20)

Moses worked through his anger with Aaron, whose other two sons had just been killed by the Lord in Leviticus 10 for stumbling into the Most Holy Place of the Tabernacle. Moses' perspective was that Aaron's remaining two sons were also disobeying the way God had said to perform the sin offering. After discussing it with Aaron, Moses' anger subsided and he was satisfied.

When they made the golden calf...

> When Moses approached the camp and saw the calf and the dancing, his anger burned and he threw the tablets out of his hands, breaking them to pieces at the foot of the mountain. And he took the calf the people had made and burned it in the fire; then he ground it to powder, scattered it on the water and made the Israelites drink it.
>
> He said to Aaron, "What did these people do to you, that you led them into such great sin?"
>
> "Do not be angry, my lord," Aaron answered. "You know how prone these people are to evil. They said to me, 'Make us gods who will go before us. As for this fellow Moses who brought us up out of Egypt, we don't know what has happened to him.' So I told them, 'Whoever has any gold jewelry, take it off.' Then they gave me the gold, and I threw it into the fire, and out came this calf!"
>
> Moses saw that the people were running wild and that Aaron had let them get out of control and so become a laughingstock to their enemies. So he stood at the entrance to the camp and said, "Whoever is for the LORD, come to me." And all the Levites rallied to him.
>
> Then he said to them, "This is what the LORD, the God of Israel, says: 'Each man strap a sword to his side. Go back and forth through the camp from one end to the other, each killing his brother and friend and neighbor.'" The Levites did as Moses commanded, and that day about three thousand of the people died. Then

Moses said, "You have been set apart to the LORD today, for you were against your own sons and brothers, and he has blessed you this day."

The next day Moses said to the people, "You have committed a great sin. But now I will go up to the LORD; perhaps I can make atonement for your sin."

So Moses went back to the LORD and said, "Oh, what a great sin these people have committed! They have made themselves gods of gold. But now, please forgive their sin—but if not, then blot me out of the book you have written."

The LORD replied to Moses, "Whoever has sinned against me I will blot out of my book. Now go, lead the people to the place I spoke of, and my angel will go before you. However, when the time comes for me to punish, I will punish them for their sin."

And the LORD struck the people with a plague because of what they did with the calf Aaron had made. (Exodus 32:19-35)

Moses' anger played out for the good and the bad. He acted decisively by destroying the golden calf and killing those responsible for worshipping the idol. He confronted Aaron about his lack of leadership, and even appealed to God to forgive them of this sin. His actions seemed appropriate and necessary, considering what had happened; however, in his anger, Moses also shattered the tablets containing the Ten Commandments. God didn't say to do that and Moses could have shown better self-control, laying them down before dealing with the Israelites. Notice what God tells him to do about it:

The LORD said to Moses, "Chisel out two stone tablets like the first ones, and I will write on them the words that were on the first tablets, which you broke. Be ready in the morning, and then come up on Mount Sinai. Present yourself to me there on top of the mountain. No one is to come with you or be seen anywhere on the mountain; not even the flocks and herds may graze in front of the mountain."

So Moses chiseled out two stone tablets like the first ones and went up Mount Sinai early in the morning, as the LORD had commanded him; and he carried the two stone tablets in his hands...

Then the LORD said to Moses, "Write down these words, for in accordance with these words I have made a covenant with you and with Israel." Moses was there with the LORD forty days and forty nights without eating bread or drinking water. And he wrote on the tablets the words of the covenant—the Ten Commandments. (Exodus 34:1-4, 27-28)

The original tablets were given to Moses by God on the mountain. (Moses didn't haul them up there.) And God himself wrote on them:

The LORD said to Moses, "Come up to me on the mountain and stay here, and I will give you the tablets of stone with the law and commandments I have written for their instruction." (Exodus 24:12)

When the LORD finished speaking to Moses on Mount Sinai, he gave him the two tablets of the covenant law, the tablets of stone inscribed by the finger of

God. (Exodus 31:18)

> Moses turned and went down the mountain with the two tablets of the covenant law in his hands. They were inscribed on both sides, front and back. The tablets were the work of God; the writing was the writing of God, engraved on the tablets. (Exodus 32:15-16)

Moses had to climb Mount Sinai with the two new tablets of stone. How heavy were they? How much extra effort was required to haul them up the mountain? Also, Moses had to write out the words again by himself. Even though Moses responded appropriately to his anger in some ways, he paid for his angry response with the tablets, by having to carry the new tablets up the mountain and then rewrite the commandments, as discipline for his lack of self control. Even if our anger is definitive and our response righteous, we have to pay attention to every detail and every interaction; otherwise, things get broken that shouldn't, or people get hurt who weren't even involved.

When they complained again about the food...

> The rabble with them began to crave other food, and again the Israelites started wailing and said, "If only we had meat to eat! We remember the fish we ate in Egypt at no cost—also the cucumbers, melons, leeks, onions and garlic. But now we have lost our appetite; we never see anything but this manna!"
>
> The manna was like coriander seed and looked like resin. The people went around gathering it, and then ground it in a hand mill or crushed it in a mortar. They cooked it in a pot or made it into loaves. And it tasted like something made with olive oil. When the dew settled on the camp at night, the manna also came down.
>
> Moses heard the people of every family wailing at the entrance to their tents. The LORD became exceedingly angry, and Moses was troubled. He asked the LORD, "Why have you brought this trouble on your servant? What have I done to displease you that you put the burden of all these people on me? Did I conceive all these people? Did I give them birth? Why do you tell me to carry them in my arms, as a nurse carries an infant, to the land you promised on oath to their ancestors? Where can I get meat for all these people? They keep wailing to me, 'Give us meat to eat!' I cannot carry all these people by myself; the burden is too heavy for me. If this is how you are going to treat me, please go ahead and kill me—if I have found favor in your eyes—and do not let me face my own ruin."
>
> The LORD said to Moses: "Bring me seventy of Israel's elders who are known to you as leaders and officials among the people. Have them come to the tent of meeting, that they may stand there with you. I will come down and speak with you there, and I will take some of the power of the Spirit that is on you and put it on them. They will share the burden of the people with you so that you will not have to carry it alone.
>
> Tell the people: 'Consecrate yourselves in preparation for tomorrow, when you will eat meat. The LORD heard you when you wailed, "If only we had meat

to eat! We were better off in Egypt!" Now the LORD will give you meat, and you will eat it. You will not eat it for just one day, or two days, or five, ten or twenty days, but for a whole month—until it comes out of your nostrils and you loathe it—because you have rejected the LORD, who is among you, and have wailed before him, saying, "Why did we ever leave Egypt?'" (Numbers 11:4-20)

Again Moses had to work things out with God, and he initially blamed God for this "trouble". He took the Israelites' complaints too personally, and thought he had to provide everything for them. Even though God was "exceedingly angry" with the Israelites, He showed compassion to Moses and gave him the help he needed. Moses was troubled, and he resolved his issue with God before it led to his own angry response.

At this point in their relationship, God shared some of his feelings about Moses when Aaron and Miriam questioned his leadership:

(Now Moses was a very humble man, more humble than anyone else on the face of the earth.)...

Listen to my words: "When there is a prophet among you, I, the LORD, reveal myself to them in visions, I speak to them in dreams. But this is not true of my servant Moses; he is faithful in all my house. With him I speak face to face, clearly and not in riddles; he sees the form of the LORD. Why then were you not afraid to speak against my servant Moses? (Numbers 12:3, 6-8)

It's obvious that Moses was growing in his ability to handle his anger. God considered him humble and faithful, which should be very encouraging to you as you grow and mature in handling your own anger. As long as you remain humble and faithful, God will be with you, even when you have to vent to him or close friends that can help with your perspective and response.

When Korah rebelled...

Korah son of Izhar, the son of Kohath, the son of Levi, and certain Reubenites—Dathan and Abiram, sons of Eliab, and On son of Peleth—became insolent and rose up against Moses. With them were 250 Israelite men, well-known community leaders who had been appointed members of the council. They came as a group to oppose Moses and Aaron and said to them, "You have gone too far! The whole community is holy, every one of them, and the LORD is with them. Why then do you set yourselves above the LORD's assembly?"

When Moses heard this, he fell facedown. Then he said to Korah and all his followers: "In the morning the LORD will show who belongs to him and who is holy, and he will have that person come near him. The man he chooses he will cause to come near him. You, Korah, and all your followers are to do this: Take censers and tomorrow put burning coals and incense in them before the LORD. The man the LORD chooses will be the one who is holy. You Levites have gone too far!"

Moses also said to Korah, "Now listen, you Levites! Isn't it enough for you that the God of Israel has separated you from the rest of the Israelite community and brought you near himself to do the work at the LORD's tabernacle and to stand before the community and minister to them? He has brought you and all your fellow Levites near himself, but now you are trying to get the priesthood too. It is against the LORD that you and all your followers have banded together. Who is Aaron that you should grumble against him?"

Then Moses summoned Dathan and Abiram, the sons of Eliab. But they said, "We will not come! Isn't it enough that you have brought us up out of a land flowing with milk and honey to kill us in the wilderness? And now you also want to lord it over us! Moreover, you haven't brought us into a land flowing with milk and honey or given us an inheritance of fields and vineyards. Do you want to treat these men like slaves? No, we will not come!"

Then Moses became very angry and said to the LORD, "Do not accept their offering. I have not taken so much as a donkey from them, nor have I wronged any of them." (Numbers 16:1-15)

Moses allowed God to take care of Korah and his followers.

When the Israelite men took Moabite women as plunder...

They fought against Midian, as the LORD commanded Moses, and killed every man. Among their victims were Evi, Rekem, Zur, Hur and Reba—the five kings of Midian. They also killed Balaam son of Beor with the sword. The Israelites captured the Midianite women and children and took all the Midianite herds, flocks and goods as plunder. They burned all the towns where the Midianites had settled, as well as all their camps. They took all the plunder and spoils, including the people and animals, and brought the captives, spoils and plunder to Moses and Eleazar the priest and the Israelite assembly at their camp on the plains of Moab, by the Jordan across from Jericho.

Moses, Eleazar the priest and all the leaders of the community went to meet them outside the camp. Moses was angry with the officers of the army—the commanders of thousands and commanders of hundreds—who returned from the battle.

"Have you allowed all the women to live?" he asked them. "They were the ones who followed Balaam's advice and enticed the Israelites to be unfaithful to the LORD in the Peor incident, so that a plague struck the LORD's people. Now kill all the boys. And kill every woman who has slept with a man, but save for yourselves every girl who has never slept with a man. (Numbers 31:7-18)

Moses had the right perspective and his anger was justified. His actions were appropriate and he demonstrated self-control by not killing the virgins.

When they grumbled again about water...

The LORD said to Moses, "Take the staff, and you and your brother Aaron gather the assembly together. Speak to that rock before their eyes and it will pour out its water. You will bring water out of the rock for the community so they and their livestock can drink."

> So Moses took the staff from the LORD's presence, just as he commanded him. He and Aaron gathered the assembly together in front of the rock and Moses said to them, "Listen, you rebels, must we bring you water out of this rock?" Then Moses raised his arm and struck the rock twice with his staff. Water gushed out, and the community and their livestock drank.
>
> But the LORD said to Moses and Aaron, "Because you did not trust in me enough to honor me as holy in the sight of the Israelites, you will not bring this community into the land I give them." (Numbers 20:7-12)

Moses struggled with yet another complaint from the Israelites. After several issues with the same person or group of people, you may allow your anger to get the best of you. That's what happened to Moses. This wasn't the first time the Israelites complained about not having any water. The first time, at Marah, the water was too bitter to drink (Exodus 15). The second time, at Rephidim, Moses struck the rock as God commanded (Exodus 17). This third time, God told Moses to speak to the rock instead of striking it. Since Moses was a bit emotionally charged toward these "rebels", he even commented, "Must we bring you water out of this rock?" His focus and credit was to himself and Aaron instead of God. Moses reacted to the situation and did not listen carefully to what God said to do. His reaction led God to prohibit him and Aaron from entering the Promised Land. We are all susceptible to reacting the way Moses did. We all have a point where we just snap and react with the flesh, and let the anger reign in our words, our tone of voice, and our punishments or ultimatums. Moses seemed to struggle with getting over this incident. God's punishment seemed harsh and unfair to Moses. Later in this same chapter, God talked about the event again:

> At Mount Hor, near the border of Edom, the LORD said to Moses and Aaron, "Aaron will be gathered to his people. He will not enter the land I give the Israelites, because both of you rebelled against my command at the waters of Meribah. Get Aaron and his son Eleazar and take them up Mount Hor. Remove Aaron's garments and put them on his son Eleazar, for Aaron will be gathered to his people; he will die there." (Numbers 20:23-26)

As that generation died off in the desert, Moses gave a long speech to the next generation, recalling the events over the last 40 years, and reminding them of all the lessons learned. During this dissertation, Moses brought up what happened at Mount Hor three different times. I would say that he hadn't let it go, nor had he resolved it with God. He blamed the Israelites that he would not cross the Jordan River and go into the Promised Land:

> But you were unwilling to go up; you rebelled against the command of the LORD your God. You grumbled in your tents and said, "The LORD hates us; so he brought us out of Egypt to deliver us into the hands of the Amorites to destroy us. Where can we go? Our brothers have made our hearts melt in fear. They say,

'The people are stronger and taller than we are; the cities are large, with walls up to the sky. We even saw the Anakites there.'"...

When the LORD heard what you said, he was angry and solemnly swore: "No one from this evil generation shall see the good land I swore to give your ancestors, except Caleb son of Jephunneh. He will see it, and I will give him and his descendants the land he set his feet on, because he followed the LORD wholeheartedly."

Because of you the LORD became angry with me also and said, "You shall not enter it, either. But your assistant, Joshua son of Nun, will enter it. Encourage him, because he will lead Israel to inherit it. And the little ones that you said would be taken captive, your children who do not yet know good from bad—they will enter the land. I will give it to them and they will take possession of it. But as for you, turn around and set out toward the desert along the route to the Red Sea." (Deuteronomy 1:26-28, 34-40)

At that time I pleaded with the LORD: "Sovereign LORD, you have begun to show to your servant your greatness and your strong hand. For what god is there in heaven or on earth who can do the deeds and mighty works you do? Let me go over and see the good land beyond the Jordan—that fine hill country and Lebanon."

But because of you the LORD was angry with me and would not listen to me. "That is enough," the LORD said. "Do not speak to me anymore about this matter. Go up to the top of Pisgah and look west and north and south and east. Look at the land with your own eyes, since you are not going to cross this Jordan. But commission Joshua, and encourage and strengthen him, for he will lead this people across and will cause them to inherit the land that you will see." (Deuteronomy 3:23-28)

But as for you, the LORD took you and brought you out of the iron-smelting furnace, out of Egypt, to be the people of his inheritance, as you now are. The LORD was angry with me because of you, and he solemnly swore that I would not cross the Jordan and enter the good land the LORD your God is giving you as your inheritance. I will die in this land; I will not cross the Jordan; but you are about to cross over and take possession of that good land. Be careful not to forget the covenant of the LORD your God that he made with you; do not make for yourselves an idol in the form of anything the LORD your God has forbidden. For the LORD your God is a consuming fire, a jealous God. (Deuteronomy 4:20-24)

It seems from Deuteronomy 3, that Moses spoke to God about the incident to a point where God said, that's enough, no more discussion about this. I've had those moments with my children, when they keep expressing that they don't understand a specific issue, but the reality is that they don't agree. Too much verbiage and discussion can stir up our anger with someone who doesn't agree with us or our decision. God had had enough, but instead of resolving his anger, Moses redirected it toward the Israelites and blamed them for his perceived injustice. This time Moses' anger was distorted. We may not agree with the punishment, but God thought it was appropriate. He did let Moses see the

Promised Land; he just couldn't enter it.

Since Moses was still struggling with this, God had to speak to him to correct his thinking. It wasn't the Israelites' fault, and God described his view of what Moses did that brought about the punishment:

> On that same day the LORD told Moses, "Go up into the Abarim Range to Mount Nebo in Moab, across from Jericho, and view Canaan, the land I am giving the Israelites as their own possession. There on the mountain that you have climbed you will die and be gathered to your people, just as your brother Aaron died on Mount Hor and was gathered to his people. This is because both of you broke faith with me in the presence of the Israelites at the waters of Meribah Kadesh in the Desert of Zin and because you did not uphold my holiness among the Israelites. Therefore, you will see the land only from a distance; you will not enter the land I am giving to the people of Israel." (Deuteronomy 32:48-52)
>
> Then Moses climbed Mount Nebo from the plains of Moab to the top of Pisgah, across from Jericho. There the LORD showed him the whole land—from Gilead to Dan, all of Naphtali, the territory of Ephraim and Manasseh, all the land of Judah as far as the Mediterranean Sea, the Negev and the whole region from the Valley of Jericho, the City of Palms, as far as Zoar. Then the LORD said to him, "This is the land I promised on oath to Abraham, Isaac and Jacob when I said, 'I will give it to your descendants.' I have let you see it with your eyes, but you will not cross over into it." (Deuteronomy 34:1-4)

Because Moses held a grudge against the Israelites, or at least had unresolved feelings toward them, God reminded him of the real reason he wasn't being permitted to enter the Promised Land. It was his disobedience. From God's perspective, Moses and Aaron "rebelled against my command" (Numbers 20), "broke faith with me" and "did not uphold my holiness with the Israelites" (Deuteronomy 32). Even though God punished Moses, He still spoke about him with favor:

> Moses was a hundred and twenty years old when he died, yet his eyes were not weak nor his strength gone...
>
> Since then, no prophet has risen in Israel like Moses, whom the LORD knew face to face, who did all those signs and wonders the LORD sent him to do in Egypt—to Pharaoh and to all his officials and to his whole land. For no one has ever shown the mighty power or performed the awesome deeds that Moses did in the sight of all Israel. (Deuteronomy 34:7, 10-12)

Moses was able to be God's spokesman and allow him to show his mighty power through Moses because of his humility and friendship with God. The openness of his emotions allowed Moses to process his anger in a healthy way, and allowed God to deal with certain situations. Most of the time, Moses showed self-control in dealing with his anger, although a couple of times he lost perspective. It's not easy dealing with your own anger, but Moses' example should provide you with hope, because God has chosen you, also, to display his mighty power. Through your interactions with other people and the many situations that can trigger your anger, God wants to listen to you, even if you're emotionally charged. His hope is that you'll let him deal with some people and provide you with the right perspective, allowing you the right response with self-control and patience.

CHAPTER SIXTEEN

Angry Men of God: Job–Angry with God

> *Speak when you are angry and you'll make the best speech you'll ever regret."*
>
> —Dr. Laurence J. Peter

All of us know the story of Job, and we usually refer to his life when we have a struggle or difficult time, or when we undergo suffering. Sometimes it helps to compare your situation with Job and think, "Well at least it's not as bad as what Job had to deal with," or something similar. Thinking of Job brings a new perspective, to think that your circumstances could be a lot worse, and it helps you find hope, courage, and the strength to persevere.

In the context of dealing with your anger, Job provided an example of what happens when anger is directed toward God. It happens to all of us, maybe more than we think. Sometimes you may deny that you really are angry with God because you assume that feeling is wrong and you shouldn't be feeling this way, since God is perfect and could never sin against you. It is true that your anger can be distorted, and not directed toward the right object or person, but if it is directed toward God, you should be honest and open about it with Him. Let's learn how to do that or how not to do it, from Job's example.

Here's how Job lived his life day-to-day:

> In the land of Uz there lived a man whose name was Job. This man was blameless and upright; he feared God and shunned evil. He had seven sons and three daughters, and he owned seven thousand sheep, three thousand camels, five hundred yoke of oxen and five hundred donkeys, and had a large number of servants. He was the greatest man among all the people of the East.
>
> His sons used to hold feasts in their homes on their birthdays, and they would invite their three sisters to eat and drink with them. When a period of feasting had run its course, Job would make arrangements for them to be purified. Early in the morning he would sacrifice a burnt offering for each of them, thinking, "Perhaps my children have sinned and cursed God in their hearts." This was Job's regular custom. (Job 1:1-5)

From God's perspective, Job was faithful, blameless, and righteous. He was living a life that was pleasing to God. Nothing in his life needed attention. That's amazing, considering that he was also successful in his livelihood, and very wealthy. He was "the greatest man among all the people of the East". It's rare to find a man such as Job anywhere. God himself even said that there was no one on earth like Job:

> Then the LORD said to Satan, "Have you considered my servant Job? There is no one on earth like him; he is blameless and upright, a man who fears God and shuns evil." (Job 1:8)

Then Job had a challenging day unlike any other he had faced in his entire life:

- One day when Job's sons and daughters were feasting and drinking wine at the oldest brother's house, a messenger came to Job and said, "The oxen were plowing and the donkeys were grazing nearby, and the Sabeans attacked and made off with them. They put the servants to the sword, and I am the only one who has escaped to tell you!" (Job 1:13-15)
- While he was still speaking, another messenger came and said, "The fire of God fell from the heavens and burned up the sheep and the servants, and I am the only one who has escaped to tell you!" (Job 1:16)
- While he was still speaking, another messenger came and said, "The Chaldeans formed three raiding parties and swept down on your camels and made off with them. They put the servants to the sword, and I am the only one who has escaped to tell you!" (Job 1:17)
- While he was still speaking, yet another messenger came and said, "Your sons and daughters were feasting and drinking wine at the oldest brother's house, when suddenly a mighty wind swept in from the desert and struck the four corners of the house. It collapsed on them and they are dead, and I am the only one who has escaped to tell you!" (Job 1:18-19)

Your livelihood, most of your possessions (except for the land), and all of your children are gone in a single day! Only people who experience natural disasters can relate. A tsunami, a hurricane, or a tornado could wipe out your house, but probably not all of your children, unless they are all in the house. Apart from our homes, much of our wealth is in electronic form, which probably wouldn't be wiped out by a localized natural disaster. Even with the 2004 tsunami in the Indian Ocean that caused incredible damage and tremendous loss of life, the wealthy of those affected areas of the world probably had their main residences located far from the coastline. Even if a vacation home was lost, the impact would not be anything near what Job experienced. How did he respond?

> At this, Job got up and tore his robe and shaved his head. Then he fell to the ground in worship and said: "Naked I came from my mother's womb, and naked I will depart. The LORD gave and the LORD has taken away; may the name of the LORD be praised." In all this, Job did not sin by charging God with wrongdoing. (Job 1:20-22)

Job didn't charge God with wrongdoing, which would have been the natural reaction to anger triggered by these events. Based on his life, Job would naturally feel an injustice had been done to him. The cultural thinking at that time connected prosperity with living right, and trouble or bad events to not living right, or living a sinful life. Since Job's life was impeccable, there would be no justifiable reason for these events to happen to him on the same day. If Job had only lost his camels, then his anger might be directed toward the Chaldeans, or his limited security to protect his servants, but these events were independent of each other. Since the Sabeans and the Chaldeans probably didn't conspire together against Job, and because the odds of two natural disasters occurring on the same day are so high, Job would naturally direct his thoughts toward God. It wasn't just a coincidence.

If little things can trigger your anger, such as a traffic inconvenience, mistreatment, dissatisfaction with a customer service representative, or even a child's immaturity that forces you to change your schedule or make you late, how would you react to a day like Job's? Many of us wouldn't be able to function as we tried to process the day's events. Who would see to proper burial of all the servants? What about planning the details of all the funerals for your own children? With your livelihood stolen or destroyed, how would you pay the bills and creditors? We would need others to help, and probably counseling to sort out our emotions. After dealing with the shock, our minds would naturally follow a logical train of thought and begin to ask, "Why?" We would try to figure out what caused these events and what could we have done to prevent them, or at least prevent all of them from happening in the same day.

We have no indication that Job did any of that, but it's hard to imagine that none of those thoughts would have crossed his mind. He did tear his robe, shave his head, and fall to the ground in worship. Tearing his robe would be a physical sign of remorse, grief, or righteous indignation. Shaving his head would be a sign of mourning. Falling to the ground would be a natural response to the overwhelming news, but he also worshiped, which is commendable. It took some time for Job to shave his head. As he was shaving his head, I'm sure the tears flowed as he thought about his children, the last interactions he had with them, and how he was going to go on with life. Job's thoughts centered on God as he processed the events of the day, and he responded with a spiritual, mature view. Everything Job had came from God and then God decided to take it all away. God has the right to do that. God can still be praised for who he is, regardless of how his choices affect our lives. You know, our anger wouldn't be triggered very often if we would respond to life events the way Job did on that day.

Job responded righteously even though he didn't know that Satan had initiated the entire chain of events. With 20/20 hindsight, you can sometimes counsel other people with a different perspective about their life events by recalling, "I remember when _____ happened to me, but here's what I learned from it." You can do that with yourself when you get another curveball or disappointment in life. Even though Job didn't realize it was Satan, it's good for us to remember it. Not only did Satan have to ask God for permission, but God even limited what Satan could do to Job:

> "Does Job fear God for nothing?" Satan replied. "Have you not put a hedge around him and his household and everything he has? You have blessed the work of his hands, so that his flocks and herds are spread throughout the land. But now stretch out your hand and strike everything he has, and he will surely curse you to your face."
> The LORD said to Satan, "Very well, then, everything he has is in your power, but on the man himself do not lay a finger." Then Satan went out from the presence of the LORD. (Job 1:9-12)

Remembering that Satan is the real enemy should help us process the frustrations, irritations, and disappointments throughout our day. Remember that Satan is the one who's really angry:

> Then war broke out in heaven. Michael and his angels fought against the dragon, and the dragon and his angels fought back. But he was not strong enough, and they lost their place in heaven. The great dragon was hurled down—that ancient serpent called the devil, or Satan, who leads the whole world astray. He was hurled to the earth, and his angels with him... Therefore rejoice, you heavens and you who dwell in them! But woe to the earth and the sea, because the devil has gone down to you! He is filled with fury, because he knows that his time is short...
> Then the dragon was enraged at the woman and went off to wage war against the rest of her offspring—those who keep God's commands and hold fast their testimony about Jesus. (Revelation 12:7-9, 12, 17)

Remembering this about Satan is easier said than done, because we're just not that spiritual 24/7. Plus, our Creator gave us the capacity to experience anger, so anger is going to happen. The proper perspective, however, can help us "respond" instead of "react" to the situation at hand. Job was going to experience that opportunity on a different day.

Round two began on another day. We don't know how much time elapsed between the two days, but Satan approached God again:

> Then the LORD said to Satan, "Have you considered my servant Job? There is no one on earth like him; he is blameless and upright, a man who fears God and shuns evil. And he still maintains his integrity, though you incited me against him to ruin him without any reason."
> "Skin for skin!" Satan replied. "A man will give all he has for his own life. But now stretch out your hand and strike his flesh and bones, and he will surely curse you to your face."
> The LORD said to Satan, "Very well, then, he is in your hands; but you must spare his life."
> So Satan went out from the presence of the LORD and afflicted Job with painful sores from the soles of his feet to the crown of his head. Then Job took a piece of broken pottery and scraped himself with it as he sat among the ashes. (Job 2:3-8)

Even Job's wife struggled with his suffering, which affected her. They were her children, too. Life had to be harder since that first day. It was her 9/11 and Satan had been her terrorist. Maybe she kept it together through the first ordeal, but we really don't know how she processed it, or how she responded. We do know how she responded to the second day:

> His wife said to him, "Are you still maintaining your integrity? Curse God and die!"
> He replied, "You are talking like a foolish woman. Shall we accept good from God, and not trouble?"
> In all this, Job did not sin in what he said. (Job 2:9-10)

Since she asked Job, "Are you still maintaining your integrity?" maybe she was critical of his initial response, or maybe she was commenting on his current state of mind after several days of nursing him. Maybe she finally reached her breaking point as she had to deal with a husband incapable of providing for her. She had become the caretaker and she would just rather have him die so that she could move on with her life. I can relate to some of those feelings, as my wife and I have cared for my father living in our house since 2000, while we raise our three teenage children. Being a caretaker requires sacrifice, some loss of privacy, and a deeper capacity to love and show mercy as those we care for age. It is not easy, and I've discovered trigger points to my own anger that I never knew I had. Even though he had not sinned to this point, Job was about to experience that same thing.

How bad was it for Job? When his friends came to see him and provide support, they were shocked at what they saw:

> When they saw him from a distance, they could hardly recognize him; they began to weep aloud, and they tore their robes and sprinkled dust on their heads.

> Then they sat on the ground with him for seven days and seven nights. No one said a word to him, because they saw how great his suffering was. (Job 2:12-13)

> My body is clothed with worms and scabs, my skin is broken and festering. (Job 7:5)

> I go about blackened, but not by the sun; I stand up in the assembly and cry for help. I have become a brother of jackals, a companion of owls. My skin grows black and peels; my body burns with fever. (Job 30:28-30)

We don't know how long Job suffered with his physical ailments. It was at least seven days, because that's how long his friends had been there, but it could have been much longer. At some point, Job snapped. He had reached his breaking point and had had enough. Without any clear explanation as to the reason for his suffering, Job made his own conclusions, and reacted with an anger that took divine intervention to resolve.

> After this, Job opened his mouth and cursed the day of his birth...
> "I have no peace, no quietness; I have no rest, but only turmoil." (Job 3:1, 26)

Satan was right about Job. He did curse and he did have a negative attitude towards God. Job handled that first day and kept his heart right. Even with the added suffering of his own body, he accepted this new trouble, as he explained to his wife. But when it went on day after day without relief, and no explanation as to its cause or what he was supposed to change to take it away, Job snapped. What does it take for you to break? What are your emotional hot buttons? We all have pet peeves about how we like things done and what irritates us, but do you know when you are triggered? Is it when you are fatigued, stressed, financially strapped, or simply depressed? Can you continue to love people and be patient with them when they are angry at you? Do you still have self-control with your children when they are emotionally charged towards you? Or do you allow your emotions to heat up in response? We may not know all of our trigger points, but Satan and God know them very well. It's important to know them yourself, because that knowledge will allow you to understand and respond to your anger in a healthy, spiritual way. As Job wrestled with the "Why?", he probably felt the same way the author expressed in these Psalms:

> O God, why have you rejected us forever? Why does your anger smolder against the sheep of your pasture? (Psalms 74:1)

> Will the Lord reject forever? Will he never show his favor again? Has his unfailing love vanished forever? Has his promise failed for all time? Has God forgotten to be merciful? Has he in anger withheld his compassion? (Psalms 77:7-9)

With no relief in sight for his physical ailments, Job had to resolve that this may be his life for the rest of his days, and he could not accept it. He could accept the events of the first day, because he could start over and progress toward a better future. He could even accept the second day with the idea that it, too, would not last. He would eventually get to feeling better, become healthy again, and start rebuilding. However, Job could not accept the idea of continuing with life as a bed-ridden soul in intensive care with constant pain and no relief…ever. Have you ever been challenged in this way, when you are dealt circumstances that change your life for years to come? An unexpected pregnancy, death of a family member, job loss, divorce, serious health issue, or other challenging life events may leave you tempted to react as Job did.

Let's look at Job's emotional state after his anger had been triggered:

"Teach me, and I will be quiet; show me where I have been wrong. How painful are honest words! …Is there any wickedness on my lips? Can my mouth not discern malice?" (Job 6:24-25a, 30)

Like a slave longing for the evening shadows, or a hired laborer waiting to be paid, so I have been allotted months of futility, and nights of misery have been assigned to me. When I lie down I think, 'How long before I get up?' The night drags on, and I toss and turn until dawn….
Remember, O God, that my life is but a breath; my eyes will never see happiness again. (Job 7:2-4, 7)

I despise my life; I would not live forever. Let me alone; my days have no meaning. (Job 7:16)

Why do you not pardon my offenses and forgive my sins? (Job 7:21)

Even if I summoned him and he responded, I do not believe he would give me a hearing. He would crush me with a storm and multiply my wounds for no reason…
Even if I were innocent, my mouth would condemn me; if I were blameless, it would pronounce me guilty. (Job 9:16-17, 20)

If I say, 'I will forget my complaint, I will change my expression, and smile,' I still dread all my sufferings, for I know you will not hold me innocent. Since I am already found guilty, why should I struggle in vain? (Job 9:27-29)

If only there were someone to mediate between us, someone to bring us together, someone to remove God's rod from me, so that his terror would frighten me no more. Then I would speak up without fear of him, but as it now stands with me, I cannot. (Job 9:33-35)

I loathe my very life; therefore I will give free rein to my complaint and speak out in the bitterness of my soul. I say to God: Do not declare me guilty, but tell me what charges you have against me…

> You bring new witnesses against me and increase your anger toward me; your forces come against me wave upon wave. Why then did you bring me out of the womb? I wish I had died before any eye saw me. If only I had never come into being, or had been carried straight from the womb to the grave! (Job 10:1-2, 17-19)

> I cry out to you, God, but you do not answer; I stand up, but you merely look at me. You turn on me ruthlessly; with the might of your hand you attack me. (Job 30:20-21)

How would you describe Job's state of mind? He hated his life. He struggled to understand why God would allow this to happen to him. He didn't feel he could resolve it with God without a mediator, because God had been silent. Job didn't see anything in his life that was sinful or wrong, which would justify his "punishment". His life no longer had any meaning, and he felt he would never see happiness again. Job remembered the way life was and it tore at his soul:

> How I long for the months gone by, for the days when God watched over me, when his lamp shone on my head and by his light I walked through darkness! Oh, for the days when I was in my prime, when God's intimate friendship blessed my house, when the Almighty was still with me and my children were around me, when my path was drenched with cream and the rock poured out for me streams of olive oil. (Job 29:2-6)

Job thought that God had something against him, that God would not forgive him, and that God continued to be angry with him for no reason. Obviously, Job's anger was distorted, because he perceived that these "injustices" were directed toward him by God. Job felt justified to complain, become bitter, and voice his frustrations with his friends. No one could console him or change his perspective. He made up his mind that his views were accurate and justified. If you've ever been in that state of mind, you can relate to Job. It's not a good place to be.

When you're in Job's state of mind, no one can talk to you or reason with you. No amount of logic or hope for the future can turn your course. Job's friends had a distorted view, too. They were convinced that Job had sinned, but was not willing to admit it.

> Why has your heart carried you away, and why do your eyes flash, so that you vent your rage against God and pour out such words from your mouth? (Job's friend Eliphaz in Job 15:12-13)

Their thoughts were the same as expressed in this proverb:

> A person's own folly leads to their ruin, yet their heart rages against the

LORD. (Proverbs 19:3)

As the friends argued with Job, maybe they became angry, too. After many chapters of bantering and arguing with Job, his friends stopped trying to persuade him. After listening to these discussions, a young man named Elihu also became angry:

> So these three men stopped answering Job, because he was righteous in his own eyes. But Elihu son of Barakel the Buzite, of the family of Ram, became very angry with Job for justifying himself rather than God. He was also angry with the three friends, because they had found no way to refute Job, and yet had condemned him. Now Elihu had waited before speaking to Job because they were older than he. But when he saw that the three men had nothing more to say, his anger was aroused. (Job 32:1-5)

Elihu shared his thoughts with the whole group for six chapters in Job 32-37. His main focus was on God and who he is. Elihu thought Job had lost perspective, and should have been more careful how he spoke about God and his purposes. Directionally, Elihu had the right idea, and before Job could reply, God intervened and personally confronted Job in Job 38-41. Maybe God knew that Job wouldn't listen to Elihu, either, and needed divine intervention to see clearly.

> Then Job replied to the LORD: "I know that you can do all things; no purpose of yours can be thwarted. You asked, 'Who is this that obscures my plans without knowledge?' Surely I spoke of things I did not understand, things too wonderful for me to know. "You said, 'Listen now, and I will speak; I will question you, and you shall answer me.' My ears had heard of you but now my eyes have seen you. Therefore I despise myself and repent in dust and ashes." (Job 42:1-6)

God also dealt with Job's three friends, as their perspective was also distorted about the events in Job's life. He didn't address Elihu's dissertation. Maybe the young man had some things on right.

> After the LORD had said these things to Job, he said to Eliphaz the Temanite, "I am angry with you and your two friends, because you have not spoken the truth about me, as my servant Job has. So now take seven bulls and seven rams and go to my servant Job and sacrifice a burnt offering for yourselves. My servant Job will pray for you, and I will accept his prayer and not deal with you according to your folly. You have not spoken the truth about me, as my servant Job has." So Eliphaz the Temanite, Bildad the Shuhite and Zophar the Naamathite did what the LORD told them; and the LORD accepted Job's prayer. (Job 42:7-9)

Once Job saw God clearly, he could see the right perspective and he changed his heart. God brought about good from Satan's evil desires. Satan was right about Job and the conditions that would cause Job to snap and get angry toward God. God used the situation to help Job grow and become more mature. He may be doing that in your life, too. God may allow Satan to take you to your breaking point, too, but only to help you mature and become even more faithful and content, no matter what the circumstances. The Apostle Paul called it "the secret of being content in any and every situation" (Philippians 4:12). Paul admitted that he had to learn it and so will you. Sometimes, like Job, you don't learn it, and God has to allow the situation to continue until you do learn it.

> After Job had prayed for his friends, the LORD restored his fortunes and gave him twice as much as he had before. All his brothers and sisters and everyone who had known him before came and ate with him in his house. They comforted and consoled him over all the trouble the LORD had brought on him, and each one gave him a piece of silver and a gold ring.
> The LORD blessed the latter part of Job's life more than the former part. He had fourteen thousand sheep, six thousand camels, a thousand yoke of oxen and a thousand donkeys. And he also had seven sons and three daughters. (Job 42:10-13)

CHAPTER SEVENTEEN

Angry Men of God: Samson—It's Their Problem

There was never an angry man that though his anger unjust.
—St. Francis DeSales

As a strong-willed person, Samson got whatever he wanted, including a wife from Israel's enemies, the Philistines. During the seven-day wedding feast, Samson made a wager with 30 Philistines to solve a riddle. The winner would receive 30 linen garments and 30 sets of clothes.

> On the fourth day, they said to Samson's wife, "Coax your husband into explaining the riddle for us, or we will burn you and your father's household to death. Did you invite us here to steal our property?"
> Then Samson's wife threw herself on him, sobbing, "You hate me! You don't really love me. You've given my people a riddle, but you haven't told me the answer."
> "I haven't even explained it to my father or mother," he replied, "so why should I explain it to you?" She cried the whole seven days of the feast. So on the seventh day he finally told her, because she continued to press him. She in turn explained the riddle to her people.
> Before sunset on the seventh day the men of the town said to him,
> "What is sweeter than honey? What is stronger than a lion?"
> Samson said to them,
> "If you had not plowed with my heifer, you would not have solved my riddle."
> Then the Spirit of the LORD came powerfully upon him. He went down to Ashkelon, struck down thirty of their men, stripped them of everything and gave their clothes to those who had explained the riddle. Burning with anger, he returned to his father's home. And Samson's wife was given to one of his companions who had attended him at the feast. (Judges 14:15-20)

So what caused Samson's anger? He probably felt manipulated and cheated, and he probably held a grudge against his wife, since he left the feast without her. It's obvious that he didn't resolve any of these emotions, and didn't reconcile with the Philistines or his wife. God in his wisdom warns in

Ephesians about not resolving conflicts because they are a deadly source of anger, and can cause further damage, even if you try to forget about them and get a good night's sleep.

> Therefore each of you must put off falsehood and speak truthfully to your neighbor, for we are all members of one body. "In your anger do not sin": Do not let the sun go down while you are still angry, and do not give the devil a foothold. (Ephesians 4:25-27)

Paul's letter quotes Psalm 4 from the Old Testament:

> Tremble and do not sin; when you are on your beds, search your hearts and be silent. (Psalm 4:4)

Some people interpret this Scripture the same way a comedian would:

> Never go to bed angry, stay up and fight. (Phyllis Diller)

I don't think that's what God had in mind when Paul wrote his book to the church in the city of Ephesus. There's no benefit in allowing an argument to continue with escalating emotions, more hurt feelings, and fatigued bodies. We all know how easily hurtful words or actions can occur when we are angry:

> Now the son of an Israelite mother and an Egyptian father went out among the Israelites, and a fight broke out in the camp between him and an Israelite. The son of the Israelite woman blasphemed the Name with a curse; so they brought him to Moses...
> Then the LORD said to Moses: "Take the blasphemer outside the camp. All those who heard him are to lay their hands on his head, and the entire assembly is to stone him. Say to the Israelites: 'Anyone who curses their God will be held responsible; anyone who blasphemes the name of the LORD is to be put to death. The entire assembly must stone them. Whether foreigner or native-born, when they blaspheme the Name they are to be put to death...
> Then Moses spoke to the Israelites, and they took the blasphemer outside the camp and stoned him. The Israelites did as the LORD commanded Moses. (Leviticus 24:10-11, 13-16, 23)

I don't think the son of the Egyptian father went out with the intent of killing an Israelite. It was probably a racial comment or prejudiced statement that stirred someone's anger. Rather than resolving it, the discussion escalated into an argument, out-of-control emotions became physical, and the Israelite was killed. When two people don't agree on an emotional issue that triggers someone's anger, there is tremendous benefit from ongoing discussion to resolve the hurt feelings, to correct the distorted perceptions, and to humbly confess the overreactions and ask forgiveness.

Samson didn't follow this godly principle, and even though he stayed away for awhile, the same emotions were simply in hibernation, waiting to "wake up" with the next conflict.

> Later on, at the time of wheat harvest, Samson took a young goat and went to visit his wife. He said, "I'm going to my wife's room." But her father would not let him go in.
>
> "I was so sure you hated her," he said, "that I gave her to your companion. Isn't her younger sister more attractive? Take her instead."
>
> Samson said to them, "This time I have a right to get even with the Philistines; I will really harm them." So he went out and caught three hundred foxes and tied them tail to tail in pairs. He then fastened a torch to every pair of tails, lit the torches and let the foxes loose in the standing grain of the Philistines. He burned up the shocks and standing grain, together with the vineyards and olive groves.
>
> When the Philistines asked, "Who did this?" they were told, "Samson, the Timnite's son-in-law, because his wife was given to his companion." So the Philistines went up and burned her and her father to death. Samson said to them, "Since you've acted like this, I swear that I won't stop until I get my revenge on you." He attacked them viciously and slaughtered many of them. Then he went down and stayed in a cave in the rock of Etam.
>
> The Philistines went up and camped in Judah, spreading out near Lehi. The people of Judah asked, "Why have you come to fight us?"
>
> "We have come to take Samson prisoner," they answered, "to do to him as he did to us."
>
> Then three thousand men from Judah went down to the cave in the rock of Etam and said to Samson, "Don't you realize that the Philistines are rulers over us? What have you done to us?"
>
> He answered, "I merely did to them what they did to me." (Judges 15:1-11)

Note how the "devil's foothold" played out:

1. When Samson found out that his wife had been given to another man, he said, "This time I have a right to get even with the Philistines; I will really harm them." He burned their fields.

2. Philistines responded by burning the woman and her father to death.

3. Samson's response, "Since you've acted like this, I swear that I won't stop until I get my revenge on you." He viciously slaughtered many Philistines. It seems that the angrier Samson became, the more Philistines he killed. Sometimes athletes can think that getting mad will enhance athletic performance, particularly in a contact sport such as football or rugby. From Gary Chapman's book, *Anger– Handling a Powerful Emotion in a Healthy Way:*

"Does getting mad enhance athletic performance? No, says a psychologist who works with Olympic athletes. 'Research indicates that anger and aggression are actually associated with a sense of defeat. Contrary to what was once believed, venting anger doesn't lead to catharsis, it simply leads to more anger'".[35]

Note: I didn't know what catharsis meant either, so here you go… purging or relieving of emotional tensions.

4. Philistines' response, "We have come to take Samson prisoner…to do to him as he did to us."
5. Samson's reply, "I merely did to them what they did to me."

Now Samson's thinking was completely distorted. He justified his response and thought he had the "right to get even". After many other people suffered, both Samson and the Philistines rationalized their actions by claiming the other party started it. The "blame game" never ends. We see this often with children, but it also plays out with adults, especially with family or extended family relationships. These unresolved feelings and conflicts create anger, mistrust, unforgiveness, bitterness, or even hatred, sometimes lasting for years. Even if your anger comes from a very small issue (as when Samson's wife ruined his riddle), it's critical that you get completely resolved and reconciled to avoid more damage in the future. Many other people will suffer. You have to get rid of all of it.

"When anger arises, think of the consequences."
—Confucius

"Men are like steel: when they lose their temper, they lose their worth."
—Chuck Norris

"When I am right, I get angry. Churchill gets angry when he is wrong. So we were often angry at each other."
—Charles De Gaulle

Fortunately, God gives us the direction we need at the beginning and end of Ephesians 4, the same chapter that speaks about unresolved anger:

> Be completely humble and gentle; be patient, bearing with one another in love (Ephesians 4:2)

> Get rid of all bitterness, rage and anger, brawling and slander, along with every form of malice. Be kind and compassionate to one another, forgiving each other, just as in Christ God forgave you. (Ephesians 4:31-32)

If you don't obey God's word to get rid of all bitterness, rage, and anger, you will suffer the consequences, as will other people in your life. It seems that the longer these feelings go unresolved, the more distant you feel in those relationships, and the more justified you feel about not resolving them. Usually rationalization follows along one of these lines of thinking: "It's their fault" or, "If they hadn't _____ we wouldn't be having these problems" or, "Other people feel this way about them", or even, "They'll never change so why should I even try".

It takes a lot of courage, initiation, and maybe even time to resolve differences and hurt feelings, but it's worth the effort for a clear conscience and being able to place yourself in a position where God can bless your efforts, even if the other person is not ready or willing.

Things didn't end well for Samson. The same issues followed him in his dysfunctional relationships with yet another woman, Delilah, and the Philistines. Through several attempts to find his source of strength, the Philistines tied up Samson in a variety of ways:

- Seven new bowstrings
- Brand new ropes
- Fabric made from seven braids of his hair

But each attempt failed and Samson easily broke the binds and escaped their grasp. With each challenge, Samson seemed to enjoy the competition. Eventually, Samson revealed the secret to Delilah and ended up being captured by the Philistines, blinded, and taken as a prisoner. God did grant Samson's last prayer as he brought down the foreign-god temple built for the Philistine god, Dagon, and killed many more Philistines.

From his birth as a Nazirite, which was intended to set him apart for God's work, Samson struggled to fulfill God's plan for him. Instead of leading Israel to defeat the Philistines completely, Samson seemed to tolerate them and simply kill some through his own strength. His unresolved anger and personal unrighteousness limited how much he could influence others for Godly purposes, as the book of James states regarding anger:

> Human anger does not produce the righteousness that God desires. (James 1:20 NLT)

CHAPTER EIGHTEEN

Angry Men of God: Saul-Unresolved

A man is about as big as the things that make him angry.
—Winston Churchill

Saul is often remembered for his volatile relationship with David, as he loved to hear David's soothing music or send him victoriously into battle. But he was also afraid and jealous of David's success, to the point of trying to kill him more than once. Saul's anger and rage almost killed his son, Jonathan, and it did kill many other innocent people, all because Saul's anger was unresolved with David. More than once, Saul appeared to have resolved it, but like an alcoholic who only changes based on his latest AA meeting, Saul reverted back to the uncontrolled madman in pursuit of the object of his anger.

Before we look into his relationship with David, let's look at Saul when he had angry episodes long before he met David. Sometimes Saul's anger was definitive, as when he heard what Nahash, the Ammonite, said to the people of Jabesh Gilead.

> Nahash the Ammonite went up and besieged Jabesh Gilead. And all the men of Jabesh said to him, "Make a treaty with us, and we will be subject to you."
> But Nahash the Ammonite replied, "I will make a treaty with you only on the condition that I gouge out the right eye of every one of you and so bring disgrace on all Israel."
> The elders of Jabesh said to him, "Give us seven days so we can send messengers throughout Israel; if no one comes to rescue us, we will surrender to you."
> When the messengers came to Gibeah of Saul and reported these terms to the people, they all wept aloud. Just then Saul was returning from the fields, behind his oxen, and he asked, "What is wrong with everyone? Why are they weeping?" Then they repeated to him what the men of Jabesh had said.
> When Saul heard their words, the Spirit of God came powerfully upon him, and he burned with anger. He took a pair of oxen, cut them into pieces, and sent the pieces by messengers throughout Israel, proclaiming, "This is what will be done to the oxen of anyone who does not follow Saul and Samuel." Then the terror of the LORD fell on the people, and they came out together as one. When Saul mustered them at Bezek, the men of Israel numbered three hundred thousand and those of Judah thirty thousand.

> They told the messengers who had come, "Say to the men of Jabesh Gilead, 'By the time the sun is hot tomorrow, you will be rescued.'" When the messengers went and reported this to the men of Jabesh, they were elated. They said to the Ammonites, "Tomorrow we will surrender to you, and you can do to us whatever you like."
> The next day Saul separated his men into three divisions; during the last watch of the night they broke into the camp of the Ammonites and slaughtered them until the heat of the day. Those who survived were scattered, so that no two of them were left together. (1 Samuel 11:1-11)

Saul was just anointed king of Israel because the people had asked for a king. Moved by the Holy Spirit, Saul felt an injustice was committed that needed a righteous response. In order to inspire others to fight, Saul threatened to burn their oxen if the people of Israel did not follow him and Samuel into battle. I'd say his people skills were not fully developed, but the Scriptures say that "the terror of the Lord fell on the people." They responded in force to battle and destroyed the Ammonites. Saul took action and God blessed his action, even though Saul was a little strong-handed. He could have taken a different approach by praying about it, remaining humble and self-controlled, and then simply asking God how to proceed against the Ammonites. In this case it turned out okay, as the Ammonites were destroyed.

Another example of Saul's anger was his reaction to Jonathan eating honey, when he had told the men, "Cursed be anyone who eats food before evening comes, before I have avenged myself on my enemies!" (1 Samuel 14:24). This happened right after Jonathan had inspired a great victory over the Philistines. After God did not answer Saul's prayer, the soldiers drew lots and Jonathan's issue came to light. Saul was focused on his command being disobeyed, and even though Jonathan was his son, his punishment must be death. Saul's men had to convince him not to kill Jonathan.

Looking at this situation from our historical point of view, we can easily see that Saul was overreacting. Of course, we would never react like that! How childish and immature. Talk about majoring in the minors, Saul did just that. He was emotionally charged and offended about one of his soldiers ignoring his command, even though it was his son. We would never make such a quick judgment without thinking things through, or pronounce judgment and appropriate "sentencing" without asking questions and understanding all the facts. Of course we have done that, and more than once.

What was going on in Saul's heart? Well, consider that he had just made an unspiritual decision in 1 Samuel 13, when he made the sacrifice before battle without waiting for Samuel. When Samuel arrived, he corrected Saul's thinking and said, "You have done a foolish thing…and your kingdom will not endure." (1 Samuel 13:13-14) Did Saul feel angry or discouraged from that conflict? Did he resolve it with Samuel? It doesn't appear that Saul did anything. Have you ever had conflict that left you feeling unresolved, whether with your own feelings or with the other person? In those situations, aren't you a little more sensitive than normal, a little more emotional and reactive? Aren't you more prone to overreact when something goes the opposite of the way you want it?

Having the presence of mind to know when your heart is still troubled, and not totally resolved, is half the battle. The other half is being willing to take the time to get resolved. That could mean some extra prayer time to regain your perspective on the issue and an appropriate response, or a follow-up conversation with the person, or getting some advice from a trusted friend. It could mean the difference between threatening to punish or making light of unexpected honey, as fitting for Jonathan's "sweet" victory. Saul's inability to handle his own anger in a healthy, productive way would be a snare to him throughout his life.

This brings us to Saul's relationship to David. With a history of not resolving issues in his own heart, and reacting with uncontrolled impulses to perceived or real injustices, is it any wonder that Saul struggled in his relationship with David? But initially, David brought peace to Saul's tortured soul through music and song. David's musical abilities, honed in the pastures of Israel as a shepherd, became medicine to Saul and a drug without which he couldn't live.

> "Whenever the spirit from God came on Saul, David would take up his lyre and play. Then relief would come to Saul; he would feel better, and the evil spirit would leave him." (1 Samuel 16:23)

Yet after David defeated Goliath and became even more successful in battle, he became a threat to Saul. Instead of resolving his anger through God or a trusted friend like Samuel, Saul's distorted view led him to try to kill David himself:

> When the men were returning home after David had killed the Philistine, the women came out from all the towns of Israel to meet King Saul with singing and dancing, with joyful songs and with timbrels and lyres. As they danced, they sang:
> > "Saul has slain his thousands,
> > and David his tens of thousands."
>
> Saul was very angry; this refrain displeased him greatly. "They have credited David with tens of thousands," he thought, "but me with only thousands. What more can he get but the kingdom?" And from that time on Saul kept a close eye on David. The next day an evil spirit from God came forcefully on Saul. He was prophesying in his house, while David was playing the lyre, as he usually did. Saul had a spear in his hand and he hurled it, saying to himself, "I'll pin David to the wall." But David eluded him twice. Saul was afraid of David, because the LORD was with David but had departed from Saul. So he sent David away from him and gave him command over a thousand men, and David led the troops in their campaigns. In everything he did he had great success, because the LORD was with him. When Saul saw how successful he was, he was afraid of him. (1 Samuel 18:6-15)

He also tried to take David's life through the Philistines:

> Saul said to David, "Here is my older daughter Merab. I will give her to you in marriage; only serve me bravely and fight the battles of the LORD." For Saul said to himself, "I will not raise a hand against him. Let the Philistines do that!"... When Saul realized that the LORD was with David and that his daughter Michal loved David, Saul became still more afraid of him, and he remained his enemy the rest of his days. (1 Samuel 18:17, 28-29)

David wasn't the source or cause of Saul's anger, but David's life made Saul afraid. Sometimes our angry responses come from fear. Our teenager makes a bad decision and we "lose it" because of our fear of the future if they continue along this line of thinking. We begin viewing a co-worker with a critical eye because she is handling her work better than we, and we are afraid that we could lose our jobs or be overlooked for the next promotion. Our spouses do not communicate to us about some detail in our lives (third time this month), and we respond in anger because we are afraid they will never change this habit, thus producing a life that for us is unlivable.

Saul's inability to deal with his fears about how he compared to David, or losing the kingship because of David, led him to being even <u>more afraid</u> (vs 29), and he "remained his enemy the rest of his days". Sometimes people take their unresolved fears to their graves. They miss out on so much joy and freedom that could be theirs, if only they would truly resolve the fears, and embrace God's love and plan for their lives. Don't let that happen in your relationships.

Let's take a look at how Saul's fear-driven anger toward David played out:

> Saul told his son Jonathan and all the attendants to kill David. But Jonathan had taken a great liking to David and warned him, "My father Saul is looking for a chance to kill you. Be on your guard tomorrow morning; go into hiding and stay there. I will go out and stand with my father in the field where you are. I'll speak to him about you and will tell you what I find out."
> Jonathan spoke well of David to Saul his father and said to him, "Let not the king do wrong to his servant David; he has not wronged you, and what he has done has benefited you greatly. He took his life in his hands when he killed the Philistine. The LORD won a great victory for all Israel, and you saw it and were glad. Why then would you do wrong to an innocent man like David by killing him for no reason?"
> Saul listened to Jonathan and took this oath: "As surely as the LORD lives, David will not be put to death."
> So Jonathan called David and told him the whole conversation. He brought him to Saul, and David was with Saul as before. (1 Samuel 19:1-7)

Jonathan intervened and saved David. He became a peacemaker and had to deal with Saul's unresolved anger toward David.

> Once more war broke out, and David went out and fought the Philistines. He struck them with such force that they fled before him.
> But an evil spirit from the LORD came on Saul as he was sitting in his house with his spear in his hand. While David was playing the lyre, Saul tried to pin him to the wall with his spear, but David eluded him as Saul drove the spear into the wall. That night David made good his escape. Saul sent men to David's house to watch it and to kill him in the morning. (1 Samuel 19:8-11)

Again, Saul tried to kill David with his own spear, then through his own men. This time it was Saul's daughter, Michal, who had to intervene and save David. Can you see any resemblance here with the family dynamics in dealing with an alcoholic? The alcoholic can't manage it himself, so other family members must intercede to protect other people. Saul is drunk on his own anger.

> So David hid in the field, and when the New Moon feast came, the king sat down to eat. He sat in his customary place by the wall, opposite Jonathan, and Abner sat next to Saul, but David's place was empty. Saul said nothing that day, for he thought, "Something must have happened to David to make him ceremonially unclean—surely he is unclean." But the next day, the second day of the month, David's place was empty again. Then Saul said to his son Jonathan, "Why hasn't the son of Jesse come to the meal, either yesterday or today?"
> Jonathan answered, "David earnestly asked me for permission to go to Bethlehem. He said, 'Let me go, because our family is observing a sacrifice in the town and my brother has ordered me to be there. If I have found favor in your eyes, let me get away to see my brothers.' That is why he has not come to the king's table."
> Saul's anger flared up at Jonathan and he said to him, "You son of a perverse and rebellious woman! Don't I know that you have sided with the son of Jesse to your own shame and to the shame of the mother who bore you? As long as the son of Jesse lives on this earth, neither you nor your kingdom will be established. Now send someone to bring him to me, for he must die!"
> "Why should he be put to death? What has he done?" Jonathan asked his father. But Saul hurled his spear at him to kill him. Then Jonathan knew that his father intended to kill David.
> Jonathan got up from the table in fierce anger; on that second day of the feast he did not eat, because he was grieved at his father's shameful treatment of David. (1 Samuel 20:24-34)

Saul's anger flared up at Jonathan and he accused him of siding with David. As Jonathan questioned Saul's logic, Saul threw the spear at Jonathan, which caused him to leave in fierce anger. Other people will be affected by your unresolved anger. Your spear may be your tone of voice, irritated glare, hurtful words, or even physical abuse as with Saul. These actions will often produce anger or hurt feelings, or both, in the people around you.

Now Saul heard that David and his men had been discovered. And Saul was seated, spear in hand, under the tamarisk tree on the hill at Gibeah, with all his officials standing at his side. He said to them, "Listen, men of Benjamin! Will the son of Jesse give all of you fields and vineyards? Will he make all of you commanders of thousands and commanders of hundreds? Is that why you have all conspired against me? No one tells me when my son makes a covenant with the son of Jesse. None of you is concerned about me or tells me that my son has incited my servant to lie in wait for me, as he does today."

But Doeg the Edomite, who was standing with Saul's officials, said, "I saw the son of Jesse come to Ahimelek son of Ahitub at Nob. Ahimelek inquired of the LORD for him; he also gave him provisions and the sword of Goliath the Philistine."

Then the king sent for the priest Ahimelek son of Ahitub and all the men of his family, who were the priests at Nob, and they all came to the king. Saul said, "Listen now, son of Ahitub."

"Yes, my lord," he answered.

Saul said to him, "Why have you conspired against me, you and the son of Jesse, giving him bread and a sword and inquiring of God for him, so that he has rebelled against me and lies in wait for me, as he does today?"

Ahimelek answered the king, "Who of all your servants is as loyal as David, the king's son-in-law, captain of your bodyguard and highly respected in your household? Was that day the first time I inquired of God for him? Of course not! Let not the king accuse your servant or any of his father's family, for your servant knows nothing at all about this whole affair."

But the king said, "You will surely die, Ahimelek, you and your whole family."

Then the king ordered the guards at his side: "Turn and kill the priests of the LORD, because they too have sided with David. They knew he was fleeing, yet they did not tell me."

But the king's officials were unwilling to raise a hand to strike the priests of the LORD.

The king then ordered Doeg, "You turn and strike down the priests." So Doeg the Edomite turned and struck them down. That day he killed eighty-five men who wore the linen ephod. He also put to the sword Nob, the town of the priests, with its men and women, its children and infants, and its cattle, donkeys and sheep. (1 Samuel 22:6-19)

This situation didn't stop with Jonathan. Saul accused his men and then the priests of Nob of conspiring against him, even to the point of killing them. When your anger remains unresolved, no one can please you or do it the right way. No one understands why you are overreacting, and many times they don't want to be around you to find out. Everything you see is distorted and your interpretation of events, people and their motives are also skewed. It's a lonely life.

Then David went out of the cave and called out to Saul, "My lord the king!"

> When Saul looked behind him, David bowed down and prostrated himself with his face to the ground. He said to Saul, "Why do you listen when men say, 'David is bent on harming you'? This day you have seen with your own eyes how the LORD delivered you into my hands in the cave. Some urged me to kill you, but I spared you; I said, 'I will not lay my hand on my lord, because he is the LORD's anointed.' See, my father, look at this piece of your robe in my hand! I cut off the corner of your robe but did not kill you. See that there is nothing in my hand to indicate that I am guilty of wrongdoing or rebellion. I have not wronged you, but you are hunting me down to take my life. May the LORD judge between you and me. And may the LORD avenge the wrongs you have done to me, but my hand will not touch you. As the old saying goes, 'From evildoers come evil deeds,' so my hand will not touch you.
>
> "Against whom has the king of Israel come out? Who are you pursuing? A dead dog? A flea? May the LORD be our judge and decide between us. May he consider my cause and uphold it; may he vindicate me by delivering me from your hand."
>
> When David finished saying this, Saul asked, "Is that your voice, David my son?" And he wept aloud. "You are more righteous than I," he said. "You have treated me well, but I have treated you badly. You have just now told me about the good you did to me; the LORD delivered me into your hands, but you did not kill me. When a man finds his enemy, does he let him get away unharmed? May the LORD reward you well for the way you treated me today. I know that you will surely be king and that the kingdom of Israel will be established in your hands. Now swear to me by the LORD that you will not kill off my descendants or wipe out my name from my father's family."
>
> So David gave his oath to Saul. Then Saul returned home, but David and his men went up to the stronghold. (1 Samuel 24:8-22)

Saul responded well to David sparing his life. For a moment, he had clarity about the kingship ("I know that you will surely be king"), and about whose fault it was ("I have treated you badly… and you are more righteous than I"). He stopped trying to kill David. Saul made the most progress toward getting his anger resolved after his interaction and brief discussion with David. To resolve your own anger toward someone, the first place to start is always with that person directly, and not through other people. Once the other person clarifies what they meant by their comment or their sincere motivation, your eyes are finally opened to the truth, and you can respond better. Saul was no exception. It helped talking with David. Saul expressed more of his real fears—that his descendants and family name would be wiped out. It was deeper than him just losing the kingship.

But this peace didn't last. Saul got worked up again and began pursuing David again to kill him:

> Then David crossed over to the other side and stood on top of the hill some distance away; there was a wide space between them. He called out to the army and to Abner son of Ner, "Aren't you going to answer me, Abner?"

Abner replied, "Who are you who calls to the king?"

David said, "You're a man, aren't you? And who is like you in Israel? Why didn't you guard your lord the king? Someone came to destroy your lord the king. What you have done is not good. As surely as the LORD lives, you and your men must die, because you did not guard your master, the LORD's anointed. Look around you. Where are the king's spear and water jug that were near his head?"

Saul recognized David's voice and said, "Is that your voice, David my son?"

David replied, "Yes it is, my lord the king." And he added, "Why is my lord pursuing his servant? What have I done, and what wrong am I guilty of? Now let my lord the king listen to his servant's words. If the LORD has incited you against me, then may he accept an offering. If, however, people have done it, may they be cursed before the LORD! They have driven me today from my share in the LORD's inheritance and have said, 'Go, serve other gods.' Now do not let my blood fall to the ground far from the presence of the LORD. The king of Israel has come out to look for a flea—as one hunts a partridge in the mountains."

Then Saul said, "I have sinned. Come back, David my son. Because you considered my life precious today, I will not try to harm you again. Surely I have acted like a fool and have been terribly wrong."

"Here is the king's spear," David answered. "Let one of your young men come over and get it. The LORD rewards everyone for their righteousness and faithfulness. The LORD delivered you into my hands today, but I would not lay a hand on the LORD's anointed. As surely as I valued your life today, so may the LORD value my life and deliver me from all trouble."

Then Saul said to David, "May you be blessed, David my son; you will do great things and surely triumph."

So David went on his way, and Saul returned home. (1 Samuel 26:13-25)

Saul again humbly responded to David sparing his life a second time. Saul promised, "I will not try to harm you again," and he seems to have kept that promise, although fear still seemed to rule his heart as he consulted Samuel's spirit through a woman medium:

The Philistines assembled and came and set up camp at Shunem, while Saul gathered all Israel and set up camp at Gilboa. When Saul saw the Philistine army, he was afraid; terror filled his heart. He inquired of the LORD, but the LORD did not answer him by dreams or Urim or prophets. Saul then said to his attendants, "Find me a woman who is a medium, so I may go and inquire of her."

"There is one in Endor," they said.

Samuel said to Saul, "Why have you disturbed me by bringing me up?"

"I am in great distress," Saul said. "The Philistines are fighting against me, and God has departed from me. He no longer answers me, either by prophets or by dreams. So I have called on you to tell me what to do."

Samuel said, "Why do you consult me, now that the LORD has departed from you and become your enemy? The LORD has done what he predicted through me. The LORD has torn the kingdom out of your hands and given it to one of your neighbors—to David. Because you did not obey the LORD or carry out his fierce wrath against the Amalekites, the LORD has done this to you today. The LORD will deliver both Israel and you into the hands of the Philistines, and tomorrow you and your sons will be with me. The LORD will also give the army of Israel into the hands of the Philistines." Immediately Saul fell full length on the ground, filled with fear because of Samuel's words. His strength was gone, for he had eaten nothing all that day and all that night. (1 Samuel 28:4-7, 15-20)

Although Saul never pursued David again, he went to his grave with many of his fears unresolved. The resulting anger within Saul had already done its damage and many people suffered. There were brief moments when Saul had the clarity he needed to find healing, but a lifetime pattern of impulsive behavior and angry responses left Saul with no alternative. He never found the healing that both God and Samuel wanted for him. Family members' intervention brought temporary relief, but they couldn't manage his anger for him. Even David's ability to withhold the urge to get even and kill the man who caused him many sleepless nights, came from a desire for Saul to work things out, and a desire to be righteous in his response. Sometimes the people we've hurt the most, want us to be healed more than we do.

CHAPTER NINETEEN

Angry Men of God: David—Passionate

Anger is momentary madness, so control your passion or it will control you.

—Horace

David was a passionate man. He's known for being a man after God's own heart, but his passion for life led him to write songs, cry with friends, take down a 9-foot warrior, take someone else's wife, and lead 400 men who had lost all hope for their lives to one military victory after another. At times his passion was controlled and focused with great victories for God, but at other times it led him into sin and disgrace. No one who has passion can avoid their own anger. David had anger and needed to learn how to control it.

When two brothers killed one of Saul's sons, David was angry:

> They brought the head of Ish-Bosheth to David at Hebron and said to the king, "Here is the head of Ish-Bosheth son of Saul, your enemy, who tried to kill you. This day the LORD has avenged my lord the king against Saul and his offspring." David answered Rekab and his brother Baanah, the sons of Rimmon the Beerothite, "As surely as the LORD lives, who has delivered me out of every trouble, when someone told me, 'Saul is dead,' and thought he was bringing good news, I seized him and put him to death in Ziklag. That was the reward I gave him for his news! How much more—when wicked men have killed an innocent man in his own house and on his own bed—should I not now demand his blood from your hand and rid the earth of you!" So David gave an order to his men, and they killed them. They cut off their hands and feet and hung the bodies by the pool in Hebron. But they took the head of Ish-Bosheth and buried it in Abner's tomb at Hebron. (2 Samuel 4:8-12)

David's response was immediate and decisive. He killed them on the spot. No jury. No witnesses. No prayer to God. No seeking advice from a prophet. Maybe he did exactly what God would want done. David's anger wasn't always definitive, nor did he always handle it with self-control, as shown by the example above. God intervened with David several times to help him with his anger. God taught him through other people's advice, life's lessons, and David's own desire to be righteous. We'll look at each method separately, because with the same approach, you too can learn to control your anger, even if you are a passionate person.

Advice

There are situations where we listen to advice from people who know more, or are simply better at something than we are, such as car mechanics, dentists, financial advisors, doctors, electricians, or plumbers. Sometimes we are willing to pay for that advice because we can't get what we need any other way. Sometimes we only follow the advice if we agree with it, which may need to be considered, especially if there are financial incentives at stake. Trust plays a large part in our decisions as we process the advice we hear. Do I trust this person? Do they have my best interest in mind? What ulterior motive might influence them to advise me in a particular direction? Do I need a second opinion or quote? There are several Proverbs that highlight the advantage of seeking advice:

> Listen to advice and accept discipline, and at the end you will be counted among the wise. (Proverbs 19:20)

> The way of fools seems right to them, but the wise listen to advice. (Proverbs 12:15)

When it comes to our anger, do we need advice? Are there people available that know more about handling anger than we do? Are there other people with intimate knowledge of our situation or life event that could offer invaluable advice on how we should proceed? There are counselors that provide those services for a fee. There may be friends or family members that have opinions and are willing to express them. Sometimes just hearing a different perspective can help us avoid further damage, or help us to see our role in the angry exchange with another person.

David had a couple of interactions which helped him see his angry response in a different light:

> The LORD sent Nathan to David. When he came to him, he said, "There were two men in a certain town, one rich and the other poor. The rich man had a very large number of sheep and cattle, but the poor man had nothing except one little ewe lamb he had bought. He raised it, and it grew up with him and his children. It shared his food, drank from his cup and even slept in his arms. It was like a daughter to him. "Now a traveler came to the rich man, but the rich man refrained from taking one of his own sheep or cattle to prepare a meal for the traveler who had come to him. Instead, he took the ewe lamb that belonged to the poor man and prepared it for the one who had come to him." David burned with anger against the man and said to Nathan, "As surely as the LORD lives, the man who did this must die! He must pay for that lamb four times

over, because he did such a thing and had no pity."

Then Nathan said to David, "You are the man! This is what the LORD, the God of Israel, says: 'I anointed you king over Israel, and I delivered you from the hand of Saul. I gave your master's house to you, and your master's wives into your arms. I gave you all Israel and Judah. And if all this had been too little, I would have given you even more. Why did you despise the word of the LORD by doing what is evil in his eyes? You struck down Uriah the Hittite with the sword and took his wife to be your own. You killed him with the sword of the Ammonites. Now, therefore, the sword will never depart from your house, because you despised me and took the wife of Uriah the Hittite to be your own.' "This is what the LORD says: 'Out of your own household I am going to bring calamity on you. Before your very eyes I will take your wives and give them to one who is close to you, and he will sleep with your wives in broad daylight. You did it in secret, but I will do this thing in broad daylight before all Israel.'" Then David said to Nathan, "I have sinned against the LORD." (2 Samuel 12:1-13)

David's anger was definitive and justified toward the man in Nathan's parable; however, when that man turned out to be David himself, his response changed. His anger turned to humility. He didn't realize how far his heart had fallen. His sin had clouded his view and his perspective on the truth. Sometimes in my own life, I've noticed that when I'm not doing well spiritually, I'm more easily angered. I have less patience, less tolerance, and less grace toward even the normal, day-to-day interruptions and interactions with people. As you process the moments of your day when you get angry, take the time to evaluate how you are doing spiritually. Have you been more sensitive lately? Are you fatigued or low on sleep? Have you been struggling with a specific sin, or has there been more conflict in your relationships? Sometimes the problem isn't just the situation that triggered your anger; it could be indicative of your spiritual health.

David's anger was triggered another time in his life:

While David was in the wilderness, he heard that Nabal was shearing sheep. So he sent ten young men and said to them, "Go up to Nabal at Carmel and greet him in my name. Say to him: 'Long life to you! Good health to you and your household! And good health to all that is yours!

Now I hear that it is sheep-shearing time. When your shepherds were with us, we did not mistreat them, and the whole time they were at Carmel nothing of theirs was missing. Ask your own servants and they will tell you. Therefore be favorable toward my men, since we come at a festive time. Please give your servants and your son David whatever you can find for them.'"

When David's men arrived, they gave Nabal this message in David's name. Then they waited. Nabal answered David's servants, "Who is this David? Who is this son of Jesse? Many servants are breaking away from their masters these days. Why should I take my bread and water, and the meat I have slaughtered for my shearers, and give it to men coming from who knows where?"

David's men turned around and went back. When they arrived, they reported every word. David said to his men, "Each of you strap on your sword!" So they did, and David strapped his on as well. About four hundred men went up with David, while two hundred stayed with the supplies. (1 Samuel 25:4-13)

> When Abigail saw David, she quickly got off her donkey and bowed down before David with her face to the ground. She fell at his feet and said: "Pardon your servant, my lord, and let me speak to you; hear what your servant has to say. Please pay no attention, my lord, to that wicked man Nabal. He is just like his name—his name means Fool, and folly goes with him. And as for me, your servant, I did not see the men my lord sent. And now, my lord, as surely as the LORD your God lives and as you live, since the LORD has kept you from bloodshed and from avenging yourself with your own hands, may your enemies and all who are intent on harming my lord be like Nabal. And let this gift, which your servant has brought to my lord, be given to the men who follow you.
> "Please forgive your servant's presumption. The LORD your God will certainly make a lasting dynasty for my lord, because you fight the LORD's battles, and no wrongdoing will be found in you as long as you live. Even though someone is pursuing you to take your life, the life of my lord will be bound securely in the bundle of the living by the LORD your God, but the lives of your enemies he will hurl away as from the pocket of a sling. When the LORD has fulfilled for my lord every good thing he promised concerning him and has appointed him ruler over Israel, my lord will not have on his conscience the staggering burden of needless bloodshed or of having avenged himself. And when the LORD your God has brought my lord success, remember your servant."
> David said to Abigail, "Praise be to the LORD, the God of Israel, who has sent you today to meet me. May you be blessed for your good judgment and for keeping me from bloodshed this day and from avenging myself with my own hands. Otherwise, as surely as the LORD, the God of Israel, lives, who has kept me from harming you, if you had not come quickly to meet me, not one male belonging to Nabal would have been left alive by daybreak." (1 Samuel 25:23-34)

After Abigail told Nabal, he suffered a heart attack or stroke, and within two weeks he was dead.

> When David heard that Nabal was dead, he said, "Praise be to the LORD, who has upheld my cause against Nabal for treating me with contempt. He has kept his servant from doing wrong and has brought Nabal's wrongdoing down on his own head." (1 Samuel 25:39)

David needed Abigail's intervention. His anger was definitive because Nabal had sinned against him, but David's response was a bit over the top. It's never too late to get someone else's perspective on both the situation that triggered your anger, and your response to it. Even if you've already acted on your response, the advice may help you with similar events in the future. At times, I've gone back to my children or my wife and offered apologies or changed my response to the initial conflict, after I've had time to reflect, pray, and seek advice.

We all need help with our perspective of life events. If you seek advice from spiritual people, God will speak to you through their advice. Even when you don't seek it out, sometimes God will bring it to you anyway, as he did with David. We need it.

Lessons Learned

Life teaches all of us lessons. Events happen and we react. Some are small and others almost crush us. Many times there are lessons to be learned. Sometimes we learn and then forget, causing us to have to learn again. Other times we learn and never forget, because the learning was too painful. Occasionally, we never learn the lesson because we don't see it as a lesson. We remember the emotions, but the situation was not our fault, and someone else needs help, correction, or consequences. What I have found in my life is that if I react with anger, then there is usually a lesson for me. Either I made it worse because of my anger, or I didn't resolve it completely, so it continues to be triggered when a similar life event happens on another day.

When David wanted to bring the ark to Jerusalem and restore its place with God's people, he placed it on a new cart and celebrated with all his might as they made their way to the city of David:

> David again brought together all the able young men of Israel—thirty thousand. He and all his men went to Baalah in Judah to bring up from there the ark of God, which is called by the Name, the name of the LORD Almighty, who is enthroned between the cherubim on the ark. They set the ark of God on a new cart and brought it from the house of Abinadab, which was on the hill. Uzzah and Ahio, sons of Abinadab, were guiding the new cart with the ark of God on it, and Ahio was walking in front of it. David and all Israel were celebrating with all their might before the LORD, with castanets, harps, lyres, timbrels, sistrums and cymbals.
>
> When they came to the threshing floor of Nakon, Uzzah reached out and took hold of the ark of God, because the oxen stumbled. The LORD's anger burned against Uzzah because of his irreverent act; therefore God struck him down, and he died there beside the ark of God.
>
> Then David was angry because the LORD's wrath had broken out against Uzzah, and to this day that place is called Perez Uzzah. David was afraid of the LORD that day and said, "How can the ark of the LORD ever come to me?" (2 Samuel 6:1-9)

David's anger was triggered by the huge disappointment in wanting to be closer to God, which he planned to accomplish by having the ark closer to him in Jerusalem. When Uzzah was killed, David thought the same fate awaited anyone who got too close to the ark. His perception was distorted because he didn't understand the real reason why God reacted that way. He misunderstood when Uzzah was suddenly killed for trying to do a good thing, not letting the ark fall off the cart. Later, David was encouraged by God's love and blessings when the ark was at Obed-Edom's house, and so he moved the ark to Jerusalem. Somehow David must have figured out that the real problem was Uzzah moved the ark in a different way than God had told Moses to move it. That's not too much different from what happens when we misinterpret someone's words, actions, or motives. We perceive an event one way, make a conclusion about the injustice or hurt feelings it causes, and then react in anger. After clarifying it through God's word, David felt differently and responded better:

> Then David summoned Zadok and Abiathar the priests, and Uriel, Asaiah, Joel, Shemaiah, Eliel and Amminadab the Levites. He said to them, "You are the heads of the Levitical families; you and your fellow Levites are to consecrate yourselves and bring up the ark of the LORD, the God of Israel, to the place I have prepared for it. It was because you, the Levites, did not bring it up the first time that the LORD our God broke out in anger against us. We did not inquire of him about how to do it in the prescribed way." So the priests and Levites consecrated themselves in order to bring up the ark of the LORD, the God of Israel. And the Levites carried the ark of God with the poles on their shoulders, as Moses had commanded in accordance with the word of the LORD. (1 Chronicles 15:11-15)

As David reflected on the mistakes that caused God's reaction and his own angry response, he blamed the Levites for not transporting the ark according to God's word. But he also "owned" his share of it by explaining, "<u>We</u> did not inquire of him about how to do it in the prescribed way." Here's the reference from Numbers 4:

> Then they are to place on it all the utensils used for ministering at the altar, including the firepans, meat forks, shovels and sprinkling bowls. Over it they are to spread a covering of the durable leather and put the poles in place. After Aaron and his sons have finished covering the holy furnishings and all the holy articles, and when the camp is ready to move, only then are the Kohathites to come and do the carrying. But they must not touch the holy things or they will die. The Kohathites are to carry those things that are in the tent of meeting. (Numbers 4:14-15)

It's good to understand what triggers your anger and to humbly accept your responsibility. Learning from those moments will help you mature and will minimize the possibility of future "triggers" when you're experiencing the same issue. Sometimes I will communicate to my wife, Kathy, or my children how I'm interpreting our interaction and their response. It helps avoid misunderstandings and clarifies events quickly, so the situation doesn't lead to angry feelings and more drama.

Be Righteous

If you are reading this book, then you have a heart that wants help with your anger. If you're seeking to handle your anger with more self-control and less damage, then that desire will lead you to be more righteous in your response. Anyone who has a desire to be righteous will have to deal with his own anger. Remember the Scripture in James that says, "Human anger does not produce the righteousness that God desires"? It's true that your anger will not produce righteousness, but your desire to be righteous can enable you to manage your anger with self-control and a calm spirit.

When Saul pursued David, I'm sure David was tempted to take revenge and kill Saul. In fact, he had two opportunities to do just that. His self-control and righteous response were motivated from his relationship with God and his convictions from God's word.

> Some urged me to kill you, but I spared you; I said, 'I will not lay my hand on my lord, because he is the LORD's anointed.' (1 Samuel 24:10)

> The LORD rewards everyone for their righteousness and faithfulness. The LORD delivered you into my hands today, but I would not lay a hand on the LORD's anointed. As surely as I valued your life today, so may the LORD value my life and deliver me from all trouble. (1 Samuel 26:23-24)

Even when his friends thought that David should kill Saul, David shared his perspective and trusted in God to deal with Saul:

> Abishai said to David, "Today God has delivered your enemy into your hands. Now let me pin him to the ground with one thrust of the spear; I won't strike him twice." But David said to Abishai, "Don't destroy him! Who can lay a hand on the LORD's anointed and be guiltless? As surely as the LORD lives," he said, "the LORD himself will strike him, or his time will come and he will die, or he will go into battle and perish. But the LORD forbid that I should lay a hand on the LORD's anointed. Now get the spear and water jug that are near his head, and let's go." (1 Samuel 26:8-11)

Don't let another person tell you how to deal with your anger unless that person is spiritually-minded, especially if her opinion includes advising you to get even or take revenge. After Saul died, David mourned by writing a lament for Saul and Jonathan. Later in his life, as David reflected on how God delivered him from Saul, he wrote Psalm 18 and focused on how personally and dramatically God answered his prayers when he was running from Saul. When your anger is caused by someone else's anger, and you're tempted to get even, seek revenge, or simply argue with that person, remember how David put his trust in God to intervene, and how he focused on righteousness in his response. It makes you wonder if Solomon wasn't thinking of his dad when he wrote the following Proverb:

> Do not say, "I'll pay you back for this wrong!" Wait for the LORD, and he will avenge you. (Proverbs 20:22)

When you learn how to control your own anger, you can help other people with their anger. That's what David did when he was returning to Jerusalem:

> Throughout the tribes of Israel, all the people were arguing among themselves, saying, "The king delivered us from the hand of our enemies; he is the one who rescued us from the hand of the Philistines. But now he has fled the country to escape from Absalom; and Absalom, whom we anointed to rule over us, has died in battle. So why do you say nothing about bringing the king back?" King David sent this message to Zadok and Abiathar, the priests: "Ask the elders of Judah, 'Why should you be the last to bring the king back to his palace, since what is being said throughout Israel has reached the king at his quarters? You are my relatives, my own flesh and blood. So why should you be the last to bring back the king?' And say to Amasa, 'Are you not my own flesh and blood? May God deal with me, be it ever so severely, if you are not the commander of my army for life in place of Joab.'"
> He won over the hearts of the men of Judah so that they were all of one mind. They sent word to the king, "Return, you and all your men." Then the king returned and went as far as the Jordan. (2 Samuel 19:9-15)

David won over the hearts of these men and they quickly resolved their differences to become united and bring the king back. You'll be amazed at what doors will open for you when you have self-control over your own emotions and especially your anger. When children are upset or angry and you respond with your own anger, they don't learn anger management. This response does, in fact, teach them the wrong way to manage anger. That's happened so many times with my children. When I respond or interact without anger, I teach my children to manage their anger better and I've seen them change more quickly and be able to discuss the issues more calmly.

David listened to others when he was angry, and learned lessons when his anger was misdirected to someone else instead of his own heart. He strove to have a righteous response when he was tempted to be angry. He truly was a passionate man after God's own heart.

CHAPTER TWENTY

Angry Men of God: Jeremiah—Life's Hard

> *Why must you be such an angry young man, when your future looks quite bright to me?*
> *How can there be such a sinister plan that could hide such a lamb, such a caring young man?*
> *You're fooling yourself if you don't believe it. You're kidding yourself if you don't believe it.*
> *Get up, get back on your feet, you're the one they can't beat and you know it.*
> *Come on, let's see what you've got, just take your best shot and don't blow it.*
>
> —Fooling Yourself (Styx)

It's one thing to experience anger when a life event happens that you didn't plan or even anticipate, as when Job lost everything and made God the object of his anger. It's a different scenario when your anger comes from something you chose to do, as when Naaman chose to see Elisha to find healing for his leprosy, or when Samson chose a woman outside of God's people. In that case, anger is often directed toward things, yourself, or other people. What if you experience anger from something God told you to do? Would you be tempted to blame God? Sometimes God's calling can be frustrating when the results don't line up with what you know God wants, or when it takes you places where you really don't want to go. Jeremiah's life was like that:

> The words of Jeremiah son of Hilkiah, one of the priests at Anathoth in the territory of Benjamin. The word of the LORD came to him in the thirteenth year of the reign of Josiah son of Amon king of Judah, and through the reign of Jehoiakim son of Josiah king of Judah, down to the fifth month of the eleventh year of Zedekiah son of Josiah king of Judah, when the people of Jerusalem went into exile. (Jeremiah 1:1-3)

Jeremiah prophesied in Jerusalem and Judah during the 41-year period from 629 to 588 BC. Different estimates move these dates a couple of years either way. The Babylonian exile and subsequent 70-year captivity began in 606 BC, and Jerusalem was destroyed in 587 BC. Research indicates Jeremiah was born anywhere from 650 to 640 BC, which places his age between 11-21 years old when God called him. It's likely that Jeremiah was a teenager with a full life ahead of him. He was the son of a priest named Hilkiah, who may have been the same priest who found the book of the Law during Josiah's reign (2 Kings 22). Jeremiah probably envisioned his life following his dad's footsteps into the priesthood. God had other plans. He was to be more than a priest. He was to be a prophet, and not just another prophet during a dark time in Israel's history. Jeremiah was to be a prophet not only to the King of Judah and Judah's people, but also a prophet to the priests.

How well would you receive a challenge from a kingdom kid or teenager in your church that hasn't seen what you've seen? Would you really listen to what this young person is saying? Would you consider that God may be speaking through this kid to address something in your heart? If you're a teenager, would you have the guts to speak to your friends' parents or your parents' friends? If God called you to challenge the status quo and declare that they have drifted and abandoned the God of their fathers, could you do it? If you did, what would happen to you? What would you say? How would you say it? What would be their reaction? It's certainly intimidating, and you would probably experience fears that you never had before. Let's see how God approached Jeremiah.

> The word of the LORD came to me, saying, "Before I formed you in the womb I knew you, before you were born I set you apart; I appointed you as a prophet to the nations."
> "Alas, Sovereign LORD," I said, "I do not know how to speak; I am too young."
> But the LORD said to me, "Do not say, 'I am too young.' You must go to everyone I send you to and say whatever I command you. Do not be afraid of them, for I am with you and will rescue you," declares the LORD.
> Then the LORD reached out his hand and touched my mouth and said to me, "I have put my words in your mouth. See, today I appoint you over nations and kingdoms to uproot and tear down, to destroy and overthrow, to build and to plant." (Jeremiah 1:4-10)
>
> "Get yourself ready! Stand up and say to them whatever I command you. Do not be terrified by them, or I will terrify you before them. Today I have made you a fortified city, an iron pillar and a bronze wall to stand against the whole land—against the kings of Judah, its officials, its priests and the people of the land. They will fight against you but will not overcome you, for I am with you and will rescue you," declares the LORD. (Jeremiah 1:17-19)

Jeremiah's initial response was doubt; he gave excuses and reasons why he couldn't follow God's plan. God didn't have a very lengthy counseling session with Jeremiah to help alleviate those fears. He addressed them, but quickly and to the point, almost as a drill sergeant in the military. God's direction was essentially, "don't be afraid, stop the excuses, you are not too young, and I'll tell you what to say." Logically, that's simple enough. Jeremiah was going to be God's spokesman. That wouldn't be difficult when pitching Weight Watchers or critiquing movies. This was different. It required challenging people's lives and their relationship with God.

In his mind, Jeremiah wasn't ready for that challenge. He wasn't prepared. His fear was real, as he undoubtedly witnessed firsthand how people reacted to the other prophets of his day, such as Habakkah and Zephaniah. Jeremiah probably knew how people would react to his message, too. God's consolation was simply, "I will be with you" and, "I will rescue you." That's not easy to believe when you've never walked with God in that way, and you don't have years of seeing God's promises come true during and after different phases in life. That didn't matter to God. He knew Jeremiah before he was in his mother's womb. God had already decided that Jeremiah could do this and would do this.

God also has tasks for you that may create for you the same fears Jeremiah battled. His message is the same for you. God is with you and that is enough. Maybe you've heard it said, "God doesn't make junk." Well, it's also true that God doesn't make bad calls, and he doesn't create a plan that's poorly designed. If God is calling you to a specific role in his kingdom, then you are the right choice!

It didn't take long for Jeremiah to realize what he was up against. God told him upfront that the people would "fight against you," but now he knew the degree to which God was implying.

> To whom can I speak and give warning? Who will listen to me? Their ears are closed so they cannot hear. The word of the LORD is offensive to them; they find no pleasure in it. But I am full of the wrath of the LORD, and I cannot hold it in. (Jeremiah 6:10-11)

At this point, Jeremiah's anger seems to be definitive and righteous. He was simply feeling what God felt toward his people. Over time, however, Jeremiah began to feel the effects of preaching to people who refused to change. He didn't want to be around them anymore, and yet he often wept for these same people. Hence, Jeremiah has been known as "the weeping prophet".

> Oh, that my head were a spring of water and my eyes a fountain of tears! I would weep day and night for the slain of my people. Oh, that I had in the desert a lodging place for travelers, so that I might leave my people and go away from them; for they are all adulterers, a crowd of unfaithful people. (Jeremiah 9:1-2)

God understood Jeremiah and provided him with more insight and clarity into the people's hearts. As Jeremiah was tempted to become angry, God helped him keep the right perspective. Israel was refusing God and had an issue with God, not Jeremiah. It would take a mature, spiritual man to continue to be

God's spokesman, but not allow it to become personal.

> "Beware of your friends; do not trust anyone in your clan. For every one of them is a deceiver, and every friend a slanderer. Friend deceives friend, and no one speaks the truth. They have taught their tongues to lie; they weary themselves with sinning. You live in the midst of deception; in their deceit they refuse to acknowledge me," declares the LORD. (Jeremiah 9:4-6)

From Jeremiah's point of view, it's hard to not take it personally when your life is threatened by the very people with whom you grew up. Temple buddies who grew up learning God's word together and playing together...were now deceiving enemies holding bad attitudes and bitterness toward Jeremiah. Some of them threatened him directly and promised to kill him if he continued with his message.

> Because the LORD revealed their plot to me, I knew it, for at that time he showed me what they were doing. I had been like a gentle lamb led to the slaughter; I did not realize that they had plotted against me, saying,
> "Let us destroy the tree and its fruit; let us cut him off from the land of the living, that his name be remembered no more." But you, LORD Almighty, who judge righteously and test the heart and mind, let me see your vengeance on them, for to you I have committed my cause.
> Therefore this is what the LORD says about the people of Anathoth who are threatening to kill you, saying, "Do not prophesy in the name of the LORD or you will die by our hands"—therefore this is what the LORD Almighty says: "I will punish them. Their young men will die by the sword, their sons and daughters by famine. Not even a remnant will be left to them, because I will bring disaster on the people of Anathoth in the year of their punishment." (Jeremiah 11:18-23)
>
> Your relatives, members of your own family—even they have betrayed you; they have raised a loud cry against you. Do not trust them, though they speak well of you. (Jeremiah 12:6)

Not only was Jeremiah preaching a message to a hostile nation, but even his own family didn't believe him. Have you ever experienced that kind of loneliness? It's not the same reaching out to a pseudo-Christian, religious world whose people have a hard time seeing their sins and their need for a savior, than retreating within a fellowship of like-minded believers who welcome your message. It's more like planting a church by yourself...in a Muslim country. Maybe you have enough heart, resilience, and commitment to do that for a two-week mission project in the summer, knowing there's an end date, but could you do it for a lifetime? Jeremiah had very few allies, except maybe a few princes, such as Ahikam, who persuaded a crowd not to kill Jeremiah, and Baruch, who scribed some of his messages. Jeremiah was lonely and felt very ineffective. Even the hope of partnering with a loving wife and children who would obey him was not an option for Jeremiah:

> Then the word of the LORD came to me: "You must not marry and have sons or daughters in this place." (Jeremiah 16:1-2)

Jeremiah began to wrestle with his emotions and his anger by asking some unanswered questions about God's patience. In Jeremiah's opinion, God should have just wiped them out!

> You are always righteous, LORD, when I bring a case before you. Yet I would speak with you about your justice: Why does the way of the wicked prosper? Why do all the faithless live at ease? You have planted them, and they have taken root; they grow and bear fruit. You are always on their lips but far from their hearts. Yet you know me, LORD; you see me and test my thoughts about you. Drag them off like sheep to be butchered! Set them apart for the day of slaughter! How long will the land lie parched and the grass in every field be withered? Because those who live in it are wicked, the animals and birds have perished. Moreover, the people are saying, "He will not see what happens to us." (Jeremiah 12:1-4)

In a sense, God agreed with Jeremiah and so reassured him of his justice while promising to discipline the Israelites for their sins:

> I will forsake my house, abandon my inheritance; I will give the one I love into the hands of her enemies...
> It will be made a wasteland, parched and desolate before me; the whole land will be laid waste because there is no one who cares. Over all the barren heights in the desert destroyers will swarm, for the sword of the LORD will devour from one end of the land to the other; no one will be safe. They will sow wheat but reap thorns; they will wear themselves out but gain nothing. They will bear the shame of their harvest because of the LORD's fierce anger. (Jeremiah 12:7, 11-13)

Although God's reassurance brought some comfort, the daily grind still took its toll on Jeremiah. God intervened to keep his servant encouraged, even comparing Jeremiah's situation to those of other godly men:

> Then the LORD said to me: "Even if Moses and Samuel were to stand before me, my heart would not go out to this people. Send them away from my presence! Let them go!" (Jeremiah 15:1)

It wasn't enough for Jeremiah. He wanted to have a better life, or at least some friends to share a quiet, relaxed time of fellowship.

> Alas, my mother, that you gave me birth, a man with whom the whole land strives and contends! I have neither lent nor borrowed, yet everyone curses me.

(Jeremiah 15:10)

But when he was left all alone with just God as a friend and support, even though he had to continue to endure the onslaught and public backlash from the Israelites, Jeremiah turned his anger toward God. It was God's issue with the nation of Israel, and yet God was unwilling to relieve Jeremiah's pain and hardships. In some ways, Jeremiah felt betrayed by God who promised Jeremiah "to be with you and rescue you". In Jeremiah's mind, that promise should have shown him some relief, and "rescue" meant having some success for all his suffering and efforts.

> LORD, you understand; remember me and care for me. Avenge me on my persecutors. You are long-suffering—do not take me away; think of how I suffer reproach for your sake...
> Why is my pain unending and my wound grievous and incurable? You are to me like a deceptive brook, like a spring that fails. (Jeremiah 15:15, 18)

In this verse, Jeremiah was not unlike us when we feel God is not doing his part in our ministry. Some of his promises may seem to have failed in our lives and we, too, begin questioning God, doubting his favor, and feeling ineffective. Our anger may come out toward people, but it may really be an issue we have with God. Sometimes I find it hard to be that honest with God, because my conscience tells me it's wrong to think that way about a loving God who has saved me. True healing can only be found if we are completely transparent and open with God about what we really think and feel. Moses did that and so did Jeremiah. God welcomes those conversations and wants to help us mature. As soon as Jeremiah's anger shifted toward God, the Lord responded with clarity and a reaffirmation of his promises.

> Therefore this is what the LORD says: "If you repent, I will restore you that you may serve me; if you utter worthy, not worthless, words, you will be my spokesman. Let this people turn to you, but you must not turn to them. I will make you a wall to this people, a fortified wall of bronze; they will fight against you but will not overcome you, for I am with you to rescue and save you," declares the LORD. "I will save you from the hands of the wicked and deliver you from the grasp of the cruel." (Jeremiah 15:19-21)

The Lord reassured Jeremiah that he would be physically rescued from his enemies. A couple of chapters later, God reminded Jeremiah that the Israelites' response was due to their own sin (i.e., not to take it personally):

> My mountain in the land and your wealth and all your treasures I will give away as plunder, together with your high places, because of sin throughout your country. Through your own fault you will lose the inheritance I gave you. I will enslave you to your enemies in a land you do not know, for you have kindled my

anger, and it will burn forever." (Jeremiah 17:3-4)

Not only did God not relieve the challenges of Jeremiah, the challenges became more intense and more difficult. The threats became reality as Jeremiah was beaten and placed in the stocks (Jeremiah 20:1-2). As Jeremiah wrestled with this, you can see his struggle even through his prayers. It's hard to imagine the unrelenting discouragements that Jeremiah faced. One moment he felt deceived by God, then reminded himself of God's promise and that God would be with him. He renewed his commitment to God, and began praising God, then remembered his suffering and cursed the day of his birth!

> You deceived me, LORD, and I was deceived; you overpowered me and prevailed. I am ridiculed all day long; everyone mocks me. Whenever I speak, I cry out proclaiming violence and destruction. So the word of the LORD has brought me insult and reproach all day long...
> But the LORD is with me like a mighty warrior; so my persecutors will stumble and not prevail. They will fail and be thoroughly disgraced; their dishonor will never be forgotten. LORD Almighty, you who examine the righteous and probe the heart and mind, let me see your vengeance on them, for to you I have committed my cause.
> Sing to the LORD! Give praise to the LORD! He rescues the life of the needy from the hands of the wicked. Cursed be the day I was born! May the day my mother bore me not be blessed!...
> Why did I ever come out of the womb to see trouble and sorrow and to end my days in shame? (Jeremiah 20:7-8, 11-14, 18)

If you have ever prayed as Jeremiah did, or at least felt the same way, you're not alone. Jeremiah lived it day after day. Good days were God-focused with clarity and confidence, and he preached a message that could not be stopped. Other days were self-focused, with discouragement and angry emotions about the life God had asked him to live for God's sake. An eternal, God-driven perspective of our lives cannot be maintained without a close connection to God, and an ability to process these types of angry emotions, even if they are directed toward God himself.

Jeremiah's openness made him more mature during those 41 years. After 23 years, Jeremiah could speak to the people without as much anger. He seemed to see clearly and not have doubts any longer:

> For twenty-three years—from the thirteenth year of Josiah son of Amon king of Judah until this very day—the word of the LORD has come to me and I have spoken to you again and again, but you have not listened. (Jeremiah 25:3)

This new attitude was even more apparent as the threats became more intense. When Jeremiah's life was threatened again, his response was quite different as a 40-something man, than when he was a teenager:

> The priests, the prophets and all the people heard Jeremiah speak these words in the house of the LORD. But as soon as Jeremiah finished telling all the people everything the LORD had commanded him to say, the priests, the prophets and all the people seized him and said, "You must die! Why do you prophesy in the LORD's name that this house will be like Shiloh and this city will be desolate and deserted?" And all the people crowded around Jeremiah in the house of the LORD. (Jeremiah 26:7-9)
>
> Then Jeremiah said to all the officials and all the people: "The LORD sent me to prophesy against this house and this city all the things you have heard. Now reform your ways and your actions and obey the LORD your God. Then the LORD will relent and not bring the disaster he has pronounced against you. As for me, I am in your hands; do with me whatever you think is good and right. Be assured, however, that if you put me to death, you will bring the guilt of innocent blood on yourselves and on this city and on those who live in it, for in truth the LORD has sent me to you to speak all these words in your hearing."
> Then the officials and all the people said to the priests and the prophets, "This man should not be sentenced to death! He has spoken to us in the name of the LORD our God." (Jeremiah 26:12-16)

That last exchange showed the courage, confidence, and straightforward manner in which Jeremiah carried himself. He had resolved that this was his life, and he was going to give it his all, no matter how it ended. Although God viewed him as "a fortified city, an iron pillar and a bronze wall to stand against the whole land" when he was a teenager, Jeremiah had truly become "a wall to this people, a fortified wall of bronze" as a middle-aged man. That is the very definition of faithfulness.

Later, Jeremiah was flogged and put in prison, but through his negotiations with King Zedekiah, he was moved to the palace prison, and given a fresh loaf of bread every day. The king's favor was short-lived, however, as men persuaded him to let them silence Jeremiah. They lowered Jeremiah into a cistern that didn't have any water, so he sank into the mud and was left there to die of starvation. God showed his faithfulness again as he moved through an Ethiopian official to rescue Jeremiah. Even as Jerusalem fell, the Babylonian King Nebuchadnezzar took care of Jeremiah, and then let him return to the Israelites who remained in Judah (Jeremiah 37-39). Jeremiah's faith and trust in God grew with each encounter because he could see God's promises being fulfilled day after day.

When a few Israelites came to Jeremiah to seek God's advice on escaping to Egypt, he continued to be God's spokesman:

> This is what the LORD Almighty, the God of Israel, says: 'As my anger and wrath have been poured out on those who lived in Jerusalem, so will my wrath be poured out on you when you go to Egypt. You will be a curse and an object of horror, a curse and an object of reproach; you will never see this place again.'
> "Remnant of Judah, the LORD has told you, 'Do not go to Egypt.' Be sure

of this: I warn you today that you made a fatal mistake when you sent me to the LORD your God and said, 'Pray to the LORD our God for us; tell us everything he says and we will do it.' I have told you today, but you still have not obeyed the LORD your God in all he sent me to tell you. So now, be sure of this: You will die by the sword, famine and plague in the place where you want to go to settle. (Jeremiah 42:18-22)

These Israelites didn't listen to Jeremiah and left for Egypt, taking Jeremiah with them. They refused to obey his message and vowed to continue burning incense to foreign gods. Jerusalem was destroyed shortly afterwards and Jeremiah continued to speak God's message to whoever would listen. Tradition says that Jeremiah died in Egypt, but not before he wrote Lamentations, which is a good summary of his life and his perspective on everything God had taught him. He was honest about the hard life God had given him, but also faithful to the Lord who had been faithful to him.

I am the man who has seen affliction by the rod of the LORD's wrath. He has driven me away and made me walk in darkness rather than light; indeed, he has turned his hand against me again and again, all day long. He has made my skin and my flesh grow old and has broken my bones. He has besieged me and surrounded me with bitterness and hardship. He has made me dwell in darkness like those long dead.

He has walled me in so I cannot escape; he has weighed me down with chains. Even when I call out or cry for help, he shuts out my prayer...

I became the laughingstock of all my people; they mock me in song all day long...

So I say, "My splendor is gone and all that I had hoped from the LORD." I remember my affliction and my wandering, the bitterness and the gall. I well remember them, and my soul is downcast within me. Yet this I call to mind and therefore I have hope:

Because of the LORD's great love we are not consumed, for his compassions never fail. They are new every morning; great is your faithfulness. I say to myself, "The LORD is my portion; therefore I will wait for him."

The LORD is good to those whose hope is in him, to the one who seeks him; it is good to wait quietly for the salvation of the LORD. It is good for a man to bear the yoke while he is young...

For no one is cast off by the Lord forever. Though he brings grief, he will show compassion, so great is his unfailing love. For he does not willingly bring affliction or grief to anyone. (Lamentations 3:1-8, 14, 18-27, 31-33)

Jeremiah had learned how to manage his anger and not allow it to make him bitter towards God. From all the discouragement, hardship, and difficulty that Jeremiah had from his teenage days to middle age, God helped him mature and work through his angry emotions, even when the emotions were directed toward God himself. God was faithful to Jeremiah, although in the beginning it didn't seem that way. Even consider what he said to other teenagers: "And it is good for people to submit at an early age to the yoke of his discipline."

Is your life hard right now? Did you choose some of your circumstances because you felt that God was directing you to do so? Maybe your decisions were based on God's direction and specific answered prayers. What if he did lead you into this life you now have, and you're frustrated? Maybe the results are not what you think God wants or expects. Maybe you think you have failed, or feel very ineffective and just angry. Your situation is definitely worth a second opinion or perspective from a spiritual friend. Maybe God just needs you to be his spokesman, regardless of how people respond. You can find resolution to your anger as Jeremiah did and admit how hard it is, but still hurt and weep for people while praising God for his promises and faithfulness.

CHAPTER TWENTY-ONE

Angry Men of God: Jonah—They Deserve It

The best remedy for a short temper is a long walk.
—Joseph Joubert

We all know the story of Jonah. We think of him running away and remember the whale, or as the NIV calls it, "a huge fish". God wanted Jonah to go to Nineveh (eastern Turkey) and preach against the sin of the Ninevites. Jonah didn't want to go, and got into a boat headed for Tarshish (southern Spain), which is on the other side of the Mediterranean Sea. Jonah selected a location as far as he could go in the opposite direction. God brought a powerful storm that almost destroyed the ship.

> Then the sailors said to each other, "Come, let us cast lots to find out who is responsible for this calamity." They cast lots and the lot fell on Jonah. So they asked him, "Tell us, who is responsible for making all this trouble for us? What kind of work do you do? Where do you come from? What is your country? From what people are you?"
> He answered, "I am a Hebrew and I worship the LORD, the God of heaven, who made the sea and the dry land."
> This terrified them and they asked, "What have you done?" (They knew he was running away from the LORD, because he had already told them so.)
> The sea was getting rougher and rougher. So they asked him, "What should we do to you to make the sea calm down for us?"
> "Pick me up and throw me into the sea," he replied, "and it will become calm. I know that it is my fault that this great storm has come upon you." (Jonah 1:7-12)

When they threw him overboard, a huge fish swallowed Jonah. While he was in the fish for three days and three nights, Jonah prayed. He promised, "What I have vowed I will make good," and God caused the fish to vomit Jonah onto dry land. When Jonah reached Nineveh, he preached and warned the people that God would destroy the city in 40 days.

When Jonah's warning reached the king of Nineveh, he rose from his throne, took off his royal robes, covered himself with sackcloth and sat down in the dust. This is the proclamation he issued in Nineveh:
"By the decree of the king and his nobles:

> Do not let people or animals, herds or flocks, taste anything; do not let them eat or drink. But let people and animals be covered with sackcloth. Let everyone call urgently on God. Let them give up their evil ways and their violence. Who knows? God may yet relent and with compassion turn from his fierce anger so that we will not perish." When God saw what they did and how they turned from their evil ways, he relented and did not bring on them the destruction he had threatened. (Jonah 3:6-10)

Did Nineveh's response come solely from Jonah's preaching? His words definitely played a part, along with God working on their hearts:

> Jonah obeyed the word of the LORD and went to Nineveh. Now Nineveh was a very large city; it took three days to go through it. Jonah began by going a day's journey into the city, proclaiming, "Forty more days and Nineveh will be overthrown." (Jonah 3:3-4)

We don't know if Jonah said anything more than, "Forty more days and Nineveh will be overthrown." If that's all he said, then that's pretty amazing. Maybe he continued to preach and persuade the entire city for days, but it could have been Jonah's appearance, after coming out of the belly of a huge fish, that added to his message.

In the late winter of 1891, the whale-ship Star of the East was in the vicinity of the Falkland Islands, when it came within sight of a whale. Two boats were dispatched with harpoons to snare and kill the beast, but the lashing of its tail capsized one of the launches, spilling the crew into the sea. All were accounted for except for a single sailor named James Bartley. Ultimately, the whale was killed and the carcass drawn aboard the vessel to begin the process of salvaging valuable resources. By the next day good progress had been made in removing the layers of blubber from the beast, so a tackle was attached to its stomach to hoist it on deck. Sailors were startled by spasmodic life within the belly of the whale, and upon further inspection the missing sailor was found.

Bartley was quite mad for two weeks, but upon recovering his senses he recounted what little he could recall of being dragged under the water. Struggling for his life, he had been drawn into a darkness within which he felt a terrible and oppressive heat. He found slimy walls that gave slightly to his touch, but he could find no exit. When his situation finally dawned on him, Bartley lost his senses completely and lapsed into a state of catatonia. This is a symptom seen most frequently in schizophrenia, characterized by muscular rigidity and mental stupor, sometimes alternating with great excitement and confusion.

During his time inside the whale, the gastric juices affected his exposed skin. His face, neck and hands were bleached a deathly white with a texture like parchment, a condition from which the skin never recovered. Bartley believed that he would probably have lived inside his house of flesh until he starved, as breathing was not a problem.

Considering that Jonah may have looked like Bartley, he may have appeared more like a ghost or a zombie. If you met someone like that who preached to you about God, you would probably repent quickly, too! Even though this story makes an entertaining anecdote and has been quoted in several Christian references, Edward B. Davis, Associate Professor of Science and History at Messiah College researched the account extensively and published an article that thoroughly disproves its authenticity.[36]

Jonah's reaction to God's mercy wasn't joy for the people or relief that maybe he could go home. It was anger:

> But to Jonah this seemed very wrong, and he became angry. He prayed to the LORD, "Isn't this what I said, LORD, when I was still at home? That is what I tried to forestall by fleeing to Tarshish. I knew that you are a gracious and compassionate God, slow to anger and abounding in love, a God who relents from sending calamity. Now, LORD, take away my life, for it is better for me to die than to live."
> But the LORD replied, "Is it right for you to be angry?"
> Jonah had gone out and sat down at a place east of the city. There he made himself a shelter, sat in its shade and waited to see what would happen to the city. Then the LORD God provided a leafy plant and made it grow up over Jonah to give shade for his head to ease his discomfort, and Jonah was very happy about the plant. But at dawn the next day God provided a worm, which chewed the plant so that it withered. When the sun rose, God provided a scorching east wind, and the sun blazed on Jonah's head so that he grew faint. He wanted to die, and said, "It would be better for me to die than to live."
> But God said to Jonah, "Is it right for you to be angry about the plant?"
> "It is," he said. "And I'm so angry I wish I were dead."
> But the LORD said, "You have been concerned about this plant, though you did not tend it or make it grow. It sprang up overnight and died overnight. And should I not have concern for the great city of Nineveh, in which there are more than a hundred and twenty thousand people who cannot tell their right hand from their left—and also many animals?" (Jonah 4:1-11)

Jonah responded in anger when God relented. Why did Jonah get angry? If God spared Nineveh, wouldn't Jonah be glad? He said that was why he ran away in the first place; he knew that God might have compassion for Nineveh and change his mind. Why would that be a negative to Jonah? Jonah even remembered Moses' description of God from Exodus 34:6. Was it because Jonah didn't want to appear to be a liar, and was concerned about what people would think? Was it because Jonah was prejudiced, and wanted something bad to happen to Nineveh, the capital of Assyria?

Jonah had every reason to feel hatred toward the Assyrians. They had taken Israel away as captives. Historically on Nineveh marbles in the 780-740 BC timeframe, is an engraved picture of captive Jews being tortured with hooks through their lips and their eyes having been put out. In every city the Assyrians conquered, they built a pyramid of human skulls. They were merciless in the barbaric slaughter of Jonah's people. Maybe some of those killed were Jonah's relatives or friends. But at this point in time, the Assyrians were humbled and repented.

God taught Jonah a lesson through a vine. Jonah became angry and would rather die, because he couldn't find comfort from the heat when the vine was gone. God asked him, "Is it right for you to be angry about the plant?" God discussed Jonah's anger with him and tried to help him discern whether it was right for him to be angry in this situation. That's good advice when your anger is stirred. First, stop and ask yourself, "Do I have a right to be angry?" Since anger occurs when one feels wronged or sees an injustice committed toward any person, then you're probably going to answer, YES! However, further reflection and consideration may yield a different answer.

So God used the vine to help Jonah understand that his anger was self-centered and focused on what he wanted, rather than what other people needed (i.e., the people of Nineveh). If the Ninevites' cruelty deserved just consequences, God was aware of that. But what if they really changed their hearts? Doesn't God's character respond with mercy, or is every convicted felon doomed, without any hope of redemption? God extended mercy to Jonah through shade, and then, in essence, asked Jonah, "Isn't it right for me to extend a greater grace to a people who need it even more than you need shade?" Jonah's self-interest led to his anger, because he felt it was justified for God to "torch" the people of Nineveh for what they had done to Israel.

Sometimes your conscience reminds you of God's mercy, but the concept of mercy is hard to embrace when the injustice caused you a lot of pain or inconvenience. If the anger was caused by an injustice to other innocent people, the desire to see the perpetrators "get what they deserve" can minimize the importance any heartfelt repentance or change within them. We can't see all the details surrounding current events and may not agree with cultural differences, but letting God be God and trusting him can help us remember that no one escapes his justice.

Over time God didn't overlook Assyria or the people of Nineveh. About 100 years later, the prophets Zephaniah and Nahum spoke about Nineveh, which wasn't so humble anymore:

> He will stretch out his hand against the north and destroy Assyria, leaving Nineveh utterly desolate and dry as the desert. Flocks and herds will lie down there, creatures of every kind. The desert owl and the screech owl will roost on her columns. Their hooting will echo through the windows, rubble will fill the doorways, the beams of cedar will be exposed. This is the city of revelry that lived in safety. She said to herself, "I am the one! And there is none besides me. (Zephaniah 2:13-15a)

> Woe to the city of blood, full of lies, full of plunder, never without victims! The crack of whips, the clatter of wheels, galloping horses and jolting chariots! Charging cavalry, flashing swords and glittering spears! Many casualties, piles

of dead, bodies without number, people stumbling over the corpses...King of Assyria, your shepherds slumber; your nobles lie down to rest. Your people are scattered on the mountains with no one to gather them. Nothing can heal you; your wound is fatal. All who hear the news about you clap their hands at your fall, for who has not felt your endless cruelty? (Nahum 3:1-3, 18-19)

God took care of Nineveh and the Assyrians, just not within the timeframe that Jonah thought he should.

CHAPTER TWENTY-TWO

Angry Men of God: Nehemiah–It's Personal

Whatever is begun in anger, ends in shame.

—Benjamin Franklin

Sometimes we feel strongly about certain causes, such as homeless shelters, domestic violence, or "Save the _____". Some issues are spiritual and some are not. When we are personally involved in these discussions or in efforts to assist or help, we are energized and enthusiastic. If conflict occurs or people or bureaucracy hinders our efforts, we can easily become emotionally charged because it concerns something about which we care deeply, and we can become angry.

Nehemiah cared about Jerusalem. He cared about God's city and how the remnant remaining in Jerusalem had survived the exile to Babylon. He cared enough to cry.

> The words of Nehemiah son of Hakaliah:
> In the month of Kislev in the twentieth year, while I was in the citadel of Susa, Hanani, one of my brothers, came from Judah with some other men, and I questioned them about the Jewish remnant that had survived the exile, and also about Jerusalem.
> They said to me, "Those who survived the exile and are back in the province are in great trouble and disgrace. The wall of Jerusalem is broken down, and its gates have been burned with fire."
> When I heard these things, I sat down and wept. For some days I mourned and fasted and prayed before the God of heaven. (Nehemiah 1:1-4)

Almost 100 years after the first exiles returned from Babylon, Nehemiah got permission to return to Jerusalem, in 444 BC. He set about to rebuild the wall and was successful, even against strong opposition that challenged his own response when other people were angry at him. As the rebuilding progressed, Nehemiah faced several situations that stirred his anger. Let's see how he responded:

> Now the men and their wives raised a great outcry against their fellow Jews. Some were saying, "We and our sons and daughters are numerous; in order for us to eat and stay alive, we must get grain." Others were saying, "We are mortgaging our fields, our vineyards and our homes to get grain during the

famine." Still others were saying, "We have had to borrow money to pay the king's tax on our fields and vineyards. Although we are of the same flesh and blood as our fellow Jews and though our children are as good as theirs, yet we have to subject our sons and daughters to slavery. Some of our daughters have already been enslaved, but we are powerless, because our fields and our vineyards belong to others."

When I heard their outcry and these charges, I was very angry. I pondered them in my mind and then accused the nobles and officials. I told them, "You are charging your own people interest!" So I called together a large meeting to deal with them and said: "As far as possible, we have bought back our fellow Jews who were sold to the Gentiles. Now you are selling your own people, only for them to be sold back to us!" They kept quiet, because they could find nothing to say.

So I continued, "What you are doing is not right. Shouldn't you walk in the fear of our God to avoid the reproach of our Gentile enemies? I and my brothers and my men are also lending the people money and grain. But let us stop charging interest! Give back to them immediately their fields, vineyards, olive groves and houses, and also the interest you are charging them—one percent of the money, grain, new wine and olive oil." "We will give it back," they said. "And we will not demand anything more from them. We will do as you say." Then I summoned the priests and made the nobles and officials take an oath to do what they had promised. I also shook out the folds of my robe and said, "In this way may God shake out of their house and possessions anyone who does not keep this promise. So may such a person be shaken out and emptied!" At this the whole assembly said, "Amen," and praised the LORD. And the people did as they had promised. (Nehemiah 5:1-13)

Nehemiah pondered the issue, and then responded. He showed self-control and firmness without giving full vent to his anger. He tried to persuade the people based on their own relationships with God, rather than order them to change. He also provided accountability, making them take an oath to do what they had promised. Nehemiah was very thorough with the details, understanding the effect of human nature to lose the conviction of the moment.

After the wall was rebuilt, Nehemiah addressed several other issues before returning to the king of Babylon in 432 BC. He registered all the people and confirmed the priesthood through accurate family records; he worked with Ezra, the priest, to begin teaching the people God's word again and they all celebrated the Festival of Tabernacles; he oversaw a collective time of confessing, weeping and recommitting of lives to follow the Lord God with all their hearts; he helped orchestrate and lead the dedication of the new wall with singing and the appointment of the Levites, musicians, and gatekeepers.

Nehemiah probably felt good about the accomplishments and reforms that he had initiated and set up. He believed the remnant of Israelites had the structure and commitment in place to live according to what God wanted. He had other men of similar conviction in place to hold them accountable, so he could return to his role with the king of Babylon.

While he was away, another issue arose involving someone who had opposed the rebuilding, and had caused Nehemiah a great deal of heartache:

> Before this, Eliashib the priest had been put in charge of the storerooms of the house of our God. He was closely associated with Tobiah, and he had provided him with a large room formerly used to store the grain offerings and incense and temple articles, and also the tithes of grain, new wine and olive oil prescribed for the Levites, musicians and gatekeepers, as well as the contributions for the priests.
> But while all this was going on, I was not in Jerusalem, for in the thirty-second year of Artaxerxes king of Babylon I had returned to the king. Some time later I asked his permission and came back to Jerusalem. Here I learned about the evil thing Eliashib had done in providing Tobiah a room in the courts of the house of God. I was greatly displeased and threw all Tobiah's household goods out of the room. I gave orders to purify the rooms, and then I put back into them the equipment of the house of God, with the grain offerings and the incense. (Nehemiah 13:4-9)

When Nehemiah came back to Jerusalem, he might have been prompted by his desire to see how the city and remnant were doing. He still cared about Jerusalem. It seems that he learned about the issue with Tobiah after arriving in Jerusalem, and he dealt with it quickly by throwing out Tobiah's belongings. While he was there, other issues were brought to his attention:

> I also learned that the portions assigned to the Levites had not been given to them, and that all the Levites and musicians responsible for the service had gone back to their own fields. So I rebuked the officials and asked them, "Why is the house of God neglected?" Then I called them together and stationed them at their posts.
> All Judah brought the tithes of grain, new wine and olive oil into the storerooms. I put Shelemiah the priest, Zadok the scribe, and a Levite named Pedaiah in charge of the storerooms and made Hanan son of Zakkur, the son of Mattaniah, their assistant, because they were considered trustworthy. They were made responsible for distributing the supplies to their fellow Levites.
> Remember me for this, my God, and do not blot out what I have so faithfully done for the house of my God and its services. (Nehemiah 13:10-14)

Nehemiah rebuked the officials for not giving the Levites their assigned portions, so they could provide for their families. He found trustworthy men and put them in charge. It seems that Nehemiah began to feel that his efforts may have been in vain, because he asked God to not blot out "what I have so faithfully done for the house of my God and its services". Have you ever felt that way about something into which you poured so much time and effort? What if something about which you feel deeply, something for which you sacrificed, begins to crumble or fall apart? It was your idea, you were the driving force, and other people committed to keep it going, but they didn't. Would you feel like your efforts were a failure? Would you be tempted to be angry at the people you left in charge? Would you feel that maybe God wasn't doing his part? Why else would Nehemiah ask God not to "blot it out" as if God caused the problems, or just let them happen?

It didn't stop there. Nehemiah saw other issues:

> In those days I saw people in Judah treading winepresses on the Sabbath and bringing in grain and loading it on donkeys, together with wine, grapes, figs and all other kinds of loads. And they were bringing all this into Jerusalem on the Sabbath. Therefore I warned them against selling food on that day. People from Tyre who lived in Jerusalem were bringing in fish and all kinds of merchandise and selling them in Jerusalem on the Sabbath to the people of Judah. I rebuked the nobles of Judah and said to them, "What is this wicked thing you are doing—desecrating the Sabbath day? Didn't your ancestors do the same things, so that our God brought all this calamity on us and on this city? Now you are stirring up more wrath against Israel by desecrating the Sabbath."
> When evening shadows fell on the gates of Jerusalem before the Sabbath, I ordered the doors to be shut and not opened until the Sabbath was over. I stationed some of my own men at the gates so that no load could be brought in on the Sabbath day. Once or twice the merchants and sellers of all kinds of goods spent the night outside Jerusalem. But I warned them and said, "Why do you spend the night by the wall? If you do this again, I will arrest you." From that time on they no longer came on the Sabbath. Then I commanded the Levites to purify themselves and go and guard the gates in order to keep the Sabbath day holy.
> Remember me for this also, my God, and show mercy to me according to your great love. (Nehemiah 13:15-22)

Nehemiah addressed the Sabbath Day violations. He warned the people, then ordered doors to be shut and not opened until Sabbath was over. Then Nehemiah stationed his own men. He even threatened to arrest the violators. At the end of the Sabbath, he again called on God to remember him and show him mercy. What would make Nehemiah think that God wouldn't show him mercy? Nehemiah hadn't done anything wrong. I usually think of showing mercy to someone who may deserve punishment or consequences, but needs mercy. Maybe Nehemiah thought God would hold him accountable for how things went in Jerusalem after he left. Maybe he felt that since he initiated the whole endeavor, rebuilding the wall and the reforms, he was responsible. And from his perspective, he had failed and needed mercy. Can you relate?

If this was happening in Nehemiah's heart, then his anger could more easily be triggered, and his patience could be thinner if the situation was left unresolved. It happens to us when our hard work and planning go for nothing, or are unappreciated. Here are a few examples: You work hard to clean the house for a special event, then come home the next day only to find the house in disarray again; your project at work gets derailed by people not doing what they promised; you help a family member or friend deal with an issue, only to see them repeat the same mistake you told them to avoid. What happened next could have been predicted if the above description fits Nehemiah's state of mind:

> Moreover, in those days I saw men of Judah who had married women from Ashdod, Ammon and Moab. Half of their children spoke the language of Ashdod or the language of one of the other peoples, and did not know how to speak the language of Judah. I rebuked them and called curses down on them. I beat some of the men and pulled out their hair. I made them take an oath in God's name and said: "You are not to give your daughters in marriage to their sons, nor are you to take their daughters in marriage for your sons or for yourselves. Was it not because of marriages like these that Solomon king of Israel sinned? Among the many nations there was no king like him. He was loved by his God, and God made him king over all Israel, but even he was led into sin by foreign women. Must we hear now that you too are doing all this terrible wickedness and are being unfaithful to our God by marrying foreign women?"
>
> One of the sons of Joiada son of Eliashib the high priest was son-in-law to Sanballat the Horonite. And I drove him away from me.
>
> Remember them, my God, because they defiled the priestly office and the covenant of the priesthood and of the Levites. (Nehemiah 13:23-29)

Nehemiah rebuked them; he called curses down on them; he beat some of the men and pulled out their hair! A little over the top, don't you think? Where's the Nehemiah that showed the patience, self-control, and ability to win over the hearts of the Israelites? It definitely was a serious issue and they needed help to repent, but beating them and pulling out their hair? It just seems from Nehemiah's response, although full of conviction and absolutely right, that he took their actions as a personal assault on him, rather than on their relationship with God. Did he take it too personally? Maybe. The people definitely needed ongoing help to keep their hearts close to God, and be sensitive to what's right and wrong. Nehemiah couldn't fix that while living in Babylon.

When things become personal, your anger can be triggered. And when it is, your response can be more emotionally charged and damaging. This often happens in a marriage when one spouse feels he has not been considered or respected, when details are forgotten, promises broken, or the same issue continues to be a problem. Recently I saw a bumper sticker that brought this point home to me:

"He who angers you controls you."
"He who angers you conquers you."

When you feel your anger being stirred, take the time to consider what triggered it. Although it may involve you, it wasn't necessarily meant as a personal assault. It may have to do with the character or circumstances of the other person or people involved. Since you can't control their emotions, schedule, priorities, or their relationship with God, respond to the facts rather than the emotions.

CHAPTER TWENTY-THREE

Angry Men of God: The Twelve–Pretentious

Pretension–The downside of being better than everyone else is that people tend to assume you're pretentious.
—Demotivational poster
at www.despair.com

There were several incidents that made the disciples angry. Before considering these events, let's first summarize the teacher/disciple relationship in the first century. Historically, it was commonplace for a person to be "a disciple" of a local rabbi. The Pharisees had disciples and so did John the Baptist (Mark 2:18). Understanding the process of how disciples were selected may give us some insight into why some of these events stirred the disciples' anger. Here's a good summary:

> The people of Galilee were the most religious Jews in the world at the time of Jesus. The Galilean people were more educated in the Old Testament and its application to their everyday life than most Jews. They were known for their great reverence for Scripture and their passionate desire to be faithful to it. They resisted the pagan influences of Hellenism far more than did their Judean counterparts. When the great revolt against the pagan Romans and their collaborators (66-74 AD) finally occurred, it began among the Galileans. Schools were associated with the local synagogue in first century Galilee and each community would hire a teacher or "rabbi" for the school. While this teacher was responsible for the education of the village, he had no special authority in the synagogue itself. Children began their study at age 4-5 years old in *Beth Sefer* (elementary school). The teaching focused primarily on the Torah, emphasizing both reading and writing Scripture. Large portions were memorized and it was likely that many students knew the entire Torah by memory by the time this level of education was completed.
> The best students continued their study in *Beth Midrash* (secondary school) while also learning a trade from their family. In the secondary school, they and the adults in the village studied the Torah, the prophets and other Old Testament books. They also began to learn the interpretations of the Oral Torah to learn how to make their own applications and interpretations of the Torah. For example, God instructed Moses to have the Israelites wear tassels (Numbers 15:39) to remember God's commands and the Oral Torah would specify the length. Some of the most outstanding students would seek permission to study with a famous rabbi. If a student wanted to study with a rabbi, he would ask if he might "follow" the rabbi. The rabbi would consider the student's potential to

become like him and whether he would make the necessary commitment. It is likely that most students were turned away and would return to the family trade they learned in school. Some of course were invited to follow, which indicated the rabbi believed the potential student had the ability and commitment to become like him. It would be a remarkable affirmation of the confidence the teacher had in the student. If accepted, they would often leave home to travel with him for a lengthy period of time.

These students were called *Talmidim* in Hebrew (singular *talmid*), which is translated disciple or student. However, there is much more to being a *talmid* than what we would call a student. Instead of learning from the teacher to get a grade or complete a class, a talmid wants to be like the teacher or become what the teacher is. That meant that students were passionately devoted to their rabbi and noted everything he said or did. Their relationship was a very intense and personal system of education. As the rabbi lived and taught his understanding of the Scriptures, his students or *talmidim* listened, watched and imitated so as to become like him. They asked questions and responded when the rabbi questioned them. They followed without knowing where the rabbi was taking them because they knew that the rabbi had a good reason for bringing them to the right place for his teaching to make the most sense. Rabbis used similar teaching techniques like the use of parables. Today there still exists more than 3500 parables from first century rabbis with Jesus being among the very best. Many of them used similar themes such as landowner, king or farmer. Eventually they would become teachers passing on a lifestyle to their *talmidim*. When the teacher believed that his *talmidim* were prepared to be like him, he would commission them to become disciple makers.[37]

Consider the original twelve disciples, whom Jesus selected after praying about his decision all night, as described in Luke 6. The group included fishermen, a disrespected tax collector, a zealot, and a few disciples of John the Baptist. The book of Acts describes them as "unschooled, ordinary men", which is why their courage and Scripture application astonished the rulers, elders, and teachers of the law. These men weren't the best students coming out of *Beth Sefer*. Maybe a couple of them continued their study in *Beth Midrash*, but we really don't know. Andrew and Philip were disciples of John the Baptist before following Jesus, which says something about their desire to be, spiritually, something more than a typical Galilean Jew. They initiated with Jesus and introduced Peter and Nathanael to him.

> When the two disciples heard him say this, they followed Jesus. Turning around, Jesus saw them following and asked, "What do you want?"
> They said, "Rabbi" (which means "Teacher"), "where are you staying?"
> "Come," he replied, "and you will see."
> So they went and saw where he was staying, and they spent that day with him. It was about four in the afternoon.
> Andrew, Simon Peter's brother, was one of the two who heard what John had said and who had followed Jesus. The first thing Andrew did was to find his

> brother Simon and tell him, "We have found the Messiah" (that is, the Christ). And he brought him to Jesus.
> Jesus looked at him and said, "You are Simon son of John. You will be called Cephas" (which, when translated, is Peter).
> The next day Jesus decided to leave for Galilee. Finding Philip, he said to him, "Follow me."
> Philip, like Andrew and Peter, was from the town of Bethsaida. Philip found Nathanael and told him, "We have found the one Moses wrote about in the Law, and about whom the prophets also wrote—Jesus of Nazareth, the son of Joseph."
> "Nazareth! Can anything good come from there?" Nathanael asked.
> "Come and see," said Philip.
> When Jesus saw Nathanael approaching, he said of him, "Here truly is an Israelite in whom there is no deceit."
> "How do you know me?" Nathanael asked.
> Jesus answered, "I saw you while you were still under the fig tree before Philip called you."
> Then Nathanael declared, "Rabbi, you are the Son of God; you are the king of Israel." (John 1:37-49)

Although these original four disciples spent several days with Jesus, as described in John 1, there didn't seem to be the whole-hearted commitment typically seen with *talmidim*, because they went back to fishing, their previous livelihood. In fact, after some time, Jesus officially called them to follow:

> As Jesus walked beside the Sea of Galilee, he saw Simon and his brother Andrew casting a net into the lake, for they were fishermen. "Come, follow me," Jesus said, "and I will send you out to fish for people." At once they left their nets and followed him. When he had gone a little farther, he saw James son of Zebedee and his brother John in a boat, preparing their nets. Without delay he called them, and they left their father Zebedee in the boat with the hired men and followed him. (Mark 1:16-20)

News spread rapidly concerning Jesus when he did miracles or had a confrontation with other rabbis. Think of the honor the disciples must have felt being approached and selected by Jesus. And yet later, they still went back to their nets. However, after the following event, there isn't any record of them returning to fishing, until after Jesus was crucified. They may have been temporary talmidim up to this point, but they became full-time *talmidim!*

> When he had finished speaking, he said to Simon, "Put out into deep water, and let down the nets for a catch." Simon answered, "Master, we've worked hard all night and haven't caught anything. But because you say so, I will let down the nets." When they had done so, they caught such a large number of fish that their nets began to break. So they signaled their partners in the other boat to come and help them, and they came and filled both boats so full that they

began to sink. When Simon Peter saw this, he fell at Jesus' knees and said, "Go away from me, Lord; I am a sinful man!" For he and all his companions were astonished at the catch of fish they had taken, and so were James and John, the sons of Zebedee, Simon's partners. Then Jesus said to Simon, "Don't be afraid; from now on you will fish for people." So they pulled their boats up on shore, left everything and followed him. (Luke 5:4-11)

As we look at the things that made the disciples angry, consider the mindset they may have had:

- We are not typical Galilean Jews.
- We have been selected and chosen by the most knowledgeable rabbi, who even does miracles!
- Even though we weren't the best in school, we are the best in his eyes.
- He believes we can become like him!
- We may be able to do miracles too...can you imagine?
- With his help, we will be the most respected, the most successful men from our hometowns.
- We must learn everything we can from him, and our time with him must be devoted to having him teach us and help us become like him

Keep in mind that there were many more disciples who followed Jesus from time to time. In Luke 9, Jesus continued to call people to follow him and some initiated with him. In Luke 10, Jesus sent seventy-two of them out in pairs to preach in every town and place where he was about to go. In John 6, many of his disciples turned back and no longer followed him, when his teaching became too hard or required too much sacrifice. There was an always-changing circle of "disciples" who wanted to be *talmidim*, but who didn't last. Even the seventy-two were all given the ability to drive out demons and heal people as described in Luke 10. After returning from being successful in driving out demons (what a rush that would be), the way Jesus encouraged them would cement in their minds what an incredible opportunity they were experiencing:

> Then he turned to his disciples and said privately, "Blessed are the eyes that see what you see. For I tell you that many prophets and kings wanted to see what you see but did not see it, and to hear what you hear but did not hear it." (Luke 10:23-24)

It wasn't like my co-worker sarcastically describing his job, "Living the

Dream." At that moment, for these men, it really couldn't get any better. But the twelve men who were with Jesus during his last week on earth were different from the others since the beginning. Not only did they have the special privilege to be chosen away from their day jobs and given special abilities to drive out demons and heal people, there was a moment during Jesus' ministry where they were singled out among the small crowd of believers. That moment came on a mountain:

> One of those days Jesus went out to a mountainside to pray, and spent the night praying to God. When morning came, he called his disciples to him and chose twelve of them, whom he also designated apostles. (Luke 6:12-13)

These twelve weren't just selected from the Jewish men in their hometown, but from a group who was walking with Jesus and learning from him. They were being honored among their peers as special, and now given a new name, "apostle". This selection would immediately elevate them to a different status within that small group of believers. How would that type of honor affect you? Wouldn't you be a little tempted to feel, "I'm one of the best," and begin viewing yourself differently, believing your God-given talents or strengths were now spiritual and perhaps "better" than someone else's gifts?. What about when Peter, James and John were the only ones from this select group of twelve to go up on the mountain of transfiguration, to go into the house to raise a dead girl to life, and to be his inner circle in the Garden of Gethsemane? These were probably not the only instances when Jesus had special time with these three men. They may have viewed themselves as better or more deserving than the other nine.

If you believe the disciples were thinking along these lines, then also consider their desire to learn from Jesus. They were the *talmidim* and needed as much time with Jesus as possible. With every new miracle and healing, the crowds increased to a point that these talmidim appear to be more like body guards and security for crowd control. Occasionally, Jesus specifically called them away for some rest, only to be confronted with yet another crowd, crying out with needs that exhausted the strongest among them. Is it any wonder that the following situations stirred their anger?

(1) Disciples rebuked people for bringing children to Jesus

> People were bringing little children to Jesus for him to place his hands on them, but the disciples rebuked them. When Jesus saw this, he was indignant. He said to them, "Let the little children come to me, and do not hinder them, for the kingdom of God belongs to such as these. Truly I tell you, anyone who will not receive the kingdom of God like a little child will never enter it." And he took the children in his arms, placed his hands on them and blessed them. (Mark 10:13-16)

Why would the disciples be angry with people who brought children, even babies (Luke 18:15), to have Jesus touch them, bless them, and pray for them? (Matthew 19:13) It is such an honor for people to think so well of you that they want your involvement with their children. Did the disciples think that it was a waste of time for Jesus, because he had more important things to do? Maybe they saw the benefit of healing people, but most of these children were probably healthy, so what was the point of spending time with them? At least the adults were learning when Jesus taught the crowds, but most of the children were just playing and not even paying attention! Jesus was indignant and used the moment to teach them about the spiritual lesson from a child's heart.

(2) Disciples rebuked blind men for interrupting Jesus

> As Jesus approached Jericho, a blind man was sitting by the roadside begging. When he heard the crowd going by, he asked what was happening. They told him, "Jesus of Nazareth is passing by."
> He called out, "Jesus, Son of David, have mercy on me!"
> Those who led the way rebuked him and told him to be quiet, but he shouted all the more, "Son of David, have mercy on me!"
> Jesus stopped and ordered the man to be brought to him. When he came near, Jesus asked him, "What do you want me to do for you?"
> "Lord, I want to see," he replied.
> Jesus said to him, "Receive your sight; your faith has healed you." Immediately he received his sight and followed Jesus, praising God. When all the people saw it, they also praised God. (Luke 18:35-43)

> As Jesus and his disciples were leaving Jericho, a large crowd followed him. Two blind men were sitting by the roadside, and when they heard that Jesus was going by, they shouted, "Lord, Son of David, have mercy on us!"
> The crowd rebuked them and told them to be quiet, but they shouted all the louder, "Lord, Son of David, have mercy on us!"
> Jesus stopped and called them. "What do you want me to do for you?" he asked.
> "Lord," they answered, "we want our sight."
> Jesus had compassion on them and touched their eyes. Immediately they received their sight and followed him. (Matthew 20:29-34)

After Jesus healed the first blind man, the disciples left Jericho only to be confronted by two more blind men with the same request. Word probably got around fast on how to have blindness healed. Since a large crowd followed them out of Jericho and "the crowd" rebuked them, we're not sure that it was the disciples who tried to stop the blind men from interrupting the procession. In both situations, Jesus didn't confront the lack of compassion in his disciples or the crowd. He simply healed the men and allowed their changed life to be the lesson.

(3) James and John earned the name "sons of thunder"

James and John had their own anger issues, as shown by the following incident. When Jesus selected them on the mountain as part of the twelve apostles, he gave them the name Boanerges, which means "sons of thunder" (Mark 3:17).

> As the time approached for him to be taken up to heaven, Jesus resolutely set out for Jerusalem. And he sent messengers on ahead, who went into a Samaritan village to get things ready for him; but the people there did not welcome him, because he was heading for Jerusalem. When the disciples James and John saw this, they asked, "Lord, do you want us to call fire down from heaven to destroy them?" But Jesus turned and rebuked them. Then he and his disciples went to another village. (Luke 9:51-56)

There must have been several other episodes when the brothers earned that "sons of thunder" name, because they were selected before this incident with the Samaritans. Jesus' response was immediate and described as a rebuke. He wouldn't tolerate their intolerance and condemnation of the Samaritans.

(4) The apostles wondered who among them was the greatest

The twelve apostles often became angry and argued about which of them would be considered "the greatest" in Jesus' kingdom. The argument started at different times and circumstances throughout their three-year ministry with Jesus. Once, James and John had their mother ask Jesus to let her sons be on his right and left in his kingdom. Another time the disciples initiated the question with Jesus. They argued about it just walking down the road and even when they discussed who might betray him at the Last Supper:

> When the ten heard about this, they became indignant with James and John. Jesus called them together and said, "You know that those who are regarded as rulers of the Gentiles lord it over them, and their high officials exercise authority over them. Not so with you. Instead, whoever wants to become great among you must be your servant, and whoever wants to be first must be slave of all. For even the Son of Man did not come to be served, but to serve, and to give his life as a ransom for many." (Mark 10:41-45)
>
> They came to Capernaum. When he was in the house, he asked them, "What were you arguing about on the road?" But they kept quiet because on the way they had argued about who was the greatest.
> Sitting down, Jesus called the Twelve and said, "Anyone who wants to be first must be the very last, and the servant of all."
> He took a little child whom he placed among them. Taking the child in his arms, he said to them, "Whoever welcomes one of these little children in my name welcomes me; and whoever welcomes me does not welcome me but the one who sent me." (Mark 9:33-37)

> At that time the disciples came to Jesus and asked, "Who, then, is the greatest in the kingdom of heaven?"
> He called a little child to him, and placed the child among them. And he said: "Truly I tell you, unless you change and become like little children, you will never enter the kingdom of heaven. Therefore, whoever takes the lowly position of this child is the greatest in the kingdom of heaven. And whoever welcomes one such child in my name welcomes me." (Matthew 18:1-5)

> In the same way, after the supper he took the cup, saying, "This cup is the new covenant in my blood, which is poured out for you. But the hand of him who is going to betray me is with mine on the table. The Son of Man will go as it has been decreed. But woe to that man who betrays him!" They began to question among themselves which of them it might be who would do this.
> A dispute also arose among them as to which of them was considered to be greatest. Jesus said to them, "The kings of the Gentiles lord it over them; and those who exercise authority over them call themselves Benefactors. But you are not to be like that. Instead, the greatest among you should be like the youngest, and the one who rules like the one who serves. For who is greater, the one who is at the table or the one who serves? Is it not the one who is at the table? But I am among you as one who serves. You are those who have stood by me in my trials. And I confer on you a kingdom, just as my Father conferred one on me, so that you may eat and drink at my table in my kingdom and sit on thrones, judging the twelve tribes of Israel. (Luke 22:20-30)

As you can tell from these passages, the first twelve disciples struggled with comparison and competition among themselves to discern who was the "greatest". Did it really matter who was the greatest? It would have been interesting to listen in on their reasoning and arguments. Maybe someone had accomplished an amazing healing, whereas someone else successfully argued a ceremonial washing debate with another rabbi. Maybe level of commitment was the basis for comparison. Maybe their perceived special treatment by Jesus gave them adequate proof of their status (i.e., Others weren't asked to go up the mountain with him!). You can understand why the other ten were so upset with James and John. The issue wasn't resolved, and continued to find its way into their conversations, even during the Last Supper, when Jesus explained his final few days with them!

Through the three years with his *talmidim*, Jesus addressed the issue with the same, repeated lesson. He used children as examples and even asked them about it when they argued privately. It doesn't appear that Jesus became angry or indignant with them. He just calmly instructed them again and again. There is something good about wanting to be the best spiritually and able to lead others. Jesus was careful not to squash that desire, even during the Passover meal. As Jesus reiterated the "the greatest will serve" speech, he told them they would <u>all</u> sit on thrones, judging the twelve tribes of Israel! Wouldn't this lead each disciple to envision himself on a throne equal to all the others? What greater honor could be conferred on a Galilean Jew?

Even in this context of being *talmidim*, Jesus used the same lesson to address the natural issue that would arise when they matured to a point that they had their own talmidim. He used the Pharisees as the example of what not to be:

> "Everything they do is done for people to see: They make their phylacteries wide and the tassels on their garments long; they love the place of honor at banquets and the most important seats in the synagogues; they love to be greeted with respect in the marketplaces and to be called 'Rabbi' by others.
> But you are not to be called 'Rabbi,' for you have one Teacher, and you are all brothers. And do not call anyone on earth 'father,' for you have one Father, and he is in heaven. Nor are you to be called instructors, for you have one Instructor, the Messiah. The greatest among you will be your servant. For those who exalt themselves will be humbled, and those who humble themselves will be exalted." (Matthew 23:5-12)

This educational system was going to be different. They were not going to become individual "rabbis" with their own following. They were supposed to consider each other as brothers, from the same family, and with the same Father. It's amazing to see Jesus' perseverance with them through this issue of character. He's the same with you when your character flaws are limiting your spiritual effectiveness in the lives of the people around you.

(5) Disciples rebuked Mary for wasting perfume

> Six days before the Passover, Jesus came to Bethany, where Lazarus lived, whom Jesus had raised from the dead. Here a dinner was given in Jesus' honor. Martha served, while Lazarus was among those reclining at the table with him. Then Mary took about a pint of pure nard, an expensive perfume; she poured it on Jesus' feet and wiped his feet with her hair. And the house was filled with the fragrance of the perfume.
> But one of his disciples, Judas Iscariot, who was later to betray him, objected, "Why wasn't this perfume sold and the money given to the poor? It was worth a year's wages." He did not say this because he cared about the poor but because he was a thief; as keeper of the money bag, he used to help himself to what was put into it.
> "Leave her alone," Jesus replied. "It was intended that she should save this perfume for the day of my burial. You will always have the poor among you, but you will not always have me." (John 12:1-8)

> Now the Passover and the Festival of Unleavened Bread were only two days away, and the chief priests and the teachers of the law were scheming to arrest Jesus secretly and kill him. "But not during the festival," they said, "or the people may riot."
> While he was in Bethany, reclining at the table in the home of Simon the Leper, a woman came with an alabaster jar of very expensive perfume, made of pure nard. She broke the jar and poured the perfume on his head.

> Some of those present were saying indignantly to one another, "Why this waste of perfume? It could have been sold for more than a year's wages and the money given to the poor." And they rebuked her harshly.
> "Leave her alone," said Jesus. "Why are you bothering her? She has done a beautiful thing to me. The poor you will always have with you, and you can help them any time you want. But you will not always have me. She did what she could. She poured perfume on my body beforehand to prepare for my burial. Truly I tell you, wherever the gospel is preached throughout the world, what she has done will also be told, in memory of her." (Mark 14:1-9)

Have you ever thought about these events as separate occurrences? One was six days before the Passover, and the other was "only two days away". Both were in Bethany, but the first had Martha serving (probably at her house); whereas, the second occurred at Simon the Leper's house. At the first event, Mary was pouring perfume on Jesus' feet, but in the second, "a woman" was breaking the jar of perfume and pouring the remaining contents on Jesus' head. The fragrance would have soaked his clothes and remained with him during the next 48 hours, when he was beaten, flogged, and crucified. My guess is that even the Roman soldiers could have smelled the perfume, as they gambled for his clothes at the foot of the cross.

Maybe Mary took to heart Jesus' words during the first event, "It was intended that she should save this perfume for the day of my burial." If they were two separate events by the same woman named Mary, it's a testimony to her heart. Over the four days between events, maybe she thought about her sacrifice of giving *some* perfume and comparing that sacrifice to Jesus' sacrifice. Even if she didn't totally comprehend the magnitude of his death, she decided to go back and give it all. He was worth it and she wanted to give it. Jesus noticed this level of sacrifice by making sure her story would be preached around the world…in memory of her.

If Judas Iscariot was the only one objecting during the first event, it seems that he wasn't alone in objecting the second time. The objectors' anger caused them to "rebuke her harshly". The Greek word "rebuke" means "to snort with anger". It was used to describe the snorting of horses. Their response brought a swift and pointed rebuke from Jesus. He wasn't going to tolerate such a rash and improper judgment from a worldly point of view, especially since he had just corrected them on the same issue four days earlier. The woman's heart was outstanding and more spiritual than the disciples.

(6) Peter struck with his sword

Jesus must have known this was coming from what he told the apostles in Luke 22:

> "Simon, Simon, Satan has asked to sift all of you as wheat. But I have prayed for you, Simon, that your faith may not fail. And when you have turned

back, strengthen your brothers."
But he replied, "Lord, I am ready to go with you to prison and to death."
Jesus answered, "I tell you, Peter, before the rooster crows today, you will deny three times that you know me."
Then Jesus asked them, "When I sent you without purse, bag or sandals, did you lack anything?"
"Nothing," they answered.
He said to them, "But now if you have a purse, take it, and also a bag; and if you don't have a sword, sell your cloak and buy one. It is written: 'And he was numbered with the transgressors'; and I tell you that this must be fulfilled in me. Yes, what is written about me is reaching its fulfillment." The disciples said, "See, Lord, here are two swords."
"That's enough!" he replied. (Luke 22:31-38)

With the increased agitation and friction between Jesus and the Pharisees and the teachers of the law, the disciples must have imagined how this was going to play out. Several times they had seen Jesus slip away from being stoned to death, so it was obvious that a spiritual showdown was coming. As the events unfolded after the last dinner together, the disciples wrestled with not seeing Jesus again, and their emphatic resolution that they were "ready to die with him". Their turmoil only intensified with Jesus' prayer and their exhaustion in the Garden of Gethsemane. They were prepared for a fight and willing for it to be a fight to the death. When the moment came, the disciples reacted:

Going at once to Jesus, Judas said, "Greetings, Rabbi!" and kissed him.
Jesus replied, "Do what you came for, friend."
Then the men stepped forward, seized Jesus and arrested him. With that, one of Jesus' companions reached for his sword, drew it out and struck the servant of the high priest, cutting off his ear.
"Put your sword back in its place," Jesus said to him, "for all who draw the sword will die by the sword. Do you think I cannot call on my Father, and he will at once put at my disposal more than twelve legions of angels? But how then would the Scriptures be fulfilled that say it must happen in this way?" (Matthew 26:49-54)

Then Simon Peter, who had a sword, drew it and struck the high priest's servant, cutting off his right ear. (The servant's name was Malchus.) Jesus commanded Peter, "Put your sword away! Shall I not drink the cup the Father has given me?" (John 18:10-11)

When Jesus' followers saw what was going to happen, they said, "Lord, should we strike with our swords?" And one of them struck the servant of the high priest, cutting off his right ear. But Jesus answered, "No more of this!" And he touched the man's ear and healed him. (Luke 22:49-51)

Obviously, the apostles didn't understand that the battle was spiritual and not physical. Once they realized they couldn't "win", they fled. In their minds, their anger was justified because Jesus was right, which made it right for them to defend him. Their predisposed perception was immediately corrected by Jesus to avoid further damage and possible loss of life.

As you reflect over how Jesus helped his disciples with their anger, what did you learn? When you become angry, how would Jesus respond to you? In these examples, some moments brought an immediate, sometimes strong reaction from Jesus, while other situations brought a healing or a lesson you have heard a hundred times. Jesus reacted most strongly when the disciples' anger was negatively affecting other people. What triggers your anger and whether it's affecting other people depends on the circumstances. That's a good thing to remember when your anger is triggered. How will your response affect those around you?

The disciples changed from a tendency to argue about who was the greatest, to considering other people's needs above their own. Jesus' patience and perseverance with them allowed God to change these issues in their character. It showed in their letters, written long after Jesus died.

Outspoken, sword-wielding Peter wrote these passages years later:

> Now that you have purified yourselves by obeying the truth so that you have sincere love for each other, love one another deeply, from the heart. (1 Peter 1:22)

> To this you were called, because Christ suffered for you, leaving you an example, that you should follow in his steps.
> "He committed no sin, and no deceit was found in his mouth."
> When they hurled their insults at him, he did not retaliate; when he suffered, he made no threats. Instead, he entrusted himself to him who judges justly. (1 Peter 2:21-23)

> Finally, all of you, be like-minded, be sympathetic, love one another, be compassionate and humble. (1 Peter 3:8)

Pretentious, "Son of Thunder" John, who wanted to be on Jesus' left or right, later said the following:

> This is how we know what love is: Jesus Christ laid down his life for us. And we ought to lay down our lives for our brothers and sisters. (1 John 3:16)

> Dear friends, since God so loved us, we also ought to love one another. No one has ever seen God; but if we love one another, God lives in us and his love is made complete in us. (1 John 4:11-12)

CHAPTER TWENTY-FOUR

Someone's Angry With Me

You cannot shake hands with a clenched fist.
—Indira Gandhi

There is nothing more galling to angry people than the coolness of those on whom they wish to vent their spleen.
—Alexandre Dumas

In learning about my own anger, I've realized that one of my trigger points is having someone angry with me. It's difficult to control my emotions and respond with a gentle tone of voice, calm expression on my face, and patience to continue the discussion. My children and my spouse have been the best resources for me to change this trigger because they let me know when I'm responding with anger. It's in my tone, my facial expression, and my level of patience.

The best place to start is in Proverbs. Then listen to the experience of counselors as they share the lessons they have learned:

> Fools show their annoyance at once, but the prudent overlook an insult. (Proverbs 12:16)

> A gentle answer turns away wrath, but a harsh word stirs up anger. (Proverbs 15:1)

> A hot-tempered person stirs up conflict, but the one who is patient calms a quarrel. (Proverbs 15:18)

> Whoever loves a quarrel loves sin. (Proverbs 17:19)

> The one who has knowledge uses words with restraint, and whoever has understanding is even-tempered. (Proverbs 17:27)

> A person's wisdom yields patience; it is to one's glory to overlook an offense. (Proverbs 19:11)

> Mockers stir up a city, but the wise turn away anger. (Proverbs 29:8)

> Do not be quickly provoked in your spirit, for anger resides in the lap of fools. (Ecclesiastes 7:9)

> If a ruler's anger rises against you, do not leave your post; calmness can lay great offenses to rest. (Ecclesiastes 10:4)

As the angry person confronts you, or at least begins venting issues with you, according to these Proverbs, your goal is to overlook the anger, stay calm, be gentle, be patient, and don't overreact. Now if you can just go do that, you can skip the rest of this chapter.

You probably have a little smile or smirk on your face because you know nobody can just go and do that. It's very difficult and a person needs time to develop that expertise, wisdom, and self-control. Gary Chapman in his book, *Anger–Handling a Powerful Emotion in a Healthy Way*, talks about how to handle someone who is angry. The anger could be directed at you or someone else, or at some circumstance, but you're involved, nonetheless. He suggests seven steps:[38]

1. Listen to the story or issue—you become aware that you are in the presence of an angry person; you get the gist of the story, and the heart of why the person is angry.

2. Listen again and have the story and cause of anger repeated—you are communicating that you really are interested, and you are not condemning the anger.

3. Listen a third time and ask a few questions to clarify your understanding—you are making sure that you get all the details of the situation.

From his 30+ years of counseling experience, Gary has concluded that it usually takes three or even four rounds of listening before an angry person expresses all of their concerns. By that time, the angry person has usually begun to calm down and the intense emotions have subsided. Gary sums up these first three "listening" steps as follows:

> "If you respond to someone's anger before you have thoroughly heard his story, you will not defuse the anger. You will compound it. Inside the mind of the angry person is a deep sense that they have been wronged. He is expressing his anger to you because either you are involved or he thinks you have the power to help. When you listen to him, you are respecting his right to be angry."[39]

4. Seek to understand the situation from the angry person's point of view—ask yourself, would you be angry? It is not the time to argue about interpretation or responsibility in the situation. That would likely escalate the anger instead of resolving it.

5. Express your understanding of the other person's anger—this communicates that given the same circumstances and perspective, you would probably be angry, too. Be honest and make every attempt to connect with the person, as if these things had happened to you.
6. Share additional information that may shed light on the subject—this clarifies more facts about the situation or gives an additional perspective that may change how the angry person views it. If you share this stuff too early in the process, it will not be heard, and it will often result in a heated argument.
7. Confess and find restitution—If their anger is definitive, and you have sinned against them or hurt them, either intentionally or unintentionally, you have to be humble, accept your responsibility, and ask for forgiveness.

These seven steps will help the angry person process anger and allow you to develop a stronger and closer relationship as a result. There are some common mistakes that people make when they don't follow these steps.

Mistake #1: Becoming like the angry person—If they are yelling, then you raise your voice in order to be heard. That's like throwing gasoline on a fire. An angry person can stay angry for a long time if there is someone willing to fight with them. If the discussion is escalating, then either you're not listening (or they don't feel validated), or you've chosen sides and are engaged in an argument. Of course, God has a few comments about that kind of response:

> Whoever loves a quarrel loves sin. (Proverbs 17:19)

> A gentle answer turns away wrath, but a harsh word stirs up anger. (Proverbs 15:1)

Consider how you would handle someone asking you for help concerning a problem with a friend. As the situation is described, emotions get more intense. You're not threatened by the intensity, because it doesn't have anything to do with you. You've assumed the role of a counselor, so it's easier to just listen and relate. You can assume that same role even if the person is upset at you and comes to you with the emotions already escalated. Sometimes you can counsel another parent on how to handle an angry child, better than you can handle your own child's anger with you. Why is that? It is because you are instinctively following these seven steps, or at least the first five, which are probably the most important. Just do the same when you're the target of someone's anger.

Mistake #2: Trying to control the angry person until the emotions subside—The angry person cannot process anger if it is kept inside. If a person is angry and talking in a loud voice, at least he is trying to process that anger. A loud voice is better than physical violence. To follow the seven steps, you have to be able to look beyond the loud voice and intense emotions in order to help the person. Of course, God knew that a long time ago:

> Fools show their annoyance at once, but the prudent overlook an insult. (Proverbs 12:16)

> Do not be quickly provoked in your spirit, for anger resides in the lap of fools. (Ecclesiastes 7:9)

It may not be pleasant for a few minutes, but if you really listen, the emotions should subside. If you ask the person to calm down first before you can help, then you may end up being no help at all.

This rule of listening is particularly true with children. A child may calm down, but may also forget about the issue. That may seem like a good thing in the short term, because it brings you relief in dealing with it. But it doesn't help in the long term, because whatever set off the anger in the first place was never resolved. You may be able to go back to resolve it, but the child may not remember what was felt at the time, or think it's no big deal later. The needed lessons and different perspectives never occur, so you're just delaying the problem for another day, when the same issue triggers the child again.

An adult will not feel validated, and may not feel that you really care, if you require him to calm down first. The adult may not be able to calm down first, which is the reason you were approached for help, or at least you were seen as someone who could help.

I've made both of these mistakes as a parent, when dealing with my own children when they were angry. There is a separate chapter in this book specifically devoted to helping angry children, because there are many dynamics that have to be addressed. I've also made these mistakes with adults because I allowed my emotions to escalate, or because I was addressing the sin as the person was venting, which doesn't help.

Gary Chapman summarizes these steps and how they help an angry person:

> "Angry people need someone who cares enough to listen long enough to understand the pain. They need someone who listens carefully enough to identify with the person's anger, wisely enough to express understanding, and courageously enough to respond with a gentle, truthful answer – an answer that seeks resolution of the issue that gave rise to the anger. That is our goal: to help the angry person discover a healthy response and a constructive solution."[40]

Usually when I am tempted to respond with anger, it is because I fear the person is not going to see her role in the situation and so not become humble. Sometimes I worry that an angry state of mind will lead to more sin and negative attitudes, making the collateral damage even worse for other people who interact with the individual. This is particularly true if the situation involves my family. Many times I've had to refrain from reacting and take the time to process my own emotions before responding.

> Be still before the LORD and wait patiently for him; do not fret when people succeed in their ways, when they carry out their wicked schemes. Refrain from anger and turn from wrath; do not fret—it leads only to evil. For those who are evil will be destroyed, but those who hope in the LORD will inherit the land. (Psalms 37:7-9)

> Don't have anything to do with foolish and stupid arguments, because you know they produce quarrels. And the Lord's servant must not be quarrelsome but must be kind to everyone, able to teach, not resentful. Opponents must be gently instructed, in the hope that God will grant them repentance leading them to a knowledge of the truth, and that they will come to their senses and escape from the trap of the devil, who has taken them captive to do his will. (2 Timothy 2:23-26)

> Starting a quarrel is like breaching a dam; so drop the matter before a dispute breaks out. (Proverbs 17:14)

It's even harder to respond righteously when the angry person is someone who doesn't like you, or doesn't agree with your opinion on a specific topic or situation. When trouble comes that person's way, it's so tempting to rejoice in your heart that God has finally brought justice, because of the person's attitude towards you. Out of your own spite, you really don't want to help because you may view the circumstance as God's discipline. Consider how God directed the Israelites to respond to their enemies or people who hated them, and may have expressed anger toward them:

> If you come across your enemy's ox or donkey wandering off, be sure to return it. If you see the donkey of someone who hates you fallen down under its load, do not leave it there; be sure you help them with it. (Exodus 23:4-5)

Or consider how God counseled King Ahaz when two other kings had anger toward him:

> When Ahaz son of Jotham, the son of Uzziah, was king of Judah, King Rezin of Aram and Pekah son of Remaliah king of Israel marched up to fight against Jerusalem, but they could not overpower it.
> Now the house of David was told, "Aram has allied itself with Ephraim"; so the hearts of Ahaz and his people were shaken, as the trees of the forest are shaken by the wind.

> Then the LORD said to Isaiah, "Go out, you and your son Shear-Jashub, to meet Ahaz at the end of the aqueduct of the Upper Pool, on the road to the Launderer's Field. Say to him, 'Be careful, keep calm and don't be afraid. Do not lose heart because of these two smoldering stubs of firewood—because of the fierce anger of Rezin and Aram and of the son of Remaliah. Aram, Ephraim and Remaliah's son have plotted your ruin, saying, "Let us invade Judah; let us tear it apart and divide it among ourselves, and make the son of Tabeel king over it." Yet this is what the Sovereign LORD says:
>
> "'It will not take place, it will not happen, for the head of Aram is Damascus, and the head of Damascus is only Rezin. Within sixty-five years Ephraim will be too shattered to be a people. The head of Ephraim is Samaria, and the head of Samaria is only Remaliah's son. If you do not stand firm in your faith, you will not stand at all.'" (Isaiah 7:1-9)

God cautioned Ahaz to be careful, stay calm and not be afraid. That's where you want your heart to be when the emotions begin to charge up. God considers it "standing firm in your faith". This faith is faith that God will help you even as you're praying in the moment; faith that God will help the angry person or persons over time; and faith that your response will help provide healing rather than more anger.

Note: These are the same two kings that slaughtered many soldiers in Judah, took women and children captive, and had to be corrected by the prophet Oded for their lack of self-control, as described in the "God's Anger-No Favoritism" chapter. This time God did not allow them to capture Jerusalem. Pekah became King of Israel when Uzziah (aka Azariah) was King of Judah, and Pekah reigned for 20 years, from 752-732 BC (2 Kings 15:27). By the time Ahaz became King of Judah, it was the 17th year of King Pekah's reign in Israel (2 Kings 16:1), or 735 BC. That's when Pekah tried to attack Judah and Jerusalem, but God would not allow it. The earlier attack and slaughter occurred earlier in his reign, probably in the first few years (about 752-750 BC). In his anger, God allowed it as discipline for Judah's sin.

King David had a couple of situations that reflect his controlled response when people were angry with him:

> David and his men reached Ziklag on the third day. Now the Amalekites had raided the Negev and Ziklag. They had attacked Ziklag and burned it, and had taken captive the women and everyone else in it, both young and old. They killed none of them, but carried them off as they went on their way.
>
> When David and his men reached Ziklag, they found it destroyed by fire and their wives and sons and daughters taken captive. So David and his men wept aloud until they had no strength left to weep. David's two wives had been captured—Ahinoam of Jezreel and Abigail, the widow of Nabal of Carmel. David was greatly distressed because the men were talking of stoning him; each one was bitter in spirit because of his sons and daughters. But David found strength in the LORD his God.
>
> Then David said to Abiathar the priest, the son of Ahimelek, "Bring me

Someone's Angry With Me

the ephod." Abiathar brought it to him, and David inquired of the LORD, "Shall I pursue this raiding party? Will I overtake them?"

"Pursue them," he answered. "You will certainly overtake them and succeed in the rescue." (1 Samuel 30:1-8)

David's men were angry at him and bitter in spirit for allowing their families to be taken hostage. They even thought of stoning David, despite all the victories, blessings, and righteousness David had brought to them when they were in distress, debt, and a state of discontent (1 Samuel 22:2). Often the person who is angry with you will not remember at that moment all the positive things you have provided for them or done for them. David's reaction was to turn to God rather than bring up a different perspective. David had losses, too, and he wept with these men. He instinctively had already done the first five steps by relating to their loss and emotions.

Sometimes it's tempting to try to correct someone's emotions or overreaction because your perspective may clearly show you that the person is not being grateful. But remember that the other person feels a deep sense of being wronged or hurt by you or the circumstances where you were involved. David went to God first, then got advice and pursued it to resolve the situation. This may be a good option for you in diffusing an emotionally charged discussion. Take a break, follow David's example, and then reconvene to pursue the best option.

Another example from David's life occurred when his son Absalom led an uprising and David left Jerusalem:

> As King David approached Bahurim, a man from the same clan as Saul's family came out from there. His name was Shimei son of Gera, and he cursed as he came out. He pelted David and all the king's officials with stones, though all the troops and the special guard were on David's right and left. As he cursed, Shimei said, "Get out, get out, you murderer, you scoundrel! The LORD has repaid you for all the blood you shed in the household of Saul, in whose place you have reigned. The LORD has given the kingdom into the hands of your son Absalom. You have come to ruin because you are a murderer!"
>
> Then Abishai son of Zeruiah said to the king, "Why should this dead dog curse my lord the king? Let me go over and cut off his head."
>
> But the king said, "What does this have to do with you, you sons of Zeruiah? If he is cursing because the LORD said to him, 'Curse David,' who can ask, 'Why do you do this?'"
>
> David then said to Abishai and all his officials, "My son, my own flesh and blood, is trying to kill me. How much more, then, this Benjamite! Leave him alone; let him curse, for the LORD has told him to. It may be that the LORD will look upon my misery and restore to me his covenant blessing instead of his curse today."
>
> So David and his men continued along the road while Shimei was going along the hillside opposite him, cursing as he went and throwing stones at him

and showering him with dirt. The king and all the people with him arrived at their destination exhausted. And there he refreshed himself. (2 Samuel 16:5-14)

Obviously Shimei had some unresolved feelings toward David from the days when Saul was king. Shimei might have been influenced by Saul's attitudes toward David, or interpreted the situation himself. Instead of taking it personally and correcting Shimei's perspective, or worse, striking him down as Abishai suggested, David was humble and assumed that God was trying to communicate something for him to change. In essence, his perspective considered the possibility that Shimei had a valid concern. David decided that listening to God first was a better option. David was following step four in the process in deciding to let God deal with Shimei.

It was the right decision as shown when David returned to Jerusalem:

> When Shimei son of Gera crossed the Jordan, he fell prostrate before the king and said to him, "May my lord not hold me guilty. Do not remember how your servant did wrong on the day my lord the king left Jerusalem. May the king put it out of his mind. For I your servant know that I have sinned, but today I have come here as the first from the tribes of Joseph to come down and meet my lord the king."
> Then Abishai son of Zeruiah said, "Shouldn't Shimei be put to death for this? He cursed the LORD's anointed."
> David replied, "What does this have to do with you, you sons of Zeruiah? What right do you have to interfere? Should anyone be put to death in Israel today? Don't I know that today I am king over Israel?" So the king said to Shimei, "You shall not die." And the king promised him on oath. (2 Samuel 19:18-23)

Shimei eventually saw that his previous actions were wrong, and he came humbly to David for forgiveness. This is an example of God working with an angry person over time to change his perspective. Since David had already resolved the issue with God, he could easily forgive him but Abishai could not. Abishai's first thought was to kill Shimei, just as before. Abishai didn't handle it the way David did, and would have made a terrible mistake had he been allowed to act on his opinion.

Here's a question for you as the reader—Given how David handled Shimei's anger and his humble request after he returned to Jerusalem, what do you think about his direction to his son, Solomon, as David lay on his deathbed?

> "And remember, you have with you Shimei son of Gera, the Benjamite from Bahurim, who called down bitter curses on me the day I went to Mahanaim. When he came down to meet me at the Jordan, I swore to him by the LORD: 'I will not put you to death by the sword.' But now, do not consider him innocent. You are a man of wisdom; you will know what to do to him. Bring his gray head down to the grave in blood." Then David rested with his ancestors and was buried in the City of David. (1 Kings 2:8-10)

Was David showing his true colors about the incident? Was he trying to get even with Shimei? Did David have a change in heart as he reflected on Shimei, or was it wrong for him to instruct Solomon to kill him? David told the truth when he said, "I will not put you to death by the sword", but did he have in mind to have Solomon do it later in life, if Shimei was still alive? I'm not sure what the truth is, but in his wisdom Solomon decided to test Shimei with an oath, and when Shimei broke it, Solomon killed him.

> Then the king sent for Shimei and said to him, "Build yourself a house in Jerusalem and live there, but do not go anywhere else. The day you leave and cross the Kidron Valley, you can be sure you will die; your blood will be on your own head."
> Shimei answered the king, "What you say is good. Your servant will do as my lord the king has said." And Shimei stayed in Jerusalem for a long time.
> But three years later, two of Shimei's slaves ran off to Achish son of Maakah, king of Gath, and Shimei was told, "Your slaves are in Gath." At this, he saddled his donkey and went to Achish at Gath in search of his slaves. So Shimei went away and brought the slaves back from Gath.
> When Solomon was told that Shimei had gone from Jerusalem to Gath and had returned, the king summoned Shimei and said to him, "Did I not make you swear by the LORD and warn you, 'On the day you leave to go anywhere else, you can be sure you will die'? At that time you said to me, 'What you say is good. I will obey.' Why then did you not keep your oath to the LORD and obey the command I gave you?"
> The king also said to Shimei, "You know in your heart all the wrong you did to my father David. Now the LORD will repay you for your wrongdoing. But King Solomon will be blessed, and David's throne will remain secure before the LORD forever."
> Then the king gave the order to Benaiah son of Jehoiada, and he went out and struck Shimei down and he died. The kingdom was now established in Solomon's hands. (1 Kings 2:36-46)

A final example of anger from David's life was when his first wife Michal was angry with him. David was celebrating the ark's arrival in Jerusalem, and he was dancing with music, sacrifices, and enthusiasm. It was the party of the year!

> As the ark of the LORD was entering the City of David, Michal daughter of Saul watched from a window. And when she saw King David leaping and dancing before the LORD, she despised him in her heart...
> When David returned home to bless his household, Michal daughter of Saul came out to meet him and said, "How the king of Israel has distinguished himself today, going around half-naked in full view of the slave girls of his servants as any vulgar fellow would!" David said to Michal, "It was before the LORD, who chose me rather than your father or anyone from his house when he appointed me ruler over the LORD's people Israel—I will celebrate before the LORD. I will become even more undignified than this, and I will be humiliated in my own

eyes. But by these slave girls you spoke of, I will be held in honor." And Michal daughter of Saul had no children to the day of her death. (2 Samuel 6:16, 20-23)

Not understanding David's perspective or motive, Michal made a judgment about the king's behavior and what was "appropriate" for a king. In her mind, David had sinned, or maybe she was just jealous. She "despised him in her heart" means she felt contempt toward him. At one time, Michal loved David and helped him get away from Saul, and then they were married. After David's relationship with Saul became strained, Saul gave Michal to Paltiel, son of Laish. After Saul's death, David and Michal reunited, but it wasn't the same. Some people have estimated the separation at about ten years. When Michal reunited with David, her husband Paltiel's reaction gave valuable insight into how those 10 years affected Michal:

> So Ish-Bosheth gave orders and had her taken away from her husband Paltiel son of Laish. Her husband, however, went with her, weeping behind her all the way to Bahurim. Then Abner said to him, "Go back home!" So he went back. (2 Samuel 3:15-16)

From this brief glimpse into her 10-year marriage to Paltiel, Michal probably "wore the pants" in their household. She'd grown accustomed to running the house and telling her husband what to do and when to do it. That atmosphere can easily create a critical heart that evaluates every situation and causes one to express an opinion whether or not it is requested. If this dynamic had developed within Michal, it's not surprising that she reacted this way to David's excitement and public display of his feelings toward God in bringing the ark to Jerusalem.

How did David react to her anger? He emphasized that his motive was for God and that he was chosen by God to be king. David viewed the whole incident as between him and God, so if Michal had a problem with it, she needed to take it up with God. In his generous spirit, David blessed each person with a loaf of bread, a cake of dates, and a cake of raisins. David knew that his celebration was pure and that it wasn't for him. He chose to simply clarify his motives, and let his actions speak for themselves. He didn't argue with her or get angry with her by accusing her of other emotions, such as, "You're just mad because you didn't have a say whether you wanted to leave Paltiel" (which may have been true); or, "You've lost that loving feeling we used to have 10 years ago" (probably also true); or, "If you were close to God, honey, you wouldn't be reacting this way". Sometimes we just react and say things that really don't help, but probably actually add to the anger, but David avoided this mistake with Michal.

These examples in David's life reveal a righteous and self-controlled approach, which will produce better results. These seven steps help ensure that your perspective is accurate and that your effort will help the angry person "discover a healthy response and a constructive solution," as author Gary Chapman was noted as saying earlier.

Sometimes even with your best efforts, the person who is angry with you does not or will not change. She still speaks negatively about you or your motives, and talking with her doesn't seem to help. God is always working, so we can't give up, or take things into our own hands to seek revenge or our own brand of justice.

> Do not repay anyone evil for evil. Be careful to do what is right in the eyes of everyone. If it is possible, as far as it depends on you, live at peace with everyone. Do not take revenge, my dear friends, but leave room for God's wrath, for it is written: "It is mine to avenge; I will repay," says the Lord. (Romans 12:17-19)

> When we are cursed, we bless; when we are persecuted, we endure it; when we are slandered, we answer kindly. (1 Corinthians 4:12-13)

> Do not gloat when your enemy falls; when they stumble, do not let your heart rejoice, or the LORD will see and disapprove and turn his wrath away from them. (Proverbs 24:17-18)

In the book of Esther, an official named Haman was enraged at a Jew named Mordecai, because he wouldn't kneel down or pay Haman honor. Instead of retaliating or conspiring against Haman, Mordecai simply continued to be righteous, and prayed about the threat Haman made to destroy all the Jews. Mordecai turned to Queen Esther and trusted that God would work everything out. When King Xerxes found out about Haman's plot, he was angry, and Haman was hanged on the very gallows built for Mordecai.

Consider how Paul dealt with Alexander, the metalworker:

> Alexander the metalworker did me a great deal of harm. The Lord will repay him for what he has done. You too should be on your guard against him, because he strongly opposed our message. (2 Timothy 4:14-15)

Paul trusted God to handle Alexander, but he warned Timothy about him, possibly because Alexander had not changed his view or perspective toward Paul and his work. Maybe Alexander was losing money in his idol-making workshop because Paul opposed worshiping idols. Maybe it was something else that stirred his anger. Either way, Paul made peace in his own heart, so that Alexander's anger would not derail Paul's own spiritual walk with God.

Another example of this trust in God is in Acts 16, when Paul cast out a spirit in a slave girl that had enabled her to predict the future. As a result, her owners lost money and became angry, and Paul and Silas were unfairly treated and severely flogged. Instead of retaliating, growing bitter, or accusing the owners, Paul and Silas were found praying and singing hymns to God at midnight.

Still another example is how Peter described Jesus during his trial and crucifixion:

> When they hurled their insults at him, he did not retaliate; when he suffered, he made no threats. Instead, he entrusted himself to him who judges justly. (1 Peter 2:23)

Jesus didn't have to take things into his own hands, even though he had twelve legions of angels at his disposal (Matthew 26:53). We don't have that kind of authority, but we can learn from Jesus to entrust our lives, our reputations, our businesses, and especially our hearts, to the one who created us and is big enough to bring about justice in his own time, whether that's next month or on Judgment Day.

> A person's wisdom yields patience; it is to one's glory to overlook an offense. (Proverbs 19:11)

Often, the patience and wisdom we need can only come from God helping us through prayer. A great example of this is what happened with Nehemiah. There were people angry with Nehemiah for what he was trying to accomplish. He got permission to return to Jerusalem and begin rebuilding the wall:

> When Sanballat the Horonite and Tobiah the Ammonite official heard about this, they were very much disturbed that someone had come to promote the welfare of the Israelites. (Nehemiah 2:10)

Sanballat and Tobiah didn't seem very eager to resolve the anger in their hearts except in their own way. Their unwillingness to change caused the situation to get worse. From the beginning, Nehemiah considered God his mediator and believed God strong enough to overcome this angry opposition. Nehemiah's faith was in God and not his own justice system.

> Then I said to them, "You see the trouble we are in: Jerusalem lies in ruins, and its gates have been burned with fire. Come, let us rebuild the wall of Jerusalem, and we will no longer be in disgrace." I also told them about the gracious hand of my God on me and what the king had said to me.
> They replied, "Let us start rebuilding." So they began this good work.
> But when Sanballat the Horonite, Tobiah the Ammonite official and Geshem the Arab heard about it, they mocked and ridiculed us. "What is this you are doing?" they asked. "Are you rebelling against the king?" I answered them by saying, "The God of heaven will give us success. We his servants will start rebuilding, but as for you, you have no share in Jerusalem or any claim or historic right to it." (Nehemiah 2:17-20)

Of course this made them even angrier…

> When Sanballat heard that we were rebuilding the wall, he became angry

Someone's Angry With Me

and was greatly incensed. He ridiculed the Jews, and in the presence of his associates and the army of Samaria, he said, "What are those feeble Jews doing? Will they restore their wall? Will they offer sacrifices? Will they finish in a day? Can they bring the stones back to life from those heaps of rubble—burned as they are?"

Tobiah the Ammonite, who was at his side, said, "What they are building—even a fox climbing up on it would break down their wall of stones!" (Nehemiah 4:1-3)

Nehemiah prayed...

Hear us, our God, for we are despised. Turn their insults back on their own heads. Give them over as plunder in a land of captivity. Do not cover up their guilt or blot out their sins from your sight, for they have thrown insults in the face of the builders. (Nehemiah 4:4-5)

More anger...

So we rebuilt the wall till all of it reached half its height, for the people worked with all their heart.

But when Sanballat, Tobiah, the Arabs, the Ammonites and the people of Ashdod heard that the repairs to Jerusalem's walls had gone ahead and that the gaps were being closed, they were very angry. They all plotted together to come and fight against Jerusalem and stir up trouble against it. (Nehemiah 4:6-8)

More prayer...

But we prayed to our God and posted a guard day and night to meet this threat. (Nehemiah 4:9)

More threats...

Meanwhile, the people in Judah said, "The strength of the laborers is giving out, and there is so much rubble that we cannot rebuild the wall."

Also our enemies said, "Before they know it or see us, we will be right there among them and will kill them and put an end to the work."

Then the Jews who lived near them came and told us ten times over, "Wherever you turn, they will attack us."

Therefore I stationed some of the people behind the lowest points of the wall at the exposed places, posting them by families, with their swords, spears and bows. After I looked things over, I stood up and said to the nobles, the officials and the rest of the people, "Don't be afraid of them. Remember the Lord, who is great and awesome, and fight for your families, your sons and your daughters, your wives and your homes."

When our enemies heard that we were aware of their plot and that God had frustrated it, we all returned to the wall, each to our own work. (Nehemiah 4:10-15)

His enemies tried to deceive Nehemiah, then fabricated stories that were not true to frighten the people of Judah, so in response Nehemiah prayed:

> When word came to Sanballat, Tobiah, Geshem the Arab and the rest of our enemies that I had rebuilt the wall and not a gap was left in it—though up to that time I had not set the doors in the gates—Sanballat and Geshem sent me this message: "Come, let us meet together in one of the villages on the plain of Ono."
>
> But they were scheming to harm me; so I sent messengers to them with this reply: "I am carrying on a great project and cannot go down. Why should the work stop while I leave it and go down to you?" Four times they sent me the same message, and each time I gave them the same answer.
>
> Then, the fifth time, Sanballat sent his aide to me with the same message, and in his hand was an unsealed letter in which was written:
>
> "It is reported among the nations—and Geshem says it is true—that you and the Jews are plotting to revolt, and therefore you are building the wall. Moreover, according to these reports you are about to become their king and have even appointed prophets to make this proclamation about you in Jerusalem: 'There is a king in Judah!' Now this report will get back to the king; so come, let us meet together."
>
> I sent him this reply: "Nothing like what you are saying is happening; you are just making it up out of your head."
>
> They were all trying to frighten us, thinking, "Their hands will get too weak for the work, and it will not be completed." But I prayed, "Now strengthen my hands." (Nehemiah 6:1-9)

Hired someone to intimidate Nehemiah...

> One day I went to the house of Shemaiah son of Delaiah, the son of Mehetabel, who was shut in at his home. He said, "Let us meet in the house of God, inside the temple, and let us close the temple doors, because men are coming to kill you—by night they are coming to kill you."
>
> But I said, "Should a man like me run away? Or should someone like me go into the temple to save his life? I will not go!" I realized that God had not sent him, but that he had prophesied against me because Tobiah and Sanballat had hired him. He had been hired to intimidate me so that I would commit a sin by doing this, and then they would give me a bad name to discredit me. (Nehemiah 6:10-13)

Nehemiah prayed again...

> Remember Tobiah and Sanballat, my God, because of what they have done; remember also the prophet Noadiah and how she and the rest of the prophets have been trying to intimidate me. (Nehemiah 6:14)

> So the wall was completed on the twenty-fifth of Elul, in fifty-two days. When all our enemies heard about this, all the surrounding nations were afraid and lost their self-confidence, because they realized that this work had been done with the help of our God. (Nehemiah 6:15-16)

Eventually God wins every time. You may not see it directly or even in your lifetime as Nehemiah did, but God still hears those prayers and he responds. If the angry person will not change after listening, discussing, and even seeking outside counsel or trusted friends to mediate and help bring peace, then your prayers will give the whole situation over to God and bring the peace your heart needs. If the disagreement is with a family member, neighbor, or co-worker that you're going to interact with frequently, you will have a great opportunity to love him the way God does, even if the sin is directed toward you. Keep in mind that you are probably not the only person to be the target of his anger. There may be countless others, which would reveal a deeper issue within him, either from the past, or from his character. It should stir more compassion within you to see the devastation that sin can have on someone's life.

There is another example in the Scriptures of how to respond when someone is angry with you. As Gideon was fighting against Midian, the Ephraimites became angry with him:

> Now the Ephraimites asked Gideon, "Why have you treated us like this? Why didn't you call us when you went to fight Midian?" And they challenged him vigorously.
> But he answered them, "What have I accomplished compared to you? Aren't the gleanings of Ephraim's grapes better than the full grape harvest of Abiezer? God gave Oreb and Zeeb, the Midianite leaders, into your hands. What was I able to do compared to you?" At this, their resentment against him subsided. (Judges 8:1-3)

Gideon had an interesting response to their anger. He praised them for their strengths and accomplishments, rather than dealing directly with the issue while they were emotionally charged. Although it's better to revisit the issue after the emotions have subsided in order to find resolution and healing, there's no indication that Gideon talked about it again with the Ephraimites. If you don't go back and resolve it, you're just postponing the same issue for another day, as shown when the Ephraimites had the same issue with another judge named Jephthah:

> The Ephraimite forces were called out, and they crossed over to Zaphon. They said to Jephthah, "Why did you go to fight the Ammonites without calling us to go with you? We're going to burn down your house over your head."
> Jephthah answered, "I and my people were engaged in a great struggle with the Ammonites, and although I called, you didn't save me out of their hands. When I saw that you wouldn't help, I took my life in my hands and crossed over to fight the Ammonites, and the LORD gave me the victory over them. Now why have you come up today to fight me?" (Judges 12:1-3)

Jephthah went on to fight against and defeat the Ephraimites in battle.

There's another lesson within the story of Nehemiah. Some of his problems were made worse because some people were listening to Tobiah and being deceived:

> Also, in those days the nobles of Judah were sending many letters to Tobiah, and replies from Tobiah kept coming to them. For many in Judah were under oath to him, since he was son-in-law to Shekaniah son of Arah, and his son Jehohanan had married the daughter of Meshullam son of Berekiah. Moreover, they kept reporting to me his good deeds and then telling him what I said. And Tobiah sent letters to intimidate me. (Nehemiah 6:17-19)

When listening to someone who's angry with someone else, it's better to send them to speak to that person directly, rather than get involved yourself. In Nehemiah's case, those who were listening to Tobiah could not discern the spiritual truths of everyone involved. God warns about drawing conclusions after listening to only one side of a story.

> In a lawsuit the first to speak seems right, until someone comes forward and cross-examines. (Proverbs 18:17)

A mediator is sometimes needed and helpful when both parties are open to a third party's perspective. However, if one party is not open to a "group discussion" of the issues, then that should help you discern which side is being more spiritual, and who may have the right perspective.

The last thing you can try is to give them a gift, but do so without fanfare.

> A gift given in secret soothes anger, and a bribe concealed in the cloak pacifies great wrath. (Proverbs 21:14)

CHAPTER TWENTY-FIVE

Children's Anger

Do not teach your children never to be angry; teach them how to be angry.

—Lyman Abbott

Children need help with understanding, handling, and expressing anger. The best tool available to them is your example, and how you handle your own anger. Every time you express your own anger positively, you give your children a lesson in anger management. Author Gary Chapman agrees:

> "Because of the nature of the parent-child relationship, parents are the most influential persons in developing a child's pattern of anger management. This should encourage us, because it gives us an opportunity to give our children positive anger management skills. On the other hand, this can be a frightening reality, because if we fail in this area, our children will be disadvantaged as they move into adulthood."[41]

Angry parents teach their kids that anger gets attention and brings action to solve their problems and frustrations. It's the voice of power and it gets results. The children also learn to read moods from angry parents. If the parents are in a good mood, then the children can get away with anything. If the parents are in a bad mood, then the children can't do anything right. You may not be yelling, but your kids see your eyes when you look at them, and they hear your tone when you speak to them.

"Children have never been very good at listening to their elders, but they have never failed to imitate them."

—James Baldwin

> Fathers, do not exasperate your children; instead, bring them up in the training and instruction of the Lord. (Ephesians 6:4)

In his book, *Hints on Child Training*, first published in 1891, H. Clay Trumbull, considered by many to be the founder of Sunday school, explains how correcting a child when you are angry (or as he calls it, scolding) is not helpful:

"To 'scold' is to assail or revile with boisterous speech. The word itself seems to have a primary meaning akin to that of barking or howling. Scolding is always an expression of a bad spirit and of a loss of temper… the essence of the scolding is in the multiplication of hot words in expression of strong feelings that, while eminently natural, ought to be held in better control.

If a child has done wrong, a child needs talking to; but no parent ought to talk to a child while that parent is unable to talk in a natural tone of voice, and with carefully measured words. If the parent is tempted to speak rapidly, or to multiply words without stopping to weigh them, or to show an excited state of feeling, the parent's first duty is to gain entire self-control. Until that control is secured, there is no use of the parent's trying to attempt any measure of child training."[42]

> Fathers, do not provoke your children to anger by the way you treat them. Rather, bring them up with the discipline and instruction that comes from the Lord. (Ephesians 6:4 NLT)

A grownup's tone of voice can scare children. It can create a situation where a child is not sure how it's going to play out. Any child has seen situations turn aggressive or even violent on television and in the movies, so naturally a child's mind begins to wonder, "What is my mom or dad going to do next?" In his book, *The Heart of Anger*, author Lou Priolo states the following:

> "The effect of tone of voice is so great that some experts believe it to be up to seven times more powerful in certain situations than the words themselves."[43]

Since parents are to model anger management for their children, you have to learn how to handle your own anger in healthy ways, as stated in the book *What Angry Kids Need*:

> "The most important thing you can do to raise a child who manages anger in healthy ways is to learn to do so yourself."[44]

One book called *A Volcano in My Tummy* offers worksheets and role playing lessons designed for either teachers or families to help children with their anger. The authors had an interesting final statement in their Introduction chapter:

> "We hope all who use this book will enjoy their anger and benefit from it."[45]

Now that's a different perspective, and one that I could never imagine saying about my own anger. How can you enjoy something that has the potential of causing so much damage? If we handle our anger in a healthy way, however, there is great benefit from it, because it was designed to bring about change.

In that sense, I can enjoy the benefits of the change, but I'm not sure I have learned how to enjoy the process of managing my own anger. If it's not easy for us as adults, then how much more difficult is it for children? Sometimes they can be frightened by their own anger and the feelings of losing control. Sometimes they can enjoy it because it gives them a sense of power and control. In his book *How to Really Love Your Angry Child*, author D. Ross Campbell, M.D. states:

> "I would imagine that as a parent you take a great many precautions in your home. You're careful to store toxins and poisons in a safe place. You take care to know where your child is at all times. Perhaps you even regulate what kinds of television programs your child views and what sorts of computer activities may take place. But are you aware that the greatest danger of all is the anger that dwells inside your child; that the most toxic poison out there is an unchecked, unbridled rage simmering within?"[46]
>
> "Yet the greatest and most pervasive threat to a healthy and happy life for your child is the presence of unacknowledged and mishandled anger. Its damage extends to mind, soul, spirit, and strength. We can trace virtually every problem of adult life back to that one common source."[47]

Children get angry for a multitude of reasons. If you don't understand how an angry child thinks and views the world, then it's very frustrating to try to help that child change. In his book, *The Angry Child*, author Tim Murphy describes ten traits of an angry child, based on his work as a child psychologist for over twenty years.[48] Each characteristic may exist in varying degrees within a child:

1. Makes his own misery—He sometimes intentionally provokes; rationalizes his behavior; has negative expectations from himself or others, which become self-fulfilling prophecy.
2. Can't analyze problems—She misunderstands the problems she faces and resists efforts to think things through or talk about them afterwards; has faulty reasoning which distorts the meaning of her emotions; quickly draws a conclusion from her emotions; magnifies details to support her point-of-view, and forgets those that don't support it (i.e., "I never said that").
3. Blames others for his misfortune—Someone else or something else provokes him, and anger is the only reasonable response; seems unaware that his actions can be provocative; assumes others do things on purpose to hurt him.
4. Turns bad feelings into mad feelings—She misinterprets her negative feelings such as fear, confusion, embarrassment, intimidation, rejection; needs help identifying the true feeling that "triggered" the anger.

5. Lacks empathy—He confuses other people's feelings – ("They're faking it" or "They're doing it to get me in trouble"); likes to have power over someone else or feel that he is in control; uses it as a defensive tactic to keep himself from being hurt.
6. Attacks people rather than solving problems—His aggression may scare people away or get what he wants, thereby solving his problem; believes if he is angry, he must be right and try to get even; may attack himself, as in, "I'm stupid", or "I can't do anything right".
7. Uses anger to gain power, much like bullies—Words are her power tools ("I don't know" keeps her in control of the negative information); may use criticism, belittlement or sarcasm; provokes a fight to give her a sense of power; wants to get you angry or upset.
8. Indulges in destructive self-talk—Rehearsing negative thoughts keeps him angry and intensifies his reaction.
9. Confuses anger with self-esteem—Feels negative about herself, then avoids looking at her failures or whether she is to blame; Lacks confidence to react to stress in any way other than anger. It's the only tool she knows that gives her a sense of strength; Needs realistic goals appropriate to her abilities; Lies and is dishonest in order to preserve self and avoid guilt.
10. Can be nice when they want to be—Comes and goes based on immediate need; nice behavior can be authentic or manipulative to gain control.

Understanding the trait you see in your angry child will help you address the root cause behind the anger. Don't be fooled by some of these traits as being something else. It is the child's way of dealing with anger. You should communicate to them that being angry is okay, but hurting other people or other things is not okay.

Authors Dr. John Townsend and Dr. Henry Cloud describe a child's anger in their popular book, *Boundaries*:[49]

> "Children need to be taught that anger is a friend. It was created by God for a purpose: to tell us that there's a problem that needs to be confronted. Anger is a way for children to know that their experience is different than someone else's."

Just as with an adult, a child's anger is a response to an event that created certain feelings that hurt. The feelings could be any of the following: sadness, fear, hurt, powerlessness, loneliness, confusion, disappointment, feeling of being left out, concern, being overwhelmed, impatience, rejection, frustration, worry, or embarrassment.

One technique to help a child process angry feelings is the use of the "I"

Children's Anger

statement.[50] You may have to model it for the child with an example from your own life.

I feel _____ (angry, hurt, frustrated, lonely, rejected, etc.)
When _____ (say what happened)
Because _____ (why it upsets you)
I would like _____ (what you want to happen or change)

Use of the "I" statement is especially helpful for preschool or elementary school-age children. My oldest daughter remembers this being taught in her 5th or 6th grade class. Preteens and teenagers should be able to have discussions that address the same four parts. Acknowledging and understanding their feelings helps validate their experiences. Resist offering another perspective or point-of-view until the anger has been expressed and understood. Ask what can be done to make things better, and then help the young person look at available options and possible outcomes.

It's challenging to help your child while they are expressing their anger. It may be expressed with a loud voice or emotionally charged words, but at least it's being expressed to you. Is that worse than hearing, "I don't want to talk to you!" and the slam of the bedroom door closing? I'd rather have the anger expressed verbally rather than through behavior. Author Gary Chapman summarizes it well:

> "Some parents have difficulty accepting a child's limits and imperfections in managing his anger. They want the child to be mature in his expressions of anger and are unwilling to allow the stages of immaturity. The parent who says, "Shut up. You're not going to talk to me that way. Don't ever raise your voice at me again. Do you understand?" is expecting perfection from the child. This is unrealistic. In fact, the parent is expecting of the child a level of maturity that the parent has not attained...Concentrate on the reason your child is angry, not on the way he is expressing it."[51]

> Fathers, don't exasperate your children by coming down hard on them. Take them by the hand and lead them in the way of the Master. (Ephesians 6:4 The Message)

Calmly ask questions and seek to understand what he thinks is unfair or wrong. The anger will not subside until he feels that you have heard and understood his complaint. There's tremendous benefit to seeing your child's heart and perspective as described by authors Jennifer Anne Brown and Pam Provonsha Hopkins:

> "When you can look at any experience from the child's point of view, you

will feel compelled to find ways to support such a child's grieving in healthy ways, rather than becoming a participant in his or her sometimes upsetting, angry behavior."[52]

If you don't listen, the anger will come out later as passive-aggressive behavior such as disrespect, an uncooperative spirit, delayed obedience, or other techniques to get you upset.

In their book, *Speaking the Truth in Love: How to Be an Assertive Christian*, Ruth N. Koch and Kenneth C. Haugk define passive aggression as follows:

> "It is aggression through subtlety, a shrewd and secretive way of taking action to manipulate, circumvent, or triumph over someone else in order to achieve goals. These individuals refuse to speak or act in a straight-forward manner."

Author D. Ross Campbell offers three characteristics that help recognize and identify passive-aggressive anger in our children:

1. It is irrational and illogical driven by the subconscious such as feelings, impressions and powerful emotions. Usually the child doesn't think through exactly how he will orchestrate the subtle rebellion, it just happens when the opportunity and mood arises.

2. Its purpose is primarily to upset the parents or other authority figure. The more efforts the parents put into curbing the behavior, the more determined will be the child's efforts to upset them. When the parents get upset, the child feels successful and will step up efforts to cause even more frustration.

3. Children ultimately hurt themselves the most by passive-aggressive behavior with lower grades, unfinished homework and an uncooperative spirit. More advanced stages include drugs, alcohol and even suicide."[54]

Authors Les Carter and Frank Minirth offer their perspective on passive-aggressive anger:

> "Caused by a need to have control with the least amount of vulnerability or conflict. Different from suppressed anger in that you know you are angry or frustrated; the other is denial. Evasive so that others won't bother me; frustrated yet responds with silence or 'everything's fine'; procrastinate or half-hearted when I don't want to do something; complain about people, but won't talk to them face-to-face; not cooperative knowing that it bothers the other person."[55]

A Scriptural example of passive-aggressive behavior is with Absalom, son

Children's Anger

of David. When Amnon, one of David's other sons, raped his sister, Tamar, this is what happened:

> Her brother Absalom said to her, "Has that Amnon, your brother, been with you? Be quiet for now, my sister; he is your brother. Don't take this thing to heart." And Tamar lived in her brother Absalom's house, a desolate woman.
> When King David heard all this, he was furious. And Absalom never said a word to Amnon, either good or bad; he hated Amnon because he had disgraced his sister Tamar. (2 Samuel 13:20-22)

Absalom withdrew his love from Amnon and wouldn't even talk to him.

> Two years later, when Absalom's sheepshearers were at Baal Hazor near the border of Ephraim, he invited all the king's sons to come there. Absalom went to the king and said, "Your servant has had shearers come. Will the king and his attendants please join me?"
> "No, my son," the king replied. "All of us should not go; we would only be a burden to you." Although Absalom urged him, he still refused to go but gave him his blessing.
> Then Absalom said, "If not, please let my brother Amnon come with us."
> The king asked him, "Why should he go with you?" But Absalom urged him, so he sent with him Amnon and the rest of the king's sons. (2 Samuel 13:23-27)

Absalom waited for Amnon to get drunk on wine, and then ordered his men to kill him. He urged King David to send Amnon to the sheep shearing party, knowing full well his own intention of killing him. He made no effort to resolve his anger during those two years. He had already decided that justice needed to be served, and he would be the judge, jury, and executioner.

Absalom also showed his passive-aggressive anger toward his father, David:

> In the course of time, Absalom provided himself with a chariot and horses and with fifty men to run ahead of him. He would get up early and stand by the side of the road leading to the city gate. Whenever anyone came with a complaint to be placed before the king for a decision, Absalom would call out to him, "What town are you from?" He would answer, "Your servant is from one of the tribes of Israel." Then Absalom would say to him, "Look, your claims are valid and proper, but there is no representative of the king to hear you." And Absalom would add, "If only I were appointed judge in the land! Then everyone who has a complaint or case could come to me and I would see that they receive justice."
> Also, whenever anyone approached him to bow down before him, Absalom would reach out his hand, take hold of him and kiss him. Absalom behaved in this way toward all the Israelites who came to the king asking for justice, and so he stole the hearts of the people of Israel.
> At the end of four years, Absalom said to the king, "Let me go to Hebron and fulfill a vow I made to the LORD. While your servant was living at Geshur in Aram, I made this vow: 'If the LORD takes me back to Jerusalem, I will worship

> the LORD in Hebron.'"
> The king said to him, "Go in peace." So he went to Hebron.
> Then Absalom sent secret messengers throughout the tribes of Israel to say, "As soon as you hear the sound of the trumpets, then say, 'Absalom is king in Hebron.'" Two hundred men from Jerusalem had accompanied Absalom. They had been invited as guests and went quite innocently, knowing nothing about the matter. While Absalom was offering sacrifices, he also sent for Ahithophel the Gilonite, David's counselor, to come from Giloh, his hometown. And so the conspiracy gained strength, and Absalom's following kept on increasing. (2 Samuel 15:1-12)

Absalom showed disrespect to his father, David, but not overtly or even in David's presence. He was subtle and conniving for four years. He then lied to David about some spiritual vow, knowing that because it was spiritual, David would allow him to go to Hebron, where the conspiracy could be launched. Of course, the messengers were sent in secret, allowing the real intent of Absalom's heart to be kept hidden. He knew what he was doing and planned it over several years. Absalom's passive-aggressive behavior was fueled by his unresolved anger toward his father, David. Whether it came from David's lack of action toward Amnon's rape of Tamar or something else, isn't clear. He manipulated David several times in order to achieve his goal of killing Amnon, then appointed himself King of Israel.

This type of behavior is difficult to see if you're not looking for it. If certain situations or emotions are not resolved, then passive-aggressive anger can be discovered with more questions about details and motives. Sometimes I've noticed with my own children that they may not be aware that their behavior is passive-aggressive, but I can see it through their responses to simple requests throughout the day.

Dr. Ross Campbell explains the source of anger in many children:

> "The difficult truth is that the greatest source of anger in children is a deep-rooted belief that they are not loved."[56]

It's difficult to communicate to our children that we love them unconditionally, when they are angry and may be expressing their anger with intense emotions and higher-than-normal volume. It's unpleasant to deal with poorly controlled anger, but a child has not developed the skills to handle anger, and parents can lose sight of children's immaturity by reacting. If a parent responds with her own raised volume or stirred anger, she communicates, "I do not love you when you are angry." Dr. Campbell offers three suggestions to help parents in their response[57]:

1. Loving eye contact—Avoiding eye contact takes away love. Your eyes should not show an angry look or frustration, but patient concern and love, which takes focus and self-control. A child's anger is

your opportunity to teach self-control.
2. Physical touch—This is the hardest to do when both of you are frustrated or angry, but it's critical. It's not necessarily a forced, full embrace, but a reassuring touch that communicates love or "I'm with you through this, no matter how you're feeling."
3. Personal time—This is one-on-one with patience and less pressure to "resolve things." Give the child time to work through the issues.

In our own family, passive-aggressive behavior comes out most frequently as disrespect and manipulation. There have been many times I have argued with my children and been drawn into their own manipulation of the situation. Author Lou Priolo gives a good definition of this type of behavior:

> "Manipulation...is often an attempt to gain control of another individual or situation by inciting an emotional reaction rather than a biblical response from that individual."[58]

He identifies several methods employed by these angry children to manipulate their parents:[59]

- Accusations/Criticisms—to create guilt/shame in parent in order to procrastinate/avoid obligation,
- Crying—to create embarrassment/sympathy in parent in order to change parent's mind,
- "Why" questions/Argumentative—to get parent upset/frustrated in order to procrastinate/control.

Author Tim Murphy also sees this behavior:

> "Angry kids tend to excel at creating arguments, sometimes out of thin air. Unfortunately, because they are not very good at problem-solving, the arguments they provoke are rarely productive. Starting a fight puts a child in charge, giving her a sense of power, especially if he sees you losing control of your emotions."[60]

> "Sometimes an angry child will go out of his way to start a fight for something to do. Just for the fun of it...often for no other reason than they're bored and find torment enjoyable."[61]

If you find yourself in these kinds of battles, you are not alone. Even Jesus faced situations where someone's anger led her to try to manipulate him:

> As Jesus and his disciples were on their way, he came to a village where

a woman named Martha opened her home to him. She had a sister called Mary, who sat at the Lord's feet listening to what he said. But Martha was distracted by all the preparations that had to be made. She came to him and asked, "Lord, don't you care that my sister has left me to do the work by myself? Tell her to help me!" "Martha, Martha," the Lord answered, "you are worried and upset about many things, but few things are needed—or indeed only one. Mary has chosen what is better, and it will not be taken away from her." (Luke 10:38-42)

Obviously, Martha wanted Mary's help, and her anger and frustration led her to try to manipulate Jesus, because she viewed Jesus as the cause of her problems. If he wasn't teaching right now, Mary would not be distracted and could help her. Martha played on his emotions when she said, "Lord, don't you care…" and her manipulation is evident because what she really wanted was help. Instead of simply stating her needs or requesting in a respectful manner, she tried to manipulate the Son of God. The same thing happens with your children when they don't like your command or direction and they try to manipulate you.

How did Jesus handle it? He appealed to her personal responsibility, by identifying her worry and being upset. Her emotions were not justified. He also appealed to God's will, showing that Mary's choice was better and more spiritual. We should do the same with our children by identifying sinful behavior and what the response should be, according to God's word, instead of getting caught up in arguments and persuasive distractions that aren't relevant to the reason for the angry response.

There are other examples where people tried to manipulate Jesus. As you study them, look for the same technique as Jesus disarms each one.

- Luke 20:19-26, Jesus talked about paying taxes;
- John 8:1-11, woman caught in adultery;
- Luke 2:41-52, Jesus' parents lost him at the Temple.

A child can make an appeal to a parent's command or direction with respect and a submissive heart. Author Lou Priolo provides an entire chapter to this appeal process, but I have summarized the main points below:[62]

The Appeal Process—After an instruction or command is given by the parent and acknowledged by the child, the child may request to make an appeal. To hear the appeal may or may not be granted, and it must only be presented to the parent who is giving the instruction. If the appeal is granted, it must be made with new information and only once, with respect and a submissive heart, which constitute the words, tone of voice, and body language. It helps the child learn how to graciously accept an appeal that has been denied (similar to accepting God's answer of "No" to a prayer).

Authors Les Carter and Frank Minirth offer several guidelines about how to manage your child's anger.[63] I've summarized the key points below:

- Don't overreact by giving in or responding with greater force in your tone of voice or volume. When you speak too strongly, you imply disrespect, lack of trust, and personal insecurity. When you speak to a child in a way that emphasizes your authority over his or her worth, then you keep the anger alive in that child. Realize your child is wrestling with his own emotions and immature response to authority. What's needed is a calm firmness with no need for a power struggle. This calm firmness shows the child how to disagree without being disagreeable. It avoids the emotionally charged rebuttals and debate. There's no need for further pleading or persuasion.

- Share your own experiences. A child's security will increase from your level of inner confidence as you share past or present situations. You shouldn't "dump your emotions" on a child or look to her to meet your needs. Rather, your resolve and mature outlook will make you more believable and thus more approachable. It should lower the pressure a child feels to be perfect, and allow her to approach her own emotions with more confidence.

    "Children need openness and honesty with their parents if they are to develop emotional composure, and this openness should not be a one-way window into the child's feelings. Children need to see the insides of their parents too."[64]

- Don't simply tell the child how to solve a problem; help him process it by helping evaluate the options available. You should discuss each option with the potential consequences, and then let him choose. It takes more time, but this mental process engages his mind and teaches him to think about how to respond to his emotions. Authors Jennifer Anne Brown and Pam Provonsha Hopkins offer good direction for these discussions:[65]

    1. Respectful – Is it fair? How might other people feel?
    2. Reasonable – Is it safe? Could it work?
    3. Rules – Does it break any rules?

They also offer a great summary of what to expect of these interactions based on a child's age:[66]

- Infant—"When the parent responds to an infant's cries with an empathetic facial expression and tone of voice, and verbalizes for him the primary emotion, the parent begins teaching the infant how to access, identify, and express his feelings."

- Toddler—"Part of helping them toward the goal of healthy emotional expression is to provide them with the skills they need to recognize and communicate their feelings...sad, angry, hurt, scared, and their many other feelings. Parents can also begin to teach some beginning skills in self-calming. Your toddler can learn to take deep breaths, count to three or sing a song."

- Preschool/Kindergarten—"A parent can begin teaching a child to express emotions and to problem solve."

- Early Elementary—"Parents' challenge during this time is to balance a shift from teacher to coach in a way that is consistent with their child's personality, skills, and maturity within a given situation. During this stage it is often better for the parent to be a good listener, letting the child think things through out loud, allowing her to come up with her own ideas and solutions."

- Middle Childhood—"This is the time when a parent's role begins to shift from coach to what will eventually become that of supporter in adolescence. However, it is also a time when sudden regressions in emotions, judgment, and behavior are not uncommon as children near preadolescence, and parents may find themselves needing to frequently adjust their responses to match the need."

In closing this chapter on children's anger, I want to devote a few words for adopted children. Having adopted our son from a Romanian orphanage at the age of four, we noticed his anger was different from our daughters. It seemed to be more intense, and his passive-aggressive behavior was often directed toward his adoptive mother. Author Nancy Verrier in her book *The Primal Wound* notes the same tendency:

> "It is the adoptee's actual experience of the abandonment which causes him to project the abandoning mother upon the adoptive mother. She is, after all, available, while the birth mother is not."[67]

Another author Sherrie Eldridge in her book, *Twenty Things Adopted Kids Wish Their Adoptive Parents Knew*, also identifies this characteristic:

> "I believe the adoptee's anger is directed primarily at the birth mother, with the intent of punishing her for abandonment as well as crying from the depths of the adoptee's heart for a reunion."[68]

> "The adoptee's anger is also directed at any others she believes have

played a part in the loss or are in some way obstructing a reunion, mainly the adoptive parents. Adoptive parents, especially mothers, often get the brunt of the adoptee's anger, for they are present."[69]

My son was abandoned at 18 months old, and I can only imagine the emotional scars and wounds that traumatic experience may have caused, especially with his emotional response to future hurts and disappointments. We have often discussed his adoption with him and provided him with as much information as we know concerning his past.

Author Nancy Verrier describes the adoptee as having a fear of rejection and how it influences the child's relationship with the mother:

"...instead of the Golden Rule of 'Do unto others as you would have them do unto you,' the rule of these adoptees is 'Do unto others first that which you fear they are going to do to you.' This is often what happens in the relationship with the adoptive mother, where she is tested over and over again to see if she is going to reject the child. The constant anxiety caused by the expectation of her eventual rejection and the child's need to let her know how he feels creates a cycle of rejective behavior between mother and child, which is destructive to their self-esteem and to their relationship."[70]

Author Sherrie Eldridge notes that there is a central message to an adopted child's thinking, which translates to, "I've been wronged". Sometimes this anger also comes from other messages such as, "I am lonely", "You are to blame", "I must guard against further loss," and "I am different from you."[71] Their passive-aggressive anger is displayed in similar forms as described previously; however, the frequency and intensity is noticeably higher. As both authors note:

"Adoptee anger, more often than not, crosses over into rage—primal rage, which, I believe, is born the moment the birth mother ceases to be present."[72]

"I am talking about overwhelming anger that seems to come out of nowhere and which either explodes onto the scene or is buried so that it makes one numb."[73]

The adoptee may have a difficult time bonding with and trusting other people, even family members that have consistently loved them and given to them. We noticed all of these issues with our son, along with an increased tendency to lie, shift blame, control, and be deceitful. Sometimes the anger came from hurts occurring earlier in the day, such as being bullied on the bus, having conflicts at school, or being frustrated with his learning disabilities and inability to remember details. Sometimes he didn't know what caused his anger. His Attention Deficit Hyperactivity Disorder (ADHD) adds to the challenges because the medicines that allow better mental focus also cause less appetite and more irritability. Natural supplements were helpful without the negative side effects.

Author Tim Murphy describes the characteristics for the Attention Deficit part of ADHD or "Inattention," as described in the *Diagnostic and Statistical Manual*:[74]

- Fails to attend to details or makes careless mistakes
- Has difficulty sustaining attention in tasks or play
- Does not seem to listen when spoken to directly
- Has difficulty organizing tasks and activities
- Avoids tasks that require sustained mental effort
- Loses things necessary for tasks or activities
- Is easily distracted
- Is forgetful

My son has all of these characteristics because of how his brain processes his experiences and emotions day-to-day. If you had these tendencies, how easily would you become frustrated or impatient? How frequently would those emotions be expressed through anger? Dr. Murphy sees a distinct connection:

> "Anger and aggressive behaviors are frequently seen in children with ADHD." [75]

The Scriptural foundations and counselors' guidance found throughout this book have produced significant changes in my son and in our relationship with him. They have helped him to be more honest, share his feelings more often, and resolve conflict in a healthier way. They have also helped my wife and I manage our own anger better. When discussing issues and conflicts, a calmer voice and controlled emotions have helped him resolve his own anger more quickly. The battles are not over, but we are winning the war.

EPILOGUE

Do not be angry with me if I tell you the truth.

—Socrates

Remember the quote from the book entitled *A Volcano in My Tummy*, where the authors state, "We hope all who use this book will enjoy their anger and benefit from it."?[76] Although I laughed when I first read that quote, it is true that if you handle your anger in a healthy way, it can bring about a change for the good either in you or in other people. I hope you have benefitted from this book, where the Scriptures and counselors' advice can bring about new convictions and lasting change.

Here are a few questions to ponder as you review the main sections of this book:

1. Do you see your anger any differently? Maybe your definition is anger and what it looks like has changed.

2. Is your anger usually definitive or distorted?

3. When your anger is triggered, how will you respond differently than you do today?

4. What did you learn about God's anger that surprised you? How will that affect your life?

5. What inspired you with how Jesus handled his anger?

6. Which "Angry Man of God" can you relate to the most? Why? What did you learn from his life?

7. What principle will help you the most in dealing with angry people?

8. What's one thing that will help you interact and minister to an angry child?

END NOTES

1. The Urban Dharma Newsletter March 9, 2004.
2. B. Alan Wallace, *Tibetan Buddhism from the Ground Up*, Boston: Wisdom, 1993.
3. Bashir, Shahzad. *Anger, Encyclopedia of the Qur'an*, Brill, 2007.
4. Gary Chapman, *Anger—Handling a Powerful Emotion in a Healthy Way* (Northfield Publishing, 1999), 16.
5. Chapman, 23.
6. Neil Clark Warren, *Make Anger Your Ally* (Colorado Springs: Focus on the Family Publishing, 1990), 55, 77.
7. Warren, 97.
8. Chapman, 59.
9. Adelaide Bry, *How to Get Angry Without Feeling Guilty* (MJF Books, 1976), ix.
10. Adelaide Bry, 8-9.
11. Chapman, 79.
12. Les Carter and Frank Minirth, *The Anger Workbook* (Thomas Nelson Publishers, 1993), 27-30.
13. Carter and Minirth, 24.
14. Chapman, 80-82.
15. Chapman, 51.
16. Mark P. Cosgrove, *Counseling for Anger* (Dallas: Word, 1988), 71, 95.
17. Chapman, 79.
18. Chapman, 44.
19. Chapman, 54.
20. Carter and Minirth, 8.
21. Carter and Minirth, 118-121.
22. Carter and Minirth, 175.
23. Carter and Minirth, 19.
24. Chapman, 73.
25. Carter and Minirth, 33-34.
26. J. I. Packer, *Knowing God* (InterVarsity Press, 1973), 136.
27. Stephen A. Bly, *The Surprising Side of Grace—Appreciating God's Loving Anger* (Discovery House Publishers, 1994), 10.
28. Bly, 16-19.
29. Bly, 29-35.
30. Article entitled *"Nahum: The Terrible Wrath of God,"* www.raystedman.org
31. Bly, 33.
32. *Antiquities XV*, 380 and XX, 219.
33. An article by F. F. Bruce in the book *Hard Sayings in the Bible*.

34. Chapman, 130.
35. Chapman, 79.
36. Edward B. Davis, *A Whale of a Tale: Fundamentalist Fish Stories*, 1991.
37. Article *Rabbi and Talmidim* from the website www.followtherabbi.com
38. Chapman, 184-188.
39. Chapman, 185.
40. Chapman, 192.
41. Chapman, 138.
42. H. Clay Trumbull, *Hints on Child Training* (1891), 129-131.
43. Lou Priolo, *The Heart of Anger* (Calvary Press, 1997), 57.
44. Jennifer Anne Brown and Pam Provonsha Hopkins, *What Angry Kids Need* (Parenting Press, 2008), 87.
45. Eliane Whitehouse and Warwick Pudney, *A Volcano in My Tummy* (New Society Publishers, 1996), 5.
46. D. Ross Campbell, M.D. with Rob Suggs, *How to Really Love Your Angry Child* (Life Journey, 2003), 10-11.
47. Campbell, 19.
48. Tim Murphy, Ph.D. and Loriann Hoff Oberlin, *The Angry Child* (Three Rivers Press, 2001), 45.
48. Dr. John Townsend and Dr. Henry Cloud, *Boundaries* (Zondervan, 1992), 72.
50. Whitehouse and Pudney, 46.
51. Chapman, 146.
52. Brown and Hopkins, 85-86.
53. Ruth N. Koch and Kenneth C. Haugk, *Speaking the Truth in Love: How to Be an Assertive Christian* (St. Louis: Stephen Ministries, 1992), 22.
54. Campbell, 79-80.
55. Carter and Minirth, 32.
56. Campbell, 13.
57. Campbell, 57-61.
58. Priolo, 125.
59. Priolo, 126.
60. Murphy, 148.
61. Murphy, 156-57.
62. Priolo, 163-172.
63. Carter and Minirth, 189-206.
64. Carter and Minirth, 202.
65. Brown and Hopkins, 62.
66. Brown and Hopkins, 110-119.
67. Nancy Verrier, *The Primal Wound* (Gateway Press, Inc., 1993), 55.
68. Sherrie Eldridge, *Twenty Things Adopted Kids Wish Their Adoptive Parents Knew* (Bantam Dell, 1999), 63.

69. Eldridge, 64-65.
70. Verrier, 86.
71. Eldridge, 63-65.
72. Eldridge, 63.
73. Verrier, 192.
74. Murphy, 119.
75. Murphy, 116.
76. Eliane Whitehouse and Warwick Pudney, *A Volcano in My Tummy* (New Society Publishers, 1996), 5.

www.ingramcontent.com/pod-product-compliance
Lightning Source LLC
Chambersburg PA
CBHW070053080526
44586CB00013B/1043